HD 6283 SAR

Age Discrimination In Employment

Age
Discrimination
In Employment

MALCOLM SARGEANT

GOWER

Published by
Gower Publishing Limited
Gower House
Croft Road
Aldershot
Hampshire GU11 3HR
England

Ashgate Publishing Company
Suite 420
101 Cherry Street
Burlington, VT 05401-4405
USA

Malcolm Sargeant has asserted his moral right under the Copyright, Designs and Patents Act, 1988, to be identified as the author of this work.

British Library Cataloguing in Publication Data
Sargeant, Malcolm
   Age discrimination in employment
   1. Age discrimination in employment 2. Ageism 3. Age discrimination – Law and legislation – Great Britain
   I. Title
   331.3'98133

   ISBN-13: 9780566087745

Library of Congress Cataloging-in-Publication Data
Sargeant, Malcolm.
   Age discrimination in employment / by Malcolm Sargeant.
      p. cm.
   Includes bibliographical references and index.
   ISBN-13: 978-0-566-08774-5 (alk. paper)
   ISBN-10: 0-566-08774-X (alk. paper)
   1. Age discrimination in employment. 2. Age discrimination in employment--Law and legislation. 3. Age and employment. I. Title.

   HD6279.S37 2006
   331.3'98133--dc22

                                                              2006024185

Printed and bound in Great Britain by TJ International Ltd, Padstow, Cornwall

Contents

List of Tables

CHAPTER 1

Age Discrimination

A feature of the Employment Equality (Age) Regulations 2006[1] is that they are not limited to one particular age group. Unlike, say, the Age Discrimination in Employment Act 1967 in the United States, they apply to all age groups and all perceived ages. It is likely, however, that most of the litigation will concern older workers who suffer discrimination. This is because firstly, they appear more likely to suffer from age discrimination and secondly, because the consequences of such discrimination are potentially more severe than for young workers. As will be shown here, the consequences of a person in their 50s losing a job are serious because it is likely that such a person will never be able to get back into the labour market at a comparable level. This is less likely to be the case with young workers, who have the opportunity of time to retrain and restart. This is not to underestimate the detrimental impact of age discrimination upon young or indeed other-age workers or to deny that it takes place. The age at which one can be viewed as an older worker can start as low as the 30s for women workers returning after a career break. Discrimination against all ages is considered in this book (see for example Chapter 4), but there is inevitably a concentration upon the issues surrounding older workers.

AGE DISCRIMINATION

Age discrimination has, of course, both an institutional and an individual perspective. A report by the Equality Authority of Ireland stated:

> *Ageism involves an interlinked combination of institutional practices, individual attitudes and relationships. Institutional practices in this context can be characterised by:*
>
> - *the use of upper age limits to determine provision or participation;*
>
> - *segregation where older people are not afforded real choices to remain within their communities;*
>
> - *a failure to take account of the situation, experience or aspirations of older people when making decisions, and a failure to seek to*

---

1   SI 2006/1031

ensure benefit to them as a result of an overemphasis on youth and youth culture; and

- *inadequate provision casting older people as burdens or dependants.*

Institutional practices can shape, and be shaped by, individual attitudes based on stereotypes of older people as dependent, in decline or marginal. Some of these practices can also have a detrimental impact on an older person's sense of self worth.[2]

These are some institutional manifestations of age discrimination. To a degree they are based upon group stereotypes. Upper age limits are imposed for health care and for employment purposes, for example, because of assumptions that it is correct to treat older people less favourably than others, perhaps because of an idea that such people have outlived the useful part of their lives and that society should somehow allocate its resources to those that have something left to contribute. Older people may be segregated and regarded as a burden or a drain on the resources of the community. There is no attempt in these practices to differentiate one older person from another. Like all discrimination it can accept that there are exceptions to the general rule, but the general rule results in treatment relying upon an unacceptable criterion. In this case the criterion is the chronological age of the group. One of the arguments in this book is that this institutional discrimination continues in the European Union and the United Kingdom and it is, in part, actually legitimised by the Framework Directive on Equal Treatment and Employment[3] and the Employment Equality (Age) Regulations 2006.

Individuals' lives are defined by age:

Our lives are defined by ageing: the ages at which we can learn to drive, vote, have sex, buy a house, or retire, get a pension, travel by bus for free. More subtle are the implicit boundaries that curtail our lives: the safe age to have children, the experience needed to fill the boss's role, the physical strength needed for some jobs. Society is continually making judgements about when you are too old for something – and when you are too old.[4]

---

2   *Implementing Equality for Older People* (2004)
3   Directive 2000/78/EC OJ L303/16 2.12.2000
4   *How Ageist is Britain?* (2005)

One survey showed that some 59 per cent of respondents reported that they had been discriminated against on the basis of age during their careers.[5] In a further survey, this time of retired trade union members, almost one-third claimed to have suffered age discrimination and one in 12 claimed to have been harassed for reasons connected to their chronological age.[6] One of the respondents recounted this story:

> I was a lecturer in journalism for over 11 years until I was forced to retire last year, despite having no wish to do so. I was told just before my 65th birthday that I would be compulsorily retired at the end of the summer term.
>
> The college, with its usual efficiency, left it too late to advertise for a replacement and they could not find a suitable applicant. At the eleventh hour, as desperation set in, I was asked to stay on. I was very happy to do so because I enjoyed my work and I was very efficient at my job.
>
> I would have been content to carry on for another two or three years and I assumed that, having breached their strict code of retirement at 65, the college would be pleased for me to do so. However, in April last year I was informed that my job was again going to be advertised and I would be forced to retire when a replacement was found. I told the personnel department that it was unfair because they had been more than ready to ignore their mandatory retirement rule when it suited them. They refused and the job was advertised, again at a late hour, and this time they found a suitable candidate although this did not happen until three weeks before the end of the summer term, so I was kept in suspense until shortly before I was due to start my holidays.

There is a sense of frustration in this letter. An experienced and active individual is ejected from employment and almost discarded as a result of the application of a rule based upon a chronological age rather than the merits of the individual. One in three respondents to a further survey said that the over-70s were regarded as incompetent and incapable and that more people reported suffering age discrimination than any other form of discrimination.[7] Sufficient surveys are reported on in this book to show that decisions are taken on the basis of an individual's age, particularly in relation to employment. One way of reducing this discrimination is to

---

5   *Tackling age discrimination in the workplace* (2005)
6   Survey carried out by Malcolm Sargeant in 2003; partly written up in Sargeant (2004) and in *The Lecturer* 11 February 2004; see Chapter 3
7   *How Ageist is Britain?* (2005)

make institutional discrimination unlawful in order to make individual discrimination unacceptable.

IS AGE DISCRIMINATION DIFFERENT?

Age discrimination might be different from other forms of discrimination because there is no discrete group that has its own membership. Everyone has some age[8] and old age is a state that the majority of the population will reach at some time. As the US Supreme Court stated:

> Old age does not define a 'discrete and insular' group…in need of 'extraordinary protection from the majoritarian political process'. Instead, it marks a stage that each of us will reach if we live out our normal span.[9]

Age discrimination in employment is often portrayed as protecting older workers from being discriminated against in comparison to younger workers. Certainly this comparison is one aspect of such discrimination. In the United States it is only those who are aged over 40 who form a protected class. Those under this age level do not receive any protection from the Age Discrimination in Employment Act 1967 (see Chapter 6). Even in the United States, however, the distinction is not just between the young and the old. It might help a court to infer discrimination, but it is not conclusive. Discrimination on the basis of age can take place between two people within the protected class.[10]

A report by the Education and Employment Committee of the House of Commons[11] stated that age discrimination was a complicated issue. It was different to other forms of discrimination because, firstly, it could affect anyone, unlike other measures on sex, race and disability, and secondly, because it was also more difficult to identify than discrimination on other grounds. In the United Kingdom and indeed in the rest of the European Union, age discrimination regulation applies to workers of all age groups. Thus, young workers will be protected in the same way that older workers may be. Presumably a 20-year-old will be able to complain about their treatment in comparison to a 25-year-old as well as the more obvious 60-year-old comparing themselves to the treatment of a much younger worker. It seems likely, however, that it is the

---

8   See Friedman (1984)

9   *Massachusetts Board of Retirement v Murgia*; taken from Jolls (1996)

10   *O'Connor v Consolidated Coin Caterers Corp*

11   House of Commons Education and Employment Committee *Age Discrimination in Employment* Seventh Report Session 2000-01 HC 259

older worker who is more likely to suffer from discrimination on the grounds of their chronological age.[12]

The Government's 1998 consultation document[13] stated, at para 2.10:

It is hard to define age discrimination succinctly. The consultation made it clear that there can be both direct and indirect forms of age discrimination in employment. The most obvious forms are where people held strong, stereotypical views about a person's capabilities to do a job or to be developed because of their age.

The Government's consultation document did not try to identify discrete groups. Rather it considered the manifestations of discrimination as they affect large numbers of workers. The fault with this approach is that it fails to identify solutions which might be age specific. The solutions to discrimination against workers under the age of 21 might be different to those concerning discrimination against workers over 65 years of age. There is an implicit assumption in this book that there are identifiable groups against whom age discrimination takes place: these are younger workers and older workers. The issues are different as between discrimination against different groups as exemplified by one survey of young people (see Chapter 3) and their experiences of discrimination. This is particularly true when one considers the consequences of discrimination. For a young worker it can mean a failed job application or a missed promotion opportunity. For an older worker it can mean the end of their working life (see Chapter 4). It is a fault of EU and national policy that the statutory measures taken are blind to this difference.

In a comparative analysis of age discrimination in the European Community the following definitions were offered:

Direct discrimination: measures targeted at older workers based solely on grounds of age, and on no other factors, such as abilities or health. These measures use specific age limits to exclude older workers from, for example, training and employment schemes, or from applying for jobs.

Indirect discrimination: measures which are not directly age-specific, but which have a disproportionately negative impact on older workers, compared with other age groups. This hidden discrimination

---

12   The Government consultation document on its code of practice on Age Diversity in Employment concluded that 'it is clear that age discrimination against older workers does exist'

13   Which preceded the voluntary Code of Practice on Age Diversity in Employment (see Chapter 2)

usually has the most widespread negative impact on older workers in employment.[14]

Older workers are defined as those of 50 years and over. There is, according to this definition, a minority of people who may face difficulties because of age-specific measures or prejudice. In this there appears to be a similarity with other recognised and unlawful forms of discrimination in employment. There is an identifiable group against whom discrimination takes place. They are not, in some circumstances, allowed to compete for opportunities on equal terms with workers outside the group.

The question perhaps should not be to what extent is age discrimination like other forms of discrimination, although this is important in identifying ways in which the subject is treated in a lesser way than say, sex or race discrimination; the question is to what extent is age intertwined with other forms of discrimination. Younger black workers may be treated differently to older black workers. There is a significant correlation between age and disability in that the older one becomes, the more likely one will become disabled (see Chapter 7). It is this intertwining, perhaps, that provides the evidence that age discrimination is based upon similar prejudices to other forms of regulated discrimination and should, therefore, be treated in a similar manner.

STEREOTYPES AND DISCRIMINATION

It has been suggested that the word 'stereotype' was first used in the eighteenth century to describe a printing process whose purpose was to duplicate pages of type.[15] The usage of the word later developed from the idea of producing further images from a stereotype into reproducing 'a standardised image or conception of a type of person'.[16] The problem with producing this 'standard image', or stereotyping, is that individuals are treated as members of a group, rather than being treated as individuals. It is the group to whom we attribute generalised characteristics, which clearly cannot possibly be the characteristics of every individual within that group.

One simple assumption, for example, might be that men are stronger than women. The result of this is that only men might be considered for physically demanding jobs, which in turn may be the higher paid jobs in certain types of employment. The outcome is that women are discriminated against in the

---

14   Drury (1993)
15   Taken from *Stereotyping* (1995)
16   This definition comes from *The Collins Dictionary and Thesaurus* 1988

selection process and end up earning less than men. The assumption is patently false. Not all men are stronger than all women. Some women will be stronger than many men and so on. The discrimination comes from the stereotyping of women in the first place. It is the allocation of a generalised characteristic to an identifiable group.

The result of employment policies based upon the age of employees is to reduce the participation rate of older people in the job market. These policies encourage them to leave the labour force and discourage them from re-joining it. They may also be responsible for older employees having fewer training opportunities than their younger colleagues. One of the reasons for this may be the stereotypical attitudes that employers have towards the abilities of employees based upon their age. In one survey of 500 companies[17] a question was asked about at what age someone would be too old to employ. Of the respondents 12 per cent considered people too old at 40, 25 per cent considered them too old at 50, 43 per cent considered them too old at 55 and 60 per cent felt they were too old at 60. The relationship of these judgements to conventional stereotypical attitudes can be shown in their answers to questions about agreeing or not agreeing with statements. Figures such as the 36 per cent who thought that older workers were more cautious, the 40 per cent who thought that they could not adapt to new technology and the 38 per cent who thought that they would dislike taking orders from younger workers suggest that stereotypical attitudes remain strong. Research indicates that there is little evidence that chronological age is a good predictor of performance.[18] An OECD study concluded:[19]

> *Age has only a marginal effect on industrial productivity and the variations in productivity within a given age group are wider than variations between one age group and another.*

The willingness of employers to attach characteristics to age groups is illustrated by a New Zealand survey covering large and small employers (Table 1.1).[20]

Older workers are more reliable, more loyal, more committed and less likely to leave than younger workers. On the other hand, older workers are more likely to resist change and have problems with technology. They may also be less flexible, less willing to train and be less creative than younger colleagues.

---

17 Taylor and Walker (1994)
18 See McEwen (1990)
19 *Demographic Ageing - consequences for social policy* (1988) cited in *Ageing and the working population and employment* EIRO 1991
20 McGregor (2002)

Table 1.1   New Zealand survey of age characteristics

Older workers are more likely to:	Agree %	Neither %	Disagree %
Be reliable	83.6	11.3	5.3
Be loyal	81.2	16.0	2.9
Be committed to the job	65.9	18.5	5.6
Be willing to stay longer in the job	61.6	32.2	6.8
Resist change	60.1	22.8	17.1
Have problems with technology	55.4	28.4	16.2
Be productive	52.5	37.4	10.1
Be less flexible	39.3	33.4	27.3
Be less willing to train	32.5	36.5	30.9
Be less promotable	32.4	41.0	26.6
Be away sick	7.1	36.8	56.2
Have lower expectations	31.3	33.6	35.0
Be less creative	22.4	43.8	33.9

The argument is not whether these characteristics are largely true or largely false, it is whether they can apply to all or most workers who are of a certain chronological age. Logic suggests that such sweeping generalisations cannot be true.

The same survey asked employers to attribute characteristics to different age groups (Table 1.2). The 45-and-over age group did not do so well. It scores highly in having leadership, strong work ethic and loyalty characteristics, but not so well in others. Similarly, young workers face prejudice based upon stereotypes. Their strengths lie in computer experience and enthusiasm, but they, according to this survey, are unlikely to have leadership qualities or a strong work ethic.

SCOPE OF AGE DISCRIMINATION

THE FRAMEWORK DIRECTIVE[21]

The Directive establishing a general framework for equal treatment in employment and occupation, of course, covers a number of other areas besides

---

21   Directive 2000/78/EC

Table 1.2 Characteristics associated with age groups: % responses from employers

Workers	15–29 yrs	30–44 yrs	45–59 yrs	60–75 yrs	All ages
Computer experience	66.9	19.9	1.1	-	12.1
Enthusiasm	35.2	28.5	3.3	0.4	32.6
High levels of motivation	14.9	48.0	6.4	0.3	30.3
Creativity	27.8	40.0	3.5	-	28.7
Innovation	20.0	48.4	5.1	-	26.5
Adaptability	29.8	35.3	10.8	0.3	23.8
Flexibility	24.5	33.1	16.5	1.2	24.7
Leadership	0.6	31.3	39.3	1.2	27.6
Strong work ethic	1.1	25.4	45.0	3.3	25.5
Loyalty to employer	0.3	10.7	50.3	10.6	28.1

age (see Chapter 4 for a more detailed consideration of the Directive).[22] The justification for the Directive generally contained in its preamble is couched in terms of fundamental rights and freedoms. In particular, paragraph 4 of the preamble states:

> The right of all persons to equality before the law and protection against discrimination constitutes a universal right recognised by the Universal Declaration of Human Rights, the United Nations Convention on the elimination of all forms of Discrimination against Women, United Nations Covenants on Civil and Political Rights and on Economic, Social and Cultural Rights and by the European Convention for the Protection of Human Rights and Fundamental Freedoms to which all Member States are signatories. Convention No 111 of the International Labour Organisation prohibits discrimination in the field of employment and occupation.

Paragraph 6 also refers to the Community Charter of Fundamental Rights. Article 1 of the Directive states that its purpose is 'the putting into effect in the Member States the principle of equal treatment' in combating discrimination on the grounds of religion or belief, disability, age or sexual orientation with regard to employment or occupation'. This is interpreted in Article 2 as meaning that 'there shall be no direct or indirect discrimination whatsoever on any of the grounds referred to in Article 1'. Harassment or an instruction to discriminate

---

22 Sexual orientation, religion or belief, disability

are also deemed to be forms of discrimination which violate the principle of equal treatment.

In contrast to this equal treatment justification, the Preamble (paragraph 8), also cites the Helsinki European Council Employment Guidelines for 2000, which called upon each Member State to give special attention to:

> *the needs of the disabled, ethnic minorities and other groups and individuals who may be disadvantaged, and develop appropriate forms of preventive and active policies to promote their integration into the labour market.*

This was further developed at subsequent Council meetings. In 2003, the guidelines called upon Member States to promote 'active ageing by fostering working conditions conducive to job retention'.

These guidelines are part of the 'Lisbon Strategy'. In March 2000 the EU Council of Ministers had agreed at the Lisbon Spring Council Meeting to adopt a strategy to raise the rate of growth and employment because of poor performance of the EU economy compared to the USA and a concern with emerging economies of Asia. The EU set itself the target of becoming 'the most dynamic and competitive knowledge-based economy in the world, capable of sustainable economic growth with more and better jobs and greater social cohesion, and respect for the environment' (see Chapter 3).

EMPLOYMENT

The ageing population

There were 59 231 900 people in the United Kingdom in mid-2002. The population of the United Kingdom is growing and ageing. The 2001 census revealed the following age breakdown:

Table 1.3   Population of the United Kingdom by age

All ages	*58.8 million*
Under 16	11.9 million
Men 16–64, women 16–59	36.1 million
Men 65+, women 60+	10.8 million

For the first time there are now more people over the age of 60 than there are children under 16. The change in the age population is noticeable when compared to the 1951 census. During this 50-year period the proportion of the population aged under 16 has fallen from 24 per cent to 20 per cent. At the same time the proportion aged 60 and over has increased from 16 per cent to 21 per cent.[23]

The average age of the population in the United Kingdom as a whole is increasing as is the average age of the economically active population. Over the 25-year period between 1996 and 2021 the proportion of people over the age of 44 years will increase from 38 per cent to 46 per cent; the 45–59 age group will increase by almost one-quarter; the 60–74 age group will increase by over one-third and the 75 years and over group will increase by 28 per cent. In contrast, the 16–29 years age group will fall by 5.7 per cent.[24] This process is a Europe-wide one, although the speed of the process is variable.[25] The number of people in the European Union aged 50–64 years is projected to increase by 6.5 million during the next ten years.[26]

The working population[27]

The total potential working population in 2003 was 36 157 000 people. This accounts for 78.1 per cent of the adult population (16+ years). Divided into age groups there is the following Table 1.4:

Table 1.4   Working population of the United Kingdom by age

Age	Percentage of total
16–24	14.0
25–49	45.1
50–SPA*	18.9
SPA and over	21.9

* State pension age; either 60 or 65 years

Some 70.1 per cent of the 50–SPA age band were in employment (6 133 000). This compares to an overall employment rate for all ages of 74.9 per cent. Almost 9 per cent of those over SPA were also continuing to work. Older workers are

23 These statistics come from the 2001 census and are to be found, like the comparisons used here, on the Office for National Statistics website at www.statistics.gov.uk

24 The immediate source was *Tackling age bias: code or law?* (1998), although the original source was ONS Monitor 10.3.98

25 See *Ageing and the Labour Market: Policies and initiatives within the European Union* (1998)

26 These and other statistics are available from Demographic Report, European Commission Office for Official Publications, September 1997, Luxembourg

27 These figures are taken from *Older Workers: Statistical Information Booklet* (2003); available on www.agepositive.gov.uk

more likely to be self-employed. The overall self-employment rate is 11.6 per cent, but the self-employment rate for the 50–SPA group is 16.7 per cent and, for those over SPA, some 24.4 per cent. The figures are even more dramatic when one looks at the gender differences. Some 22.2 per cent of men 50–SPA are self-employed and some 40.5 per cent of those over SPA. This is likely to reflect the greater difficulty that older workers have in obtaining employed positions. Long-term unemployment also affects older workers much more than other age groups. The fact that this was an increasing trend was a concern. Table 1.5 shows the increasing numbers of economically inactive men in the United Kingdom and how it had changed between 1977 and 2000.[28]

Table 1.5   Economically inactive men

Age group	Spring 1977	Spring 2000
16–24	750 000	819 000
25–34	91 000	266 000
35–44	110 000	464 000
50–64	490 000	1 321 000

The Department for Education and Employment commissioned a research project in 1996 with two main aims.[29] The first and principal aim was to identify the effect of age on economic activity. The second was to explore the characteristics of older workers. Older workers were defined as those aged 50 years or over. The main conclusions were:

1.   Older workers were less likely to be in paid work than younger groups. When they did work they were more likely to be working as self-employed or part-time.

2.   Among white-collar occupations there was a 'sharply increased' likelihood of becoming economically inactive beyond the ages of 50 and 55. An important proportion of this would be through the choice of individuals. Those in blue-collar jobs faced higher risks of unemployment and those risks became greater with age.

3.   When older workers were unemployed and claiming benefit they tended to use fewer methods of job search. Once people had become

---

28   *Age Discrimination in Employment* (2001), page xvi
29   *Characteristics of Older Workers* (1998)

unemployed, their chances of returning to paid work were much reduced if they were older than 50 years.

4.   People in their 50s appeared reluctant to say that retirement represented their main economic activity. 'Only after prompting did many concede that they had, effectively, now retired.'

5.   Another important reason for economic inactivity, and reduced hours, were the caring responsibilities of adults. By their late 60s, almost one woman in three had cared for an adult at some point in their life, as had more than one in five men.

6.   Taking all forms of inactivity together, the chances of men leaving inactivity for paid work were sharply reduced after the age of 50 years 'and were close to zero for those over 60'. For women, the chances of moving out of inactivity were much reduced after the age of 40 years and 'was particularly uncommon for those older than their late 50s'.

7.   The more recently that older workers had received employer-paid training, the more likely they were to be in paid work.

The clear picture that one obtains from the research and analysis in this report is that the subject of potential disadvantages suffered by older workers is a complex one. People do not leave the workforce merely because of age discrimination, nor do substantial numbers leave involuntarily. Nevertheless, the report makes clear that older workers are disadvantaged compared to younger workers. They are at a greater risk of exiting the workforce permanently and they do find it much more difficult, if not impossible, to re-enter the workforce. There is enough evidence put forward in this publication to show that one of the reasons for this are discriminatory practices used by employers. Indeed this was a conclusion accepted by the Government in its subsequent consultation document and the Code of Practice on Age Diversity in Employment (see Chapter 2). The House of Lords Select Committee on Economic Affairs[30] was told[31], in confirmation of this, that:

> despite the research findings that age has no net effect on workers performance, when supervisors and managers are asked to rate the performance of workers, they consistently rate the performance of older workers below that of younger workers.

---

30   *Aspects of the Economics of an Ageing Population* (2003)
31   Dr Philip Taylor Executive Director, Cambridge Interdisciplinary Research Centre on Ageing

EDUCATION

Isolating age discrimination in the workplace does not resolve all the issues relating to age discrimination at work. It must result, sometimes, in only the symptoms being treated, rather than the underlying causes. Age discrimination in employment occurs when an older person is refused training which will give them access to work. It also occurs when the older person is discriminated against in the receipt of healthcare when the outcome is to limit the length of their working life. Although this book is concerned with only age discrimination in employment it is worth considering the related discrimination that may take place in other areas that has an effect on the ability of people to take and continue in employment.

The Regulations do recognise that age discrimination in vocational training and higher education, at least, is closely connected to age discrimination in employment.[32] Access to education and vocational training is an important element in helping with access to jobs and subsequent career progression.

The concept of lifelong learning is inextricably linked to issues concerned with age. Lifelong learning implies further training or education for individuals throughout their lives. It is concerned with those that finish their standard education without sufficient skills and it is also concerned with providing, or updating, individuals with further skills and knowledge throughout their working lives.

Individuals will enter the educational system as mature adults for a variety of purposes, which may be connected with personal development or merely the pleasure of learning. Many, however, enter in order to enhance their job/career prospects. One important aspect is concerned with such economic needs, as suggested in the Dearing Report (1997):

> From this point of view, lifelong learning is a key instrument in developing a competitive, multi-skilled workforce.

Mature students

Mature students are generously defined by the DfEE as those aged 21 years and over at undergraduate level and 25 years and over at postgraduate level. Significant numbers of people take part in education at all age levels. Table 1.6 illustrates the diversity of the ages of those accepted into higher education in

---

32   See Regulations 20 and 23 of the Employment Equality (Age) Regulations 2006

Table 1.6   Age of accepted applicants into higher education (percentages of total)[33]

Age	2001	2002	2003	2004	2005
20 and under	78.59	77.80	77.52	77.82	78.07
21–24	11.09	11.73	11.80	11.72	11.46
25–39	8.37	8.47	8.62	8.47	8.46
40 plus	1.95	2.01	2.06	1.99	2.01

2002 and the changes that have taken place since 2001. It also illustrates the relatively small numbers of older people that enter higher education.

For there to be an issue about lifelong learning and age discrimination in employment, it needs to be shown that a proportion of the mature students in higher education are there to increase their prospects either with their current employer, if they have one, or with a new employer. If the motivation of students is increasing their employability then the relevance of the existence of age discrimination in employment becomes important. Employability here means the ability to obtain the desired employment, the ability to stay in the desired employment and the ability to progress within an individual's employment.

A survey for the Dearing Committee[34], carried out in 1997, had a sample that consisted of 79 per cent of the students over the age of 25 studying part-time. Of these part-timers, some 62 per cent were female. The report stated that the majority of mature students study part-time and did not (even when they existed) receive a maintenance grant. The survey also found that, for almost half of the students surveyed, the most important reasons for entering higher education were job related.

Older people are less likely to take part in organised learning. The 1997 National Adult Learning Survey showed that only 9 per cent of 50–59-year-olds compared with 17 per cent of all adults had taken taught learning with future work in mind.[35]

The data on age and training is unambiguous: older people have less access to training, at all occupational levels. This is on top of the fact that they will generally have fewer qualifications than their younger counterparts, because

---

33   The figures come from the UCAS web site at www.ucas.ac.uk
34   *The National Committee of Inquiry into Adult Education* report 2 (1997); see also *Winners and Losers in an expanding system* (2001) www.niace.org.uk
35   See Schuller (2003)

they passed through the initial phase of education when it was narrower; and further compounded by those with fewer qualifications having less access.[36]

More recent evidence suggests, however, that the proportion of older people taking part in some learning is increasing, although the contrast between those under 50 years and those over this age, with the exception of non-vocational learning, is still marked (see Table 1.7).[37]

Table 1.7   Percentage of age groups reporting different types of learning

Age group	16–29	20–29	30–39	40–49	50–59	60–69	70+
Any learning	82	85	83	81	74	51	28
Taught learning	67	69	70	67	54	35	18
Self-directed learning	57	69	65	68	60	34	16
Vocational learning	76	81	79	76	65	30	6
Non-vocational learning	23	22	26	26	27	33	25

HEALTH CARE

Although less than 1 per cent of the older population is in hospital at any one time, 'older people tend to be stereotyped as a homogenous group characterised by passivity, failing physical and mental health, and dependency'.[38]

'There is a substantial body of evidence indicating that older people experience age discrimination in health care.'[39] One survey of general practitioners, by the charity Age Concern,[40] found that 77 per cent of the GPs surveyed said that age rationing occurs in the National Health Service and more than one-third stated that older patients do not enjoy the same quality of care in NHS hospitals as other patients. This was perhaps evidenced by the fact that 84 per cent of those surveyed stated that they had patients over the age of 50 who had decided to go privately for treatment that they could have received on the NHS. The GPs themselves appeared, inadvertently perhaps, to assist in this discrimination by sometimes not referring older patients to other parts of the NHS because of their age.

---

36 Ibid.
37 *National Adult Learning Survey* (2002)
38 *Age discrimination in health and social care* (2000)
39 See Robinson (2003)
40 In 2000; see www.ageconcern.org.uk

Although the NHS is tackling age discrimination, it is clear that there are issues to be faced in the provision of health care, all of which may affect an individual's employability. One Department of Health report suggests that, locally, age discrimination may manifest itself in a number of different ways, including:

- low overall rates of provision of those interventions which are relatively more important to older people – for example, hip and knee replacement, cataract surgery, occupational therapy and chiropody;

- low relative rates of access of older people to specialist services compared with younger people or refusal of particular treatments or care;

- low referral rates to particular services;

- unthinking and insensitive treatment from individual members of staff.[41]

This disadvantage suffered by older people is an important issue when one also considers the demographic change that is taking place in the population as a whole,[42] which in turn affects the ageing of the general workforce.

Of course much of this discrimination will have taken place against the very old who are even less likely to be part of the workforce, but there still continues to be a close relationship between health care and work. Total numbers of days lost through sickness are about 160 million per annum.[43] This amounted to some 8.9 days per worker each year in the public sector and some 6.5 days for those in the private sector. About 20 per cent of absenteeism consists of long-term absence and the balance short-term absence.[44] Managing this absence is an important issue for many employers and active health intervention must be part of that management process.

The link between health and work is also shown in statistics about early retirement. According to the Government Green Paper on *Working and Saving for Retirement* the mean age for men retiring in the United Kingdom is 62.6 years

---

41 *National Service Framework for Older People: Interim Report on Age Discrimination* (2002). This extract is found on p. 19 of the Report
42 See also Henwood (1990); see also information on the Kings Fund website at www.kingsfund. org.uk
43 The figure for 2002 was 166 million, according to the CBI annual absence survey 2003; information from www.guardian.co.uk
44 See www.managingabsence.org.uk although the information came from the CBI 2001 report 'Pulling Together'

and for women 61.1 years. Amongst those already retired and who had retired early some 33 per cent had retired because of illness or disability. This is further evidenced by the Middlesex survey which showed that almost 23 per cent of retired members surveyed had done so because of illness or disability.[45]

These clear links might suggest that tackling discrimination in employment without providing for measures to tackle discrimination in health care provision leads to a regulatory provision which is incomplete.

CONFUSION AND CONTRADICTION

The debate about age discrimination in the United Kingdom has become confused with debates about other issues, such as the closing of defined benefits pension schemes and the demographic change that is taking place within the European Union. The discussion is not only about whether discriminating on the grounds of chronological age is right or wrong, it is also about whether the present arrangements can cope with an ageing population. This is perhaps unfortunate because there is a debate to be had about age discrimination purely as a civil/human rights issue.[46]

There are perhaps two major arguments for introducing measures to combat age discrimination in employment: the demographic/economic argument and the equal treatment argument. They reveal a functional and non-functional approach to the issue. It is the inter-reaction of these two approaches that causes confusion when considering the practical measures to be taken.[47]

FUNCTIONAL APPROACH

The demographic/economic debate is one that has concerned the European Commission for some time. The population of the EU Member States is ageing, albeit at different rates. This ageing process is as a result of a combination of people living longer and a reducing birth rate. Concurrently with this process of an ageing population has been an increase in the number of older people exiting the workforce, so that there appears to be the prospect of a declining workforce with the responsibility of maintaining an increasing retired or unemployed older population.

---

45   Survey of retired trade unionists 2003
46   See for example, Fredman and Spencer (2003)
47   See Sargeant (2005c). See generally Sargeant (1999)

The Government objectives that result from this demographic/economic process are firstly, to 'change the culture' and raise expectations about older people; secondly, to enable and encourage over 50s to stay in work; thirdly, to help and encourage older displaced workers to re-enter work; and finally, to help older people use their skills and experience for the benefit of the wider community.[48] Apart from this last objective, the measures are therefore about encouraging older people to continue working and, as part of this, to protect them from unfair treatment based on age when they are at work.

The preamble to the Framework Directive recognises that the prohibition of age discrimination is an essential part of meeting the aims set out in the guidelines but subsequently states (paragraph 25), however, that differences in treatment may be justified under certain circumstances. Direct and indirect discrimination at work are to be made unlawful except where there is 'objective justification by a legitimate aim and the means of achieving that aim are appropriate and necessary'. Article 6 of the Directive then proposes three differences of treatment on the grounds of age that may be justifiable by 'a legitimate aim, including legitimate employment policy, labour market and vocational training objectives'. The first difference permits some positive action for specific groups including young people, older workers and those with caring responsibilities to encourage their integration into the workforce; the second allows for the fixing of minimum conditions or the giving of advantages linked to age, professional experience or seniority; the third allows a maximum recruitment age based on the training requirements of the post or the need for a reasonable period of employment before retirement.

These exceptions seem to be in opposition to any principle of equality and suggest a contradiction between the equal treatment approach and the latter approach which is perhaps a more functional one.[49]

A weakening of the principle of equal treatment in favour of a functional approach which is perceived to be better for business and better for employees in practice might be the result. This was reflected in the Government's 2003 consultation exercise which proposed a number of specific areas for possible exceptional treatment.[50] These were:

- health, safety and welfare – for example the protection of young workers;

---

48 *Winning the Generation Game* (2000)
49 See Sargeant (2005a)
50 *Equality and Diversity: Age Matters* (2003)

- the facilitation of employment planning – for example where a business has a number of people approaching retirement age at the same time;

- the particular training requirements of the post in question – for example air traffic controllers (the Government's example);

- encouraging and rewarding loyalty;

- the need for a reasonable period of employment before retirement.

There appeared to be a willingness to compromise the principle of equality in favour of perhaps more pragmatic and functional exceptions. It is likely that these exceptions are to be treated narrowly and perhaps will not result in the contradiction illustrated here. The fact that there is a possibility, however, is a matter of concern. Age discrimination in employment is to be specifically allowed to continue in certain circumstances in order to encourage the employment of older people and not to place an apparently too onerous a burden upon employers. It is obviously acceptable to regard health and safety as an exception, especially perhaps the protection of young workers, as is exemplified in the special rules contained in the Working Time Regulations 1998. Phrases such as 'the facilitation of employment planning', 'the particular training requirements of the post in question', 'encouraging and rewarding loyalty' and 'the need for a reasonable period before retirement' all suggest an approach which may, in the short term, encourage employers to employ older workers but will also limit the application of any principle of equal treatment. In the longer term, it is suggested, this may lead to a lessening of protection for such a class because there is a continued legitimisation of age discrimination in employment practices.

This debate is a functional one. It appears to have little to do with a concern about discriminatory treatment except insofar as this treatment interferes with the primary objective of keeping a greater proportion of older people in work and reducing the burden of support from the State and from a smaller workforce. If one adopts this standpoint then making age discrimination in employment unlawful makes sense unless it actually produces unwanted economic effects, for example an employer's ability to have an age diverse workforce in order to assist in long-term succession planning. Perhaps, in contrast to the treatment of discrimination on the grounds of gender, racial origin and disability, there can be justifiable exceptions to the 'principle of equality' in the treatment of age discrimination.[51]

An alternative, non-functional, justification for making age discrimination in employment unlawful is the equal treatment argument. The principle of equal treatment is mentioned in Article 1 of Directive 2000/78/EC and it is mentioned a number of times in the preamble to that Directive.[52] It is not difficult to see where this principle leads in terms of gender or race, but there is more of a problem when considering its application to age issues. Equal treatment suggests equality of treatment between parties or ensuring that one individual or group is not treated less favourably than another group. This presents real problems when considering age discrimination with the lack of a discrete group who can be judged to have been treated less favourably.

NON-FUNCTIONAL APPROACH

The non-functional approach provides that discriminatory treatment is wrong and such treatment cannot be justified on the grounds of age. Perhaps more is needed than just the concept of equal treatment, which requires that likes be treated as alike. The aim of equality, according to Fredman, is 'to give all people an equal set of alternatives from which to choose and thereby to pursue their own version of the good life'.[53] In order to achieve this there needs to be some positive action that recognises the need to cope with inter-generational cultural differences. The focus might, therefore, be on supporting individuals rather than on some equation of relative equality.

Ageing, according to John Grimley Evans,[54] comes about because people change from how they were when they were young. All differences between young and old, however, are not necessarily due to age. An example of this might be what Evans calls the 'cohort phenomena' which is the result of the different experiences of people born at different times. Older people will have been through an education and training system which is different to that experienced by young people. Perhaps, in training, older people are subjected

---

51 See *Equality and Diversity: Age Matters* (2003)
52 Clauses (1) to (6) of the preamble; there is mention of the Community's long history of supporting the principle of equal treatment between men and women, but of course action on other issues such as racial discrimination and age are much more recent initiatives.
53 Fredman, 'The age of equality', in Fredman and Spencer (2003), p. 43; see also Dine and Watt (1996): 'If liberalism could be said…to have a central dogma it would surely include, at least at a preliminary stage, the provision that all citizens irrespective of gender, origin or other irrelevant characteristics should have an opportunity to secure for themselves, in reliance upon their own merits and endeavours, their choice from among the goods available in a given society.'
54 'Implications of the ageing process', in Fredman and Spencer (2003), p. 12

to teaching and learning techniques experienced by the young, but not by a previous generation. As a result, the older worker may be faced with a greater challenge when experiencing training.

The important outcome of this debate is that the reasons for tackling age discrimination in employment are concerned with creating equality of opportunity for workers of all ages, although the principle does not necessarily require equal treatment in all circumstances. It is, however, a different debate to the functional one which derives from the economic/demographic issues.

Given that there are manifestations of discrimination based upon age and that there continues to be a stereotyping of the relative abilities of different groups of workers based on age, one might conclude that there is a case for treating such discrimination in the same way as the Government has tackled discrimination based upon gender and race.

Is age discrimination different, or to be treated differently, than some other forms of discrimination? The approach does appear to be different. There might be more opportunities to *differentiate* rather than *discriminate* between persons of different ages. The US Secretary of Labor commenting in 1965[55], prior to the introduction of the US Age Discrimination in Employment Act, on the existence of age discrimination stated that:

> We find no significant evidence of...the kind of dislike or intolerance that sometimes exists in the case of race, color, religion, or national origin, and which is based on considerations entirely unrelated to ability to perform a job.

He did go on to say, however, that:

> We do find substantial evidence of...discrimination based on unsupported general assumptions about the effect of age on ability...in hiring practices that take the form of specific age limits applied to older workers as a group.

Age discrimination took place then (and still does of course), but it may not create the strong emotions that are sometimes created in consideration of some other forms of discrimination. Perhaps it is the lack of these strong feelings that allows for a more functional approach to the subject.

---

55 See Eglit (1999); see also *The Older American Worker-Age Discrimination in Employment* (1965) report to the US Congress

CHAPTER 2

United Kingdom Perspectives

The process of law making can sometimes be long and sometimes complex. The Labour Government which came to power in 1997 had a commitment to taking some action on age discrimination, although it was not clear what this action would be. In the end it procrastinated by taking a voluntarist route, which few thought would succeed. At the same time the European Union had been developing its own approach to a forecast and significant ageing of the population. The result of this, amongst other measures, was the Framework Directive on Equal Treatment in Employment and Occupation[1], which included discrimination on the grounds of age amongst its provisions (see Chapter 3). The Directive allowed Member States to apply for an extension of up to three years from the original implementation date of 2 December 2003 'in order to take account of particular conditions'. The United Kingdom amongst others took an extension with the result that in the United Kingdom there was a final implementation date of December 2006.

All UK Governments, prior to the adoption of the Equal Treatment in Employment and Occupation Directive, consistently opposed all attempts to introduce legislation on any aspect of age discrimination in employment. The Labour Party had initially seemed more determined. A senior member, Ian McCartney MP, had written to the 'Association of Retired Persons Over 50' in 1995 stating that 'the next Labour Government will introduce legislation to make age discrimination illegal, just as discrimination on the grounds of race and sex are today'.[2]

Ian McCartney MP subsequently became a Minister in a Labour Government committed to a non-statutory route. In 1998, for example, a backbench Member of Parliament attempted to introduce the Employment (Age Discrimination in Advertising) Bill 1998. This was introduced by Ms Linda Perham MP and received its second reading in February 1998. It failed to make any progress because it did not receive the support of the Government. This Bill was the last of a long line of such bills introduced to make unlawful the use of age limits in recruitment advertising or recruitment and selection. Previous attempts had been by David Winnick MP in 1990 and 1996, Gwynneth Dunwoody MP in

---

1   Directive 2000/78/EC
2   Cited in House of Commons Research Paper 96/19 31 January 1996

1992, Baroness Phillips in 1989 (in the House of Lords), Barry Field MP in 1989 and Ann Clwyd MP in 1985.[3]

All these measures failed because previous Conservative Governments and the 1997 Labour Government were opposed to legislation as a solution. All Governments have accepted that age discrimination is unjustifiable and wasteful; for example Ms Ann Widdecombe MP speaking for the Conservative Government in 1993 stated that 'we are all aware that some employers discriminate on age grounds. This is wasteful and short-sighted'.[4] In 1998, Andrew Smith MP speaking on behalf of the Labour Government stated that 'unjustified age discrimination is unfair and a terrible waste of human potential'.[5]

Ms Linda Perham's Bill had been a modest measure aimed at stopping the use of overt age restrictions in recruitment advertising and the use of words in such advertisements which suggest an age dimension to the recruitment. It had not been suggested that such a measure would end age discrimination, but it was suggested that it would go some way to highlighting the issue as well as ending a wrong. That such a measure could work in practice was exemplified by the Institute of Personnel and Development, which had had a strong policy on age references in advertisements that it has carried since 1993. The Government had also instructed Job Centres not to accept vacancies that stipulated an age, but still opposed the Bill, preferring the voluntarist route.

FIRST CONSULTATION

In May 1997, the Government announced that it would consult on the best way to tackle age discrimination in employment. The results of this consultation were published in *Action on Age*.[6] A major contributor to this consultation was some research which had already been commissioned by the Department for Education and Emplyment (DfEE) in 1996. The report entitled *Characteristics of Older Workers* was published in January 1998.[7] The purpose of this report was to identify the effect of age on economic activity and to explore the characteristics of older workers, using data from the Family and Working Lives Survey. The study concluded that any 'older workers effect' becomes apparent around the age of 50 and stated that:

---

3   Information from House of Commons Research Paper 96/19 31 January 1996
4   HC 4 November 1993 col 434
5   HC 6 February 1998 col 1416
6   *Action on Age Report of the Consultation on Age Discrimination in Employment* (1998)
7   See consideration of this report in Chapter 1

Once they had become 50, the risks of leaving work to become unemployed or inactive tended to increase. And the chances of returning to paid work for those who were inactive or unemployed tended to decrease.

The most common area raised in the consultation was the difficulties that older workers had in finding jobs. Problems encountered included the use of age criteria and language in job advertisements. This was an issue borne out by the *Middlesex Survey* (see Chapter 4) and certainly other research at the time. In the late 1980s for example, the Equal Opportunities Commission monitored more than 11 000 recruitment advertisements in a variety of journals. More than 25 per cent stipulated an upper age limit, with almost two-thirds of those stating an upper[8] limit of 35 years. In the debate on her Bill (see above) Ms Perham MP referred to advertisements which used language which had a discriminatory effect, such as an advertisement in the *Independent* newspaper advertising for secretaries to join a 'young, fun team of surveyors'.[9]

A further issue mentioned in the *Action on Age* consultation was the pressure exercised on older employees whilst they were in work. There was concern about training and promotion opportunities being open to older workers and the encouragement of older workers to leave to make way for others, especially through the redundancy process when older workers, it was suggested, were more likely to be considered first.

Perhaps the most interesting part of this consultation was its incompleteness as it did not include a consideration of retirement ages or what happened to workers after normal retirement age. The issue of retirement was raised a lot during the consultation. The document, however, stated that:

This is [retirement age] outside the scope of the consultation, as like other terms and conditions of employment, retirement ages are a matter for negotiation between individual employers and their employees, or their representatives.

It is perhaps ironic that it is this lack of a national policy on retirement ages that placed the United Kingdom in the position of debating the removal of mandatory contractual retirement ages, in order to comply with the Equal Treatment in Employment Directive.

---

8   See McEwen (1990)
9   At this time the author of this book also wrote to the advertising managers of six national newspapers to ask whether they had a policy on age in recruitment advertising. None appeared to have one and, indeed, the Advertising Standards Authority confirmed that no code existed for the industry as a whole

Only a limited number of measures came out of this consultation. The action plan seemed more concerned with helping older workers cope with age discrimination rather than requiring employers to end the practice. Thus, there were a number of measures to help older workers find jobs[10] and some help with education and training, but little else apart from the removal of the upper age limit from job vacancies in Government-owned Job Centres and a consultation on a Code of Good Practice on Age Discrimination.

VOLUNTARISM V STATUTE

The issue of whether to introduce legislation or continue on a voluntarist route was considered as part of the consultation. Arguments put forward in favour of legislation included:

- social change would only take place against a background of anti-discrimination legislation;

- research indicated that both managers and employees favoured legislation;

- legislation in other countries was effective.

The majority of calls for legislation, according to the consultation report, were for a far wider piece of legislation that included more than just employment. Since legislation already existed for sex, race and disability discrimination, then it should be introduced with regard to age.

Arguments put forward against legislation included:

- employers should be free from further labour market regulation and costs;

- employers would find ways around the legislation or 'take it underground';

- legislation would be so complex that it would be 'a part measure only'.

One could imagine these arguments being used against any proposed legislation on any form of discrimination. The consultation document stated, however, that 'on balance, there was no consensus of opinion on legislation and a strong case for legislation was not made during the consultation'.[11]

---

10 Extending the New Deal for unemployed people aged 25 years and over and also for disabled people
11 *Action on Age Report*, Para 2.31

Yet, it had earlier stated that 'research findings indicated that managers and employees favoured legislation'.[12] There were some indications that employer representatives and especially human resource professionals favoured legislation. One report of an Institute of Personnel Management conference at Harrogate some years earlier suggested the following arguments in favour of legislation:[13]

- Legislation would raise the issue of age discrimination to the same level of importance as sex and race discrimination.[14]

- Legislation would demonstrate society's disapproval of morally unacceptable behaviour such as the translation of age-related stereotypes about people into decisions which have a deep affect upon people's lives.

- Legislation would empower human resource people and others to influence their colleagues who may not find age discrimination unacceptable.

- Legislation would empower older workers.

- Legislation would help businesses by reversing the practice of encouraging older workers to exit the labour force thus stopping valuable resources being thrown away.

In a survey of the membership of the Institute of Management some two-thirds of respondents supported the introduction of comprehensive legislation to prevent age discrimination at work. An even greater number (70 per cent) supported legislation to restrict the use of age in job advertisements. Support from managers and HR professionals for legislation may, of course, indicate that arguments to end discriminatory practices in their own organisations are considerably strengthened when there is legislation in existence.

Major employer organisations, however, did not support a legislative route and it may be that this deep seated opposition still manifests itself when considering the practical aspects of the 2006 Age Regulations, for example in the opposition of employer organisations to the abolition of the mandatory retirement as expressed in the 2003 consultation (see below). The Institute of Directors welcomed the Government's decision at the time not to introduce legislation and believed that such legislation would entail an unwarranted

12 Op. cit., para 2.26
13 Handley (1993); the speech was by Professor Warr of Sheffield University
14 This speech was made before the adoption of the Disability Discrimination Act 1995

restriction on an employer's right to organise their business. It also doubted whether legislation would be effective as there was little evidence that the problem had been eliminated in those countries which had introduced laws on the subject. The Institute did state that discrimination in all its forms was wrong and can be damaging to individual enterprises and the economy. It was legitimate, however, to discriminate on the basis of age on occasions when the job or situation demanded. The Confederation of British Industry (CBI) also supported a voluntary approach. Their Director of Human Resources was quoted as saying that the CBI believed that the eventual Code of Practice will 'help drive attitudinal change and achieve fair treatment for all ages in the workplace'.[15] The CBI was opposed to legislation because 'the law is a blunt instrument to change outmoded attitudes'.[16]

In contrast there was strong support for legislation from the trade union participants in the consultation. The General Secretary of the Trades Union Congress (TUC) summed up the union point of view in a 1998 statement:

> *The TUC has long been concerned that the talents and experience of many older working people are being wasted as a consequence of prejudice and misconception. We have no wish to see all aspects of the employment relationship regulated by legislation. But in the case of age discrimination we consider that legislation similar to race and sex discrimination laws would be helpful in changing attitudes.[17]*

This preference for a legislative approach was supported by the trade unions who participated in the consultation exercise,[18] such as the General and Municipal Boilermakers Union (GMB) which stated that they:

> *were disappointed that the Government has not stuck to its manifesto commitment of legislation against age discrimination, and have concerns that a voluntary approach will not be sufficient to deal with this problem.*

The Report also stated that the fact that other countries had legislation was not conclusive and the effectiveness of that legislation 'was open to interpretation'.

The outcome of all this was that the Government rejected the statutory route and decided that its role was to provide a framework in which age

---

15   Mr John Cridland, CBI press release June 1999
16   CBI press briefing 16.11.1998
17   TUC press release January 30 1998
18   Including the TGWU, the GMB, MSF, UNIFI, NUT and the GMB

discrimination could be tackled. As part of this enabling policy it proposed to publish a non-statutory Code of Good Practice on Age Discrimination in Employment.

THE CODE OF PRACTICE

In November 1998, the Government published a consultation on a *Code of Practice for Age Diversity in Employment.* It is not at all clear how a proposed code of practice on age *discrimination* in employment became a draft code of practice on age *diversity* in employment. It perhaps reflected the Government's unwillingness to take effective action against the causes of discrimination. Rather, it appeared to be concerned with encouraging employers to realise the advantages of an age-diverse workforce and encouraging those employers to adopt policies that would achieve this. Indeed the Code itself listed the 'business benefits' of replacing 'unnecessary age criteria with objective, job-related ones. In short, these benefits amounted to:

1.   having a wider choice of applicants from which to recruit

2.   managing resources more effectively by minimising turnover

3.   being able to build a more flexible, multi-skilled workforce

4.   having access to a wider range of experience and expertise

5.   developing a better motivated workforce which feels valued and is willing to contribute to business success

6.   reducing costs through increased productivity and reduced levels of absenteeism.

It is quite an impressive list, but, of course, it did not take account of all the issues surrounding age discrimination, like those concerned with objectively justifying exceptions and retirement age. It seems in retrospect an odd way of approaching the problem and perhaps suggests that the Government did not take the issue as seriously as other forms of discrimination. One assumes that it would never have suggested that the best way to end race or sex discrimination was by encouraging employers to adopt policies which would create a gender or racially diverse workforce. In those cases legislation was an important contributor to changing attitudes, but this was not thought to be the case with regard to age discrimination.

The consultation on having an age code stated that the purpose of the Code was to help employers, employees and applicants by setting a standard and showing them how to eliminate age as a criterion for employment decisions. The Code set out some guidelines with respect to six areas:

- recruitment – on the basis of skills and abilities needed

- selection – on merit based on the application form and performance at interview

- promotion – based on ability, or demonstrated potential

- training and development – encouraging all employees to take advantage

- redundancy – based upon objective job-related criteria

- retirement – ensuring fair application.

In June 1999, the final version of the Code was published.[19] This substantially consisted of a fuller version of the previous draft version from the consultation exercise. It also published a companion set of guidance notes and case studies.

WINNING THE GENERATION GAME

Winning the Generation Game was a report produced in 2000[20] which suggested that workers have been stopped from making a contribution as they grow older by, amongst other measures:

- a view among society, employers and many older people themselves that they have less to offer - often based on demonstrably false prejudices;

- perverse incentives in occupational pension regimes that encourage employees and employers to come to early retirement arrangements;

- assumptions in the benefits and employment services, which tend to 'write off' older workers.

This report was about helping people to remain active in later life, which meant not writing off or excluding people from work, leisure or community participation. It was part of a Government project on active ageing, in which the Performance and Innovation Unit of the Cabinet Office was asked to look at the implications of the trend towards economic inactivity of people between 50 years and state pension age, and to identify whether the Government should

---

19   It was further updated in 2001
20   Performance and Innovation Unit, Cabinet Office

take action. The report's conclusions are revealing. It states what is perhaps obvious to many, but not to some who make such decisions:

> *The fact is that age is not a sound basis on which to judge ability to work or learn. Even though people change as they age, they do not all change in the same way, at the same speed or the same extent. Some will change for the better and some for the worse, and that judgment will in itself be different in respect of different activities. It is essential, therefore, that people should be judged on the basis of ability and not age. Moreover, insofar as it is possible (though potentially misleading) to assess older workers as a group, evidence shows that their productivity and return to employers is no different to younger ones.*

Research, according to the report, showed that British employers held views about both young and older people 'that are not supported by objective evidence'. Employers' stereotypical views about age affected decisions about recruitment, training, promotion and 'releasing workers'. It does seem an odd reflection upon later Government consultations where the views of employers result in having an important effect upon decisions concerning the Age Regulations, for example given this report's conclusions about employers' views and given the fact that the majority of private sector employers do not employ people over the age of 60 years it does seem odd that it is the employers' views about the need to keep a mandatory retirement age that have prevailed (see below).

The report then recommended more positive action by the Government and also considered the issue of voluntarism or legislation. It stated that the evidence internationally was not conclusive, but also pointed out that it would be equally difficult to demonstrate conclusively the impact of other anti-discrimination legislation. The conclusion was that age discrimination legislation would have a 'positive effect on British culture and would build, as other discrimination Acts have, on a growing sense of public interest and concern about the issue. Most importantly the report states that 'the absence of legislation on age, when it exists for gender, race and disability, sends a powerful message that age discrimination is taken less seriously'.

The report recommended that the Government should consider introducing legislation if an evaluation of the *Code of Practice* found that it had not been effective. It also recommended that this evaluation be transparent and command confidence.

The Government did publish in full the results of the evaluation.[21] Substantial numbers of employers were surveyed through 1999 and 2000. These surveys revealed once again the stereotypical views held by many employers[22]:

> Respondents were asked to indicate whether or not the specified attributes applied to older or younger workers, to both or neither. Stability, maturity, reliability, work commitment and good managerial skills were the most frequently stated attributes of older workers, while ambition, IT skills, creativity and a willingness to relocate were attributed to younger workers.

Encouragingly, one in three companies were aware of the Code of Practice[23], but, of these, only 23 per cent had actually seen a copy. More alarmingly perhaps, only 1 per cent of companies expected to make changes as a result of the Code. The report stated that the main reason for no change taking place 'is the belief that company policy or practice is already appropriate or that it currently meets government guidelines'. Age discrimination was generally rated as less important than other types of discrimination such as race, gender or disability. According to the analysis 'the lower rating was undoubtedly due, at least in part, to its lower profile and the fact that, unlike other areas, it is not covered by legislation'. The report suggested that there was a feeling that age discrimination at work was more acceptable or was perhaps something that was inherent in the workplace. Respondents made it clear that they expected that the Code would eventually be replaced by legislation and that much needed to be done to raise awareness of the issue. 'The Code', according to the report, 'although seen as paving the way is unlikely to achieve the effect on its own.'

A good example of discrimination being inherent in the workforce is in parts of the legal profession. An article in the Law Society Gazette[24] suggested that:

> Many legal employers consider it unrealistic to be expected to give out training contracts to people in their forties. Training costs a lot of time, money and effort, which may not be worth only ten or fifteen years of work in return.

One human resources director of a large city law firm was quoted in the same article as saying:

---

21 Evaluation of the Code of Practice on Age Diversity in Employment Final Report (2001)

22 Evaluation of the Code of Practice on Age Diversity in Employment Interim Summary of Results (2000)

23 Not surprisingly, awareness was much higher in large companies where almost two-thirds knew about the Code of Practice

24 Lewis (2001)

Of course we are ageist; offering training contracts to older applicants would have serious disadvantages. Our firm likes to think we can shape trainees into our particular mould; we have a certain style, we are known for it, we have a certain way of doing things. We just can't guarantee that older trainees would espouse that style.

The final evaluation report concluded that the Code was seen as a step in the right direction, but that respondents expected that the Code would eventually become law. The authors of the report stated that 'The researchers therefore conclude from the research, that there is a small but growing level of support for age discrimination legislation.'

SECOND CONSULTATION

In December 2001, the Government published a further consultation document titled 'Towards Equality and Diversity'.[25] It was concerned with implementing the Race Directive[26] and the Framework Directive.

Apart from a general summary of the approach to implementing these Directives, the consultation document contained one chapter[27] on some specific issues relating to age. This began with the statement that 'we intend to legislate to tackle age discrimination at work and in training'. This, of course, was a major step forward, which was the result of the adoption of the Framework Directive in 2000. It was also clear, however, that the voluntarist route had failed and that the only way in which age discrimination was going to be effectively tackled was through legislation. It is impossible to know whether the UK Government would have progressed to this stage without the requirement to implement the Framework Directive.

Towards Equality and Diversity was a document which was clear in its appraisal of what was likely to come. The justification for the proposed legislation was a business one. Diversity is good for business and anti-discrimination legislation is one part of achieving that diversity. It is this approach that consistently shaped the decisions reached by the Government in its progress towards the adoption of Age Regulations. The document stated, in relation to age, that 'we need to be clear about what we trying to achieve with legislation'. The answer was to identify and prohibit unfair practices based

---

25 *Towards Equality and Diversity; Implementing the Employment and Race Directives* (2001)
26 Directive 2000/43/EC of 29 June 2000 which concerned the principle of equal treatment between persons irrespective of racial or ethnic origin
27 Chapter 15

on discriminatory attitudes or inaccurate assumptions. There was, however, recognition that there may be differences in treatment that could be justified. These include firstly those initiatives that improve the opportunities of people to enter work or training and secondly those employment practices which can be 'clearly and objectively justified'. Thus 'a key goal' of the consultation was to identify which types of treatment are acceptable and which are not. The word 'acceptable' is an interesting one and perhaps identifies what objective justification is really about. It may be that it is really a concern to find such justification for practices which are held to be acceptable and can be justified in economic/business terms. The consultation was not about how to protect the human rights of workers as such, unless those human rights coincided with a business rationale.

The main issues were identified and views were invited on them. These issues were considered to be those related to direct and indirect discrimination; recruitment, selection and promotion; training; occupational requirements[28]; pay and non-pay benefits[29]; redundancy and retirement.

There were a total of 870 responses received to the consultation.[30] Of these, 583 responses came from organisations and 287 from individuals. The responses confirmed how widespread was discrimination based upon age. Some 50 per cent of respondents had either suffered age discrimination at work or had witnessed others suffering such discrimination. This discrimination took a variety of forms:

- being forced to retire at a certain age   22 per cent;

- not being given a job they applied for   18 per cent;

- being prevented from attending training courses   17 per cent;

- being told age was a barrier to general advancement   17 per cent;

- assumptions being made about abilities due to age   15 per cent;

- being selected for redundancy because of age   13 per cent.

---

28   The consultation document stated that 'The Directive provides for narrowly defined exceptions to be made where it is a requirement for a post to be occupied by someone of a particular age.'

29   Excluding the operation of occupational pension schemes and the use of age criteria in actuarial calculations

30   *Towards Equality and Diversity: Report of Responses on Age* (2003)

According to the consultation report, there were a number of contrasting views about how far the Government should go in implementing the legislation:

- the 'age lobby' wanted legislation to cover other areas apart from employment;

- 'age and other equality organisations' were concerned that implementing the Directive by secondary legislation, rather than statute, would undermine the authority of the Directive;

- the 2006 deadline for implementation was too far away;

- 'business' was concerned about the legislation undermining workforce planning and succession management;

- 'small businesses' were concerned about potential costs and how they would get support and advice;

- trade unions needed time to review collective agreements;

- professional bodies were concerned about the effects on their own activities – there might be implications for providers of group life assurance, income protection and so on.

Respondents suggested that there were circumstances under which age discrimination could be justified. Examples given were:

- if a job required a minimum age, such as driving or bar work

    30 per cent;

- if the return on training was not cost beneficial   30 per cent;

- if the work was of a very physical nature   21 per cent;

- health and safety grounds   18 per cent;

- if the job needed life experience, such as social work   18 per cent;

- if peers of a similar age were needed, such as holiday reps

    11 per cent

The majority of respondents were opposed to the use of age as a criterion in recruitment and promotion, although they were not opposed when considering redundancy or training opportunities, for example when a person was nearing retirement.

It is worth noting here how this whole exercise seemed to be carried out as a consultation about the effects on employers and generally the practical implications. There is little discussion about individuals' human rights. This perhaps displays the functional approach (see Chapter 1) to the issue, despite its non-functional or human rights justification.

THIRD CONSULTATION

In July 2003, the Government published its next consultation, *Age Matters*.[31] Again it is interesting to consider the approach as stated in the document. The proposals aimed to:

- strike the right balance between regulating and supporting new legislation through other measures designed to achieve culture change;

- achieve as coherent an approach as possible across all the equality strands, since that should reduce costs for business and bureaucracy for individuals.

It would have been refreshing if one of the aims had been, in accordance with the Directive, to protect and promote individuals' human rights not to be discriminated against on the grounds of age. Instead, we have a pragmatic approach that seeks to balance the effectiveness of legislation with the need not to impose too much of an extra burden in terms of costs or bureaucracy.

The Government proposed that new regulations would protect a variety of people:

- people at work, including agency workers and some self-employed people;

- people who apply for work;

- office holders appointed by the Crown;

- people undertaking or applying for employment-related training;

- people undertaking or applying for courses in further and higher education;

- in some circumstances, people who have left work or one of the types of training or education mentioned above;

---

31   *Equality and Diversity: Age Matters* (2003)

- people who are members of, or apply to, trade unions or professional bodies.

Direct discrimination, defined as occurring when a decision is made on the basis of a person's chronological age, and indirect discrimination, defined as happening when a policy or practice applies to everyone but causes disadvantage to a certain age group unless there are good reasons for it, were to be made unlawful.

It will be possible to treat people differently on the grounds of age if the employer can justify doing so by reference to specific aims which are appropriate and necessary. These aims could be:

- health, welfare and safety, for example the protection of younger workers;

- facilitation of employment planning, for example where a business has a number of people approaching retirement at the same time;

- the particular training requirements of the post in question, including those that have lengthy training periods and require a high level of fitness and concentration;

- encouraging and rewarding loyalty;

- the need for a reasonable period of employment before retirement.

Certain discriminatory laws may also be capable of objective justification; for example the national minimum wage where younger people receive a different rate can be justified because it helps younger workers to find jobs in competition with older workers.

The consultation document also contained a proposal for an alternative approach to just removing the mandatory retirement age. It is worth noting that the document quotes the Green Paper *Simpicity, Security and Choice*[32] as stating that:

> Under the Directive, compulsory retirement ages are likely to be unlawful unless employers can show that they are objectively justified.

Thus, there is likely to be a need for objective justification for any rule that makes it compulsory for an individual to retire at a certain age. The majority of respondents to the consultation had been opposed to allowing employers to retire employees at a certain age. The consultation proposed that compulsory

---

32 *Simplicity, Security and Choice: Working and Saving for Retirement* (2002)

retirement age be made unlawful but that employers could require employees to retire at a default age of 70 years, without having to justify their decision. How this differs from a mandatory retirement age is difficult to comprehend. It is difficult to see how it could have been justified as a proper implementation of the Directive. How would the Government have been able to justify the age of 70 years in some future legal challenge. Why 70, rather than 69 or 71? (For further discussion on retirement age issues see Chapter 5.)

Other proposals in the consultation document were that the age restrictions on making a claim for unfair dismissal should be removed (except of course for the moment when an employee is retired) and that the age-related aspects of the basic award element of unfair dismissal compensation be removed. Perversely the Government also then proposed to keep the 20-year limit on the length of service that counts towards the basic award, thus continuing to discriminate against younger and older people. A similar approach was also proposed for statutory redundancy payments, which contained a significant age element, where half a week's pay is given for each year of service between the ages of 18 and 21 years, one week's pay[33] for each year of service between the ages of 22 and 40 years and one and a half weeks' pay for each year of service between the ages of 41 and 65 years, although there was a steep tapering off of benefits for the year before retirement age. The age limits were to be removed, but, in an astonishing piece of parsimony the Government proposed changing the payment to one week's pay per year of service for everyone. This had the effect of removing the age differential, but potentially made the situation worse for every worker over the age of 41 years who would see their entitlement cut.[34] This appeared to be in contradiction of Article 8.2 of the Framework Directive which states that:

> The implementation of this Directive shall under no circumstances constitute grounds for a reduction in the level of protection against discrimination already afforded by Member States in the fields covered by this Directive.

In addition, the consultation proposed making provision for employers to be able to justify recruitment upper age limits which could be objectively justifiable (it is interesting that the document did not refer to minimum age limits) and also seniority practices which otherwise may be indirectly discriminatory. These included practices which may be based upon length of service or experience, such as longer holidays, incremental pay and long-service awards.

---

33 Subject to the statutory maximum for a week's wage
34 See Chapter 8 for what was in the final version of the Regulations

CONSULTATION RESPONSE

The response to this consultation was published in 2005.[35] This was the final statement of views before the publication of the Age Regulations. Generally, the 427 respondents welcomed the proposals to outlaw age discrimination, but there were clearly uncertainties and differences of opinion. This may be partly a result of the Government only consulting on the economic/business case for legislation, rather than any other more fundamental approach. Difficulties generally that were listed included:

- difficulties in understanding how one could justify direct discrimination and indeed the fact that it was possible in the first place;

- the proposed specific aims which might justify differences in treatment[36] were supported by employers and employer organisations, but opposed by the TUC, other than any concerned with the health and safety of young workers. This a division that repeats itself elsewhere in regard to the retirement age;

- whether there should be an upper age limit on training and education opportunities. Such upper limits were opposed by a number of organisations, including the Policy Research Centre on Ageing and Ethnicity which wanted the abolition of the upper age limit of 54 years for student loans in higher education. An opposing view was put by employers who were concerned about financing training or education within too soon a period before the employee was due to retire;

- several trade unions expressed the view that retaining a lower rate for the national minimum wage was discriminatory;

- a number of unions and others favoured extending the legislation to include goods and services.

The document also discussed issues around the retirement age, which are further discussed in Chapter 5. A majority of respondents[37] were in favour of a default retirement age, although almost two-thirds were against having that age set at 70. Some 82.4 per cent of respondent employers opposed a higher default age.

---

35 *Equality and Diversity: Age Matters Age Consultation 2003 Summary of Responses* (2005)
36 Health, safety and welfare; facilitation of employment planning; the particular training requirements of the post in question; encouraging and rewarding loyalty; the need for a reasonable period of employment before retirement
37 Yes – 51.8 per cent; no – 42.9 per cent

When it came to unfair dismissal and redundancy payments, there were a large majority of respondents in favour of removing the age aspects of redundancy payments and the basic award for unfair dismissal.[38] There was also a large majority who thought that an employer who dismisses employees on the grounds of retirement should be able to defend the dismissal as fair.[39]

Almost three-quarters of respondents were in favour of allowing employers to apply an upper age limit to recruitment if they could justify doing so by reference to aims set out in the legislation. A number of organisations responded by connecting the upper age limit to issues of retirement. If there were no mandatory retirement age, then it would be more difficult to justify having an upper age limit on recruitment. Lastly, the document looked at pay and non-pay benefits where a large majority (77.7 per cent) of respondents were in favour of a justification defence for basing some pay and benefits on length of service or experience, even though it might amount to direct discrimination.

It is self-evident that if you set the agenda in a certain context, then the responses to a consultation such as this will be within that context. The Government context was a business one which perhaps balanced the needs of the business community with its own longer-term programme of encouraging diversity in employment. In order to encourage this diversity there may need to be exceptions made to the general principle of non-discrimination. To do otherwise would, according to this standpoint, inhibit the development of an age diverse workforce. Sometimes exceptions are made, therefore, which are to the long-term benefit of the group affected by these exceptions. There is an almost irresistible attraction to this argument. There is a default retirement age in order to save the dignity of employees, so that they do not end their careers going through a disciplinary or dismissal procedure because of their failing competence. Employers are to be allowed to make exceptions to facilitate staff planning, so that young people will be able to enter workforces, albeit at the expense of the older worker. Training opportunities can be withheld from older workers because there is not enough time for the employer to gain an adequate return on their investment. How different the approach might have been if one started from a human rights perspective, where each individual has the right not to be discriminated against for reasons connected to group stereotyping.

---

38 74.3 per cent in favour of removing the age elements of the basic award; 79.1 per cent in favour of making service below the age of 18 count for the purposes of redundancy payments
39 66 per cent in favour; 30.5 per cent against

FOURTH CONSULTATION

In 2005, the Government published its draft Age Regulations which fulfilled all the fears of those who were unhappy with the business agenda being followed by the Government.

Published at a very similar time was a series of case studies of employers and the pending age discrimination legislation.[40] The report stated that many human resource managers identified a number of potential benefits from reducing age discrimination. These included 'skills and knowledge retention, organisational stability, depth of experience, better management, reduced training and recruitment costs, matching staff and customer profile, and the fact that people would no longer be written off'. Even the HR managers were of the view, however, that some discriminatory practices were acceptable. There were though mixed views about the impact of any possible abolition of the contractual retirement age, although one felt that it would help improvements in the management of older workers. Employers, according to the report, identified four areas of concern about the proposed age regulations. These were, firstly, that they should be clear so that the need for litigation was limited; secondly, that any potential conflicts between the age regulations and other areas of employment law and Government policy should be eliminated (worries included the relationship with the TUPE[41] Regulations, any prohibition on age-based pay systems and the national minimum wage); thirdly, that there should be general exemption from length-of-service awards; and lastly, that there should be comprehensive guidelines.

The draft Regulations allowed for important exceptions and included a default retirement age of 65 years. These draft Regulations and the changes which took place in the final Regulations are discussed in Chapter 8. It is worth recording here, however, the deep differences that existed between the employers and trade unions in response to the draft Regulations

Evidence that the Government had adopted an employers' agenda in dealing with age discrimination was provided by the responses to the 2005 consultation on its draft age regulations, called *Coming of Age*. The CBI stated in its response:

> *The Age Matters and Coming of Age consultations, as well as the ongoing dialogue that has been conducted with employers and other parties, have been highly beneficial in producing draft regulations*

---

40   *The age dimension of employment practices: Employer case studies* (2005)
41   Transfer of Undertakings (Protection of Employment) Regulations 1981

that take business concerns into account as well as combating age discrimination.

The Engineering Employers Federation (EEF) also responded by saying that:

The EEF is pleased to record its appreciation that the DTI has listened to many of the concerns of employers in formulating the draft Employment Equality (Age) Regulations.

In contrast, the Trades Union Congress (TUC) stated that:

The responses of the TUC and the unions to previous consultations have been effectively rejected;

whilst another trades union, NATFHE[42], stated that:

Our overall response to the draft age regulations is one of great disappointment. An opportunity to right some of the historical inequalities related to age has been largely squandered in an effort to keep those employers who are not committed to age diversity from protesting.

One of the major objections of the TUC was around the ability of employers to objectively justify continuing discriminatory practices. These were thought to be too wide and that there should be a list of specific exceptions, rather than some 'sweeping general justification', which was seen to be the Government taking the 'lazy option'. One of the specific exceptions that were included, namely the continuing justification of paying young workers a lower national minimum wage, was thought to 'constitute blatant direct discrimination against young adult workers'. There was also a major concern that employers would 'level down' employee rights and benefits in order to ensure that they were not discriminating. The TUC wanted a 'no levelling down clause' in the Regulations to stop this practice.

The CBI's major concern centred on the retirement age. Its view was that the right to retire staff at 65 years was a 'vital management tool'. Employees must not be allowed to challenge the decision to retire a person at the proper age. This was also the concern of the EEF which was concerned that employees should not be able to challenge the presumption of retirement. It was concerned that if an employer allowed some employees to work beyond retirement age that this would be used by other employees as evidence that their dismissal was for other reasons relating to the individual, apart from retirement. The rather

---

42   National Association of Teachers in Further and Higher Education

strange solution proposed by the EEF was to put the onus on the employee to prove that retirement was not the principal reason for his or her dismissal.

The CBI, in contrast to the TUC, was in favour of an exception being made for the paying of lower rates to younger workers. The CBI wanted it extended to more than the national minimum wage stating, quite correctly, that one of the odd outcomes of the Regulations was that an employer who paid more than the national minimum wage but who still treated younger workers differently would be guilty of age discrimination, whilst the employer who stuck to the national minimum wage would not be so guilty.

The Government published its summary of responses to the 2005 consultation.[43] There were altogether 392 responses. The breakdown of responses is instructive because of the Government's continued use of stating how many respondents were in favour or against particular recommendations:

Table 2.1 Responses to 2005 consultation by type of respondent

Type of respondent	Number
Business organisation	162
Public body	63
Educational	34
Trade union	35
Legal	38
Member of the public	60

Generally speaking there was a welcome for the Regulations, but disappointment from some trade unions about the weakness of the Regulations. There was a really interesting point of view raised by both Age Concern and by the Chartered Institute of Personnel Management (CIPD). This was that the tone of the consultation document was essentially negative. According to Age Concern, it accentuated the things that employers will be permitted to do, rather than on what was unlawful. Similarly, the CIPD suggested a list of what's not exempted rather than a long list of what is. The problem of course is that in contrast to other discrimination measures there is a long list of exemptions to be covered.

---

43 *Equality and Diversity Coming of Age Report on the Consultation on the draft Equality (Age) Regulations 2006* (2006)

There was particular concern about the retention of the national minimum wage. According to the report 'the unions were practically as one in their conviction that workers aged 18–21 years should be able to claim the adult rate of pay in their particular job or that age-related provisions should be done away with altogether'. This of course was not a view share by employers. Indeed the CBI argued that there should be protection for employers using age-related pay rates which were different to the levels of the national minimum wage.

Although there was a general welcome for the Regulations there was concern, according to the report, that they would 'give rise to difficulties in their implementation'. The areas of concern are shown in the summary table in the report (Table 2.2):

Table 2.2   Extent of concern about future difficulties

Question	Yes	No	No strong feelings
Will the approach to 'objective justification' cause difficulties?	136	56	46
Will the approach to service-related pay and benefits cause difficulties?	32	71	37
Will the approach to the retirement cause difficulties?	162	55	14

In contrast, the majority of respondents took a more positive view about the arrangements concerning unfair dismissal, occupational pensions and statutory redundancy payments.

One statement which concludes chapter 3 of the consultation report was:

Employers in general thought the Regulations went too far whilst unions, organisations for older people and other organisations that were not primarily employers, were of the opinion that they didn't go far enough.

European Perspectives and the Framework Directive

There is ample evidence that discrimination takes place in the EU. One EU-wide indicative survey[1] of people's perceptions of discrimination[2] found that the most often cited ground for discrimination was age (5 per cent) followed by racial or ethnic origin (3 per cent), religion or belief, physical disability, learning difficulties or mental illness (2 per cent each). In the same survey people were asked which of the following would have the most difficulty in finding a job, training or promotion:

- a person from another ethnic origin

- a person with minority beliefs

- a physically disabled person

- a person with learning difficulties

- a person under 25

- a person over 50

- a homosexual.

Some 87 per cent of respondents thought those with learning difficulties would be the most disadvantaged and some 77 per cent thought that the physically disabled would be the next most disadvantaged. In third place was the over 50-year-old; some 71 per cent thought that such a person would have less chance. There was a significant variation between countries though ranging from 17 per cent in Greece to 83 per cent in Finland. The fourth choice, for information, was the person from another ethnic origin.

This diversity between countries was also reflected in the European Survey of Working Conditions 2000[3] where about 4 per cent of those surveyed reported age discrimination at work as occurring in the previous 12 months. This ranged from only 1 per cent in Denmark to some 14 per cent in Austria.

---

1   Marsh and Sahin-Dikmen (2003)
2   In relation to racial or ethnic origin, religion or beliefs, disability, age and sexual orientation
3   Reported in *Live Longer, Work Longer* (2006)

DEMOGRAPHIC CHANGE

Current United Kingdom policy is, of course, essentially determined by the European Union. The European Commission has been concerned about the demographic change that is taking place and its impact upon the labour market and future plans for growth of the European economy. In 1995, the Commission produced a report on the demographic situation.[4] Its opening title sums up some of the prejudices about ageing, when it stated, 'Demographic ageing must not be confused with a decrepit society'. This process resulted from two major trends:

- the scope for couples to decide how many children they have and when they should have them;

- social and medical progress which has resulted in a longer lifespan and a drop in mortality.

Improvements in life expectancy was initially achieved by reducing infant mortality. Now it was being improved by people living longer, so that children who reached their first birthday were unlikely to die before the age of 60. The result of this was that just lumping together people over a certain age as 'the elderly' was unsatisfactory. There were now two distinct groups: firstly, the retired who are in full possession of their mental and physical abilities and who are well integrated into the economy; secondly, those who are really 'biologically aged' with reduced independence and high dependence upon external resources for their support. The increase in numbers in both of these groups has important outcomes. The result of this in number terms was that the number of young people aged under 20 will fall by 9.5 million (11 per cent), the number of working age people will decline by 13 million (6.4 per cent) and the number of retired adults will increase by over 37 million (50 per cent). This, of course, is partly explained by the arrival of the 'baby boomers' (born from the late 1940s to the middle 1960s) into retirement. This change will have an effect on the economy of the EU and the individual Member States.

One astonishing indicator of the economic burden resulting from demographic change internationally is to look at the ratio of the retired to workers. In the OECD area[5] the ratio in 2000 was about 38 retirees for every 100 workers. This is projected to grow by 2050 to just over 70 retirees per 100 workers. 'In Europe, this ratio is projected to be close to one retiree for every worker.'[6]

---

4   *The demographic situation in the European Union* (1995)
5   Some 35 countries in the Organisation for Economic Co-operation and Development
6   *Live Longer, Work Longer* (2006)

One solution for maintaining, or increasing growth, is to increase the level of employment. The 1995 report illustrated the issues in relation to employment in what was a clear precursor of the Lisbon Strategy adopted in 2000 (see below):

1. the proportion of active women over the age of 15 is significantly lower than the equivalent figure for men, especially amongst older age groups;

2. the young are particularly affected by unemployment;

3. the impact of early retirement means that there are only half as many workers in the 60–65 year age group as in the 55–59 year age group.

The population change for the EU was not uniform in each country, although the overall trend is common:

Table 3.1   Population growth in the EU (per cent) between 1995 and 2025

Country	Under 19 years	20–59 years	60+ years
Austria	-11.4	-3.1	+56.4
Belgium	-9.8	-6.1	+46.1
Denmark	+2.6	-3.0	+41.5
Finland	-5.2	-4.1	+66.6
France	-6.1	+0.2	+57.7
Germany	-12.1	-13.5	+51.2
Greece	-2.06	+0.5	+41.4
Ireland	-25.1	+2.7	+67.7
Italy	-19.4	-15.2	+40.7
Netherlands	-1.2	-1.2	+79.5
Portugal	-8.8	+5.0	+34.1
Spain	-17.2	-4.4	+45.3
Sweden	+1.2	+3.7	+38.1
United Kingdom	-8.2	-2.8	+43.6

For the EU as a whole, the number of young adults (25–39 years) started to decline in 2005 and the decline will accelerate (to -16 per cent between 2010 and 2030). The number of 40- to 54-year-olds will start to decline from 2010 whilst the number of people aged over 55 will grow by 9.6 per cent between 2005 and 2010, and by 15.5 per cent between 2010 and 2030.[7]

Clearly the effects of the demographic change will be felt at different times in different parts of the EU. Some countries were expecting a short-term gain in the population of working age, such as Ireland and Portugal. Other countries have a much more serious short-term problem, such as Italy and Germany where there are significant falls in the youngest age group and the working age population, combined with large increases in the older age group.

The European Commission later summed up the concerns posed by the ageing population.[8] There was:

- a relative decline of the population of working age and the ageing of the workforce;

- pressure on pension systems and public finances resulting from a growing number of retired people and a decline in the working-age population;

- a growing need for old-age care and health care – the big increase in numbers of the very old will lead to a growth in demand for formal care systems;

- a growing diversity among older people in terms of resources and needs – there will be differences in the family and housing situation, educational and health status and income and wealth which will determine the quality of life of older people;

- the gender issue – women account for almost two-thirds of the population above 65 years.

Thus, there were to be significant policy issues concerned with, firstly, the European employment strategy in order to bring about an increase in the employment rate of older workers; secondly, with social protection policies, including reversing the trend towards early retirement; thirdly, health policies which include giving special attention to medical and social research relating to ageing; and fourthly, policies concerned with discrimination and social exclusion, including measures to be taken under Article 13 of the Treaty.

The Commission's conclusions were:

---

7   Green Paper, *Confronting demographic change: a new solidarity between the generation* (2005) 94
8   *Towards a Europe for all Ages* Communication from the Commission COM(1999)

The magnitude of the demographic changes as we enter the 21ˢᵗ century will force the European Union to rethink and change outmoded practices and institutions. An active society for all ages requires a strategy which both enables and motivates older people to stay involved in working and social life. The growing number of older people constitutes a wealth of under-utilised experience and talent. They also create new needs to be met by enterprises, public organisations and NGOs.

Opportunity Age was a document published by the UK Government[9] to set out its framework strategy for managing the demographic change which is predicted for the United Kingdom. The background to this strategy, according to the document, is that: firstly, people are living longer so that the average man, by 2051, of 65 years will have a further 22 years of life compared with only 12 years in 1950; secondly, long term improvements in health mean that more people will survive until the age of 65 years; finally, there is a long-term decline in the birth rate as people choose to have fewer children or none at all. The result of this is that by 2051 people over 65 are likely to make up a quarter of the population.

Part of the strategy is to increase both the post-50 employment rate and the average retirement age. The employment rate for men between 50 and the state pension age, for example, had fallen drastically. In 1979 it was 84.1 per cent. By 1995 this figure had fallen to 63.3 per cent. The Government estimated that this drop in the employment rate resulted in 2.6 million individuals in this age group who were not working. Although this trend has now been reversed, it is still estimated that only 42 per cent of men are still in work by the age of 64 years. The Government's strategy is to have another one million older people in work as a contribution to achieving an overall employment rate of 80 per cent. There are a number of strategies designed to achieve this. One is the tackling of age discrimination and another is a 'long-term aim to consign fixed retirement ages to the past'.

THE LISBON STRATEGY

In March 2000, the EU Council of Ministers at the Lisbon Spring Council Meeting adopted a strategy to raise the rate of growth and employment. A major factor in this was the poor performance of the EU economy compared to that of the USA as well as a concern with the emerging economies of Asia.

---

9   *Opportunity Age* (2005); it is in two volumes, the first, *Meeting the challenges of ageing in the 21ˢᵗ century* outlines the policy; the second, *A social portrait of ageing* provides a snapshot of trends and evidence

The Community set itself the target of becoming 'the most dynamic and competitive knowledge-based economy in the world, capable of sustainable economic growth with more and better jobs and greater social cohesion, and respect for the environment'.

The key challenges for the EU were global competition, the forthcoming enlargement and the ageing population. Europe was more likely to be successful if it worked together rather than tackling the issue from an individual Member States perspective. It was a policy of combining economic growth with a concern to advance social cohesion. The EU wanted to be a high-productivity, high-value-added, high-employment economy, rather than a low-pay, low-productivity one, in order to maintain its commitment to social and environmental Europe.

The Lisbon Strategy called for:

1.   increasing the total employment rate to 67 per cent by 2005 and 70 per cent by 2010;
      increasing the female employment rate to 57 per cent by 2005 and 60 per cent by 2010;
      increasing the employment rate of older workers to 50 per cent by 2010;

2.   defining a multi-annual programme on adaptability of business, collective bargaining, wage moderation, improved productivity, lifelong learning, new technologies and the flexible organisation of work by 2002;

3.   removing disincentives for female labour force participation;

4.   adapting the European social model to the transformation towards the knowledge economy; facilitating social security in cross-border movement; temporary agencies directive; sustainability of pension schemes; open method of coordination in the field of social protection;

5.   eradicating poverty; social inclusion; specific target groups.

According to a review of the strategy,[10] progress had been disappointing. This had been because of the burst in the 'dot.com boom', the effects of the 11 September 2001 attacks in the USA, the increase in oil prices and the poor performance of national economies. There had been some successes as some Member States have stepped up their active labour market policies;

---

10   *Facing the challenge: the Lisbon Strategy for growth and employment* (2004)

employment rates had risen from 62.5 per cent in 1999 to 64.3 per cent in 2003. In addition seven Member States had met the interim target of a 67 per cent employment rate by 2005, and the employment of older workers had reached 41.7 per cent. The review stated that the 2010 targets, including that of a 50 per cent employment rate for older workers, were unlikely to be reached. This was partly because of new economic challenges from Asia, including India, and partly because of declining birth rates and rising life expectations. By 2050 the total working age population will be 18 per cent less than in 2005; and numbers over age 65 will have increased by 60 per cent.

The matter was also an issue at the Stockholm European Council meeting in 2002. In response to that meeting, the European Commission agreed on increasing labour force participation and promoting active ageing.[11] This report showed that 31.1 per cent of the working-age population in the EU was inactive (that is, 50 million women and 22 million men). Many of these wished to work now and, over a five-year perspective, some 56 per cent of inactive men and some 49 per cent of inactive women wished to return to work. The issue for the Commission was the availability of work of the right type and quality. The lower the quality[12] of the work then the higher the drop-out rate to inactivity. The majority of older people wished to continue working but the type of job and conditions were not available to help them do this.

Thus, changing attitudes, amongst other measures, was essential in order to raise the level of participation. The Commission concluded that:

> *Raising participation rates will not be easy, partly because it will depend on changes in cultural and socio-psychological factors, in particular attitudes to older people in employment, and partly because it will require important changes in policy instruments to achieve changes in behaviour of employers and workers.*

IMMIGRATION

One way of mitigating the effects of an ageing population is to, at least partially, fill the gaps in the labour market with immigrant workers. Many of the statistics that one reads about the ageing population do not appear to take into account the effects of inward migration. The EU's perspective is that although

---

11   Report requested by Stockholm European Council: *Increasing labour force participation and promoting active ageing* (2002)

12   Meaning lack of training, lack of job security or low pay/productivity

managed immigration will help, it will not solve the problems associated with demographic change.

Immigration is, thus, unlikely to solve the problem, but it may mitigate it. As the European Commission Green Paper on *Confronting demographic change*[13] stated:

> *Immigration from outside the EU could help to mitigate the effects of the falling population between now and 2025, although it is not enough on its own to solve all the problems associated with ageing, and it is no substitute for economic reforms.*

The same Green Paper points out that there has never been economic growth without population growth. Ways of increasing population growth include a higher birth rate and inward migration. Immigration has clearly mitigated the effects of population decline or ageing in some countries, but from an EU perspective the migration of workers from the post-2004 Member States to the rest of the EU may help some Member States like the United Kingdom, but only adds to the population decline in those migrant exporting States and makes no difference at all to overall EU statistics. Indeed, one analysis showed that about one-third of all non-nationals living in Member States were citizens of other Member States of the EU.[14]

Using immigration as the sole means of reducing the impact of ageing on the labour market is not a realistic choice. Massive increases in immigration until 2030 would be required. Estimates suggest that the annual net migration into the EU was of the order of 850 000 per annum during the 1990s. The annual inward migration necessary to keep the support ratio (4.3 persons of working age to one person aged 65 plus) at the same as in 1995 would be 15 times greater than the 1990s levels. Indeed, according to the UN estimates, by 2040–2050 in some scenarios there would be a need by the EU for net immigration equivalent to half the world's annual population growth.[15]

As the migrant population would also be ageing, it may only put off the problem rather than solve it.[16] In any case there would be other social and economic issues concerned with integration that would need to be tackled if there were to be such an increase.

13 Green Paper *Confronting demographic change: a new solidarity between generations* (2005); see also
    Green Paper *On an EU approach to managing economic migration* (2004)
14 *First annual report on migration and integration* (2004)
15 *Replacement migration: is it a solution to declining and ageing populations?* (2000)
16 *Immigration, integration and employment* (2003)

THE FRAMEWORK DIRECTIVE

The justification for Directive 2000/78/EC establishing a general framework for equal treatment in employment and occupation was Article 13 of the EC Treaty, introduced by the Treaty of Amsterdam 1998. This states simply:

> *Without prejudice to the other provisions of this Treaty and within the limits of the powers conferred by it upon the Community, the Council, acting unanimously on a proposal from the Commission and after consulting the European Parliament, may take appropriate action to combat discrimination based on sex, racial or ethnic origin, religion or belief, disability, age or sexual orientation.*

It is interesting to note that Article 13 does not confine the 'appropriate action' to that of employment only. The Framework Directive, however, only applies to 'employment and occupation' with regard to discrimination on the grounds of religion or belief, disability, age or sexual orientation. In contrast, Directive 2000/43/EC implementing the principle of equal treatment between persons irrespective of racial or ethnic origin, introduced at much the same time, was not restricted to employment.[17] This latter Directive included such matters as social security and health care, and access to and supply of goods and services, including housing.[18]

Sex discrimination was excluded from the Directive, because the Commission believed that the appropriate legal basis for such action was Article 141 EC Treaty[19], from which a number of Directives dealing with equal treatment had already been adopted.[20]

The Framework Directive has been subject to some criticism for having an outdated approach. Professor Hepple[21] stated that:

> *The main defects are that it lacks clarity and perpetuates a fragmented and inconsistent approach to different grounds of discrimination; it is limited to employment and occupation so placing a burden on employers which they cannot be expected to discharge unless corresponding duties are placed on providers of education, healthcare and transport; it is based only on negative prohibitions against direct and indirect discrimination*

---

17   For more discussion about a possible hierarchy of discrimination see Chapter 1
18   Article 3 Directive 2000/43/EC
19   See *Proposal for a Council Directive establishing a general framework for equal treatment in employment and occupation* (1999)
20   Such as Directive 76/207 EEC on the implementation of the principle of equal treatment between men and women; subsequently amended by Directive 2002/73/EC
21   Hepple (2001) at the Nuffield Foundation

and harassment rather than positive duties to promote equality; and
it focuses on individualised retrospective fault finding rather than a
strategic approach.

It is difficult not to agree with these criticisms in relation to action on age discrimination. The Framework Directive is part of a fragmented approach to discrimination as it is essentially one of three directives (race and equal treatment directives) making such discrimination unlawful. These directives are inconsistent in their scope, but sometimes search for consistency where it may not be needed. It does not impose a positive duty to end discrimination. The Directive also distinguishes between those aspects of age discrimination which are undesirable, and should, therefore, be made unlawful, and those aspects which are desirable, and should, therefore, be permitted. One study sympathetic to this approach stated

...age distinctions based upon unfair assumptions and stereotypes are
undesirable but other distinctions upon the grounds of age are rooted in
rational considerations that are not incompatible with the recognition
of individual dignity, serve valuable social and economic objectives, and
often are designed to benefit particular age groups.[22]

This, of course, is true. The difficulty is where to draw the line between those distinctions which are desirable and those which are undesirable. It is also important to accept that both sides of the dividing line consist of discriminatory measures. It is just that, according to this view, some discriminatory measures are 'rational', 'serve valuable economic and social objectives' and benefit 'particular age groups'. This illustrates the different approach to age when compared to other grounds of discrimination. It is unlikely that it would be acceptable to use terms such as these when referring to gender or race.

Despite this, the Directive is a huge leap forward and, as a result of its adoption, at least 25 countries in Europe will make some aspects of age discrimination unlawful, as well as taking action on the other grounds of disability, religion or belief and sexual orientation. As a result of this Directive, the United Kingdom has regulations which outlaw some aspects of age discrimination, only a few years after the Government firmly adopted a voluntarist and non-coercive approach.

---

22 O'Cinneide (2005)

THE PREAMBLE

In Chapter 1 there was some discussion about the contradictory approaches to age discrimination contained in the Directive. On the one hand there is a human rights/equal treatment/fundamental rights justification contained in paragraphs 1–6 of the preamble. There is then a more functional/economic/ business rationale which dominates much of the rest of the preamble. This is clearly stated in paragraph 11 which states that discrimination on the various grounds 'may undermine the objectives of the EC Treaty'. These objectives are 'a high level of employment and social protection, raising the standard of living and the quality of life, economic and social cohesion and solidarity and the free movement of persons'.

In the rest of the preamble there are a number of specific areas that are excluded[23] from the scope of the Directive and it is worth noting these. They are:

- social security and social protection schemes whose benefits are not treated as pay, nor any other form of state payment related to providing access to employment or maintaining employment (paragraph 13);

- national provisions laying down retirement ages (paragraph 14); the United Kingdom, unlike some other Member States, did not have such provisions. Apart from the state pension age, most retirement ages are a matter of individual contracts (see Chapter 5);

- the recruitment, promotion, maintenance in employment or training of an individual who is not competent, capable and available to perform the essential functions of the post concerned or to undergo the relevant training (paragraph 17).

  This was a major issue for employers in the 2003 Government consultation. There was a lot of concern that it would be difficult to dismiss older workers whose competence was failing. Indeed, keeping a default retirement age was seen as a way of not having to tackle this issue as older employees would automatically leave when this age was reached:

- the armed forces, the police, the prison or emergency services are not required to recruit or keep in employment people who do not have the required capacity to carry out the range of functions required of them (paragraph 18);

---

23 Only those that are relevant to age are listed here

- in addition each Member State is left to decide whether to apply the rules to all or part of their armed forces (paragraph 19);

- where there is a genuine and determining occupational requirement (paragraph 23) (see below);

- differences in treatment which can be justified in relation to 'legitimate employment policy, labour market and vocational training objectives' (paragraph 25) (see below).

Most of the other provisions of the preamble are reflected in the individual articles of the main text. It is worth noting that paragraph 28 states that the provisions in the Directive lay down the minimum requirements and that Member States have the option of introducing or maintaining more favourable provisions. The European Commission believes that some Member States have introduced more favourable measures and indeed 'this has involved the introduction of an entirely new, rights-based approach to anti-discrimination legislation and policy'.[24] The United Kingdom, however, has introduced its Age Regulations in accordance with the European Communities Act 1972. Section 2(2) of this Act, of course, only permits the use of Regulations to implement Community law and there are no provisions for such Regulations to go beyond the provisions of that law. Paragraph 28 also states that:

> The implementation of this Directive should not serve to justify any regression in relation to the situation which already prevails in each Member State.

This was an issue with the Government's proposals to equalise the amount of statutory compensation given for redundancy to one week's pay (subject to the statutory maximum) for each year of service, regardless of age. This replaced an age-based system which gave workers over the age of 40 more compensation than their younger colleagues, namely one and a half weeks' pay per year of service over that age. The Government's initial proposal to reduce it to one week for everyone appeared to be a regression as far as older workers made redundant were concerned.

DIRECT AND INDIRECT DISCRIMINATION

The purpose of the Directive is set out in Article 1 as being to lay down a general framework for combating discrimination and putting into effect the principle of equal treatment. This is virtually identical to Article 1 of the

---

24 *Equality and non-discrimination in an enlarged European Union* (2004)

Race Directive (2000/43/EC). It is interesting that the Commission's original proposal for Article 1 copied the model set out in the Equal Treatment Directive (76/207/EEC) and spelt out the areas to which the principle of equal treatment would apply; namely 'access to employment and occupation, including promotion, vocational training, employment conditions and membership of certain organisations'. These specific areas were moved into a separate article (Article 3) covering the scope of the Directive in the final version and replaced with a general commitment to anti-discrimination and the principle of equal treatment here.

As has been suggested elsewhere,[25] it is important to realise that the Framework Directive only provides a minimum level of protection. This minimalist approach is especially evident with regard to age.[26]

The principle of equal treatment here means, according to Article 2, that there should be no direct or indirect discrimination on the grounds of age. [27] Thus Article 2.2(a) states that direct discrimination shall be taken to occur where one person is treated less favourably than another in a comparable situation. When one relates this to age, of course, there may be a variety of problems:

- There may be an issue where one may not be comparing like with like. Is the treatment of a 20-year-old to be compared to the treatment of a 65-year-old in all circumstances (except where a legitimate exception can be objectively justified)? Perhaps the answer is yes, but there must be a certain unease that maybe the 20-year-old requires more development, training, protection and so on when compared to someone who may have been at work for 40 years plus. On the other hand perhaps this view is the result of ageist thinking and they are both employees who should not be

---

25 See Whittle (2002)

26 With regard to disability there is also, of course, an important duty on employers in Article 5 to make reasonable accommodation

27 Another aspect to this, of course, is that the principle of equal treatment can justify the equally bad treatment of a class of employees. In *Zafar v Glasgow City Council*, for example, an Employment Tribunal held that an individual had been treated less favourably than others because the individual had been subject to treatment falling far below that of a 'reasonable employer'. This presumption of less favourable treatment was not allowed to stand because, hypothetically, if the employer was not a reasonable employer, then he or she may treat all employees in an unsatisfactory way, so that it was not possible to state, therefore, that an individual had been treated less favourably. This approach to equal treatment requires employers to be consistent in their treatment of employees, not to treat them 'better' as a result of any anti-discrimination legislation. As long as all employees are treated in a similar manner, then it may not be possible to show less favourable treatment.

discriminated between, provided they are, in the Directive's words, 'in a comparable situation'.

- Another aspect is that (see Chapter 4) age groups are changeable and that during a normal lifetime one may expect to progress through a whole range of different age groups and experience different amounts and types of discrimination. As a result of this it might be difficult to assume that the interests of all in any particular age group are similar or that the experiences of those in any particular age group are similar. It may be that the 'less favourable' approach might have been better replaced with a test of someone suffering some detriment as a result of actual or perceived age.

- Age is also closely linked with other grounds of discrimination (see Chapter 7) and there may be issues concerning whether a person has been treated less favourably on the grounds of age or whether other reasons might act as a cover for age, or indeed whether age might act as a cover for something else or might act as a re-enforcer of discrimination on some other ground. It may be difficult at times to isolate an inference of age discrimination.

Examples of situations where other courts have accepted an inference of direct age discrimination have been:[28]

- a marked statistical difference in success rates for different age groups in apparently similar circumstances;

- comments that indicate an intention to discriminate;

- mismatch between formal selection criteria and those criteria applied in practice;

- language in advertisements;

- discriminatory questions asked at interview.

These, of course, are indications of discrimination that apply to other areas apart from age.

There is no need for a comparator to actually exist. Article 2(a) refers to comparison with another who 'has been or would be treated in a comparable situation'. Thus, it is possible to use a hypothetical comparator. Deciding who or

---

28 O'Cinneide (2005); drawing upon information about the Irish, Dutch and Slovakian experiences

which group is to be the hypothetical comparator may not be as straightforward as in gender or race cases.

Indirect discrimination is a more complex subject and has been an issue around which the effects of the mandatory retirement age in relation to sex discrimination has been considered by the courts in Great Britain (see below). Article 2.2(b) states that indirect discrimination is:

> *taken to occur where an apparently neutral provision, criterion or practice would put persons having a particular age at a particular disadvantage with other persons, unless*

> *(i) that provision, criterion or practice is objectively justified by a legitimate aim and the means of achieving that aim are appropriate and necessary.*

This is the same approach as in the Race Directive (2000/43/EC).

This definition is different to the original one proposed by the Commission in the 1999 document. According to the Commission, this definition was a result of the case law of the European Court of Justice in cases involving the free movement of workers,[29] in particular the decision in *O'Flynn v Adjudication Officer*. In this case the complainant was a migrant worker who was refused a funeral grant because such grants were only available to those which took place in the United Kingdom. The Court stated:

> *Unless objectively justified and proportionate to its aim, a provision of national law must be regarded as discriminatory if it is intrinsically liable to affect migrant workers more than national workers and if there is a consequent risk that it will place the former at a particular disadvantage. It is not necessary in this respect to find that the provision in question does in practice affect a higher proportion of migrant workers. It is sufficient that it is liable to have such an effect.*

Relying upon this the European Commission had proposed a definition which had said that indirect discrimination had been taken to occur when an 'apparently neutral provision, criterion or practice is liable to affect adversely a person, or persons to whom the grounds ... applies'. This definition was the subject of some debate before the House of Lords Select Committee of the EU where the Commission representative defended it as removing the need

---

29   See 1999 proposals for the Directive

to demonstrate statistically that indirect discrimination had occurred.[30] This was a view supported by others in their evidence to the Committee.[31] There were also critics of this view. Professor Hepple argued that it 'completely misunderstands what indirect discrimination is ... indirect discrimination is practiced against a group ... but cannot apply to an individual'. Mr Robin Allen is also reported as stating that the Commission had 'lost the comparative element that needs to be in there'. As a result of its deliberations, the House of Lords Select Committee stated that 'the definition of indirect discrimination as it stands is unacceptable'. It urged the Commission to adopt a definition based on that found in the Burden of Proof Directive.[32] This referred to a provision, requirement or practice which disadvantages a 'substantially higher proportion of one sex'.[33] Thus, the group element and the comparative requirement are included. In the event the Commission did change the definition to include these elements, so the definition in the Framework Directive refers to 'persons' having a particular age compared to the singular version of 'a person'.

As a result of the need to show a disparate impact as between groups, the issue of statistics is important in indirect discrimination cases. The Commission had put forward its proposals to lessen reliance upon such statistics, although the House of Lords had responded by stating that 'the courts have already shown themselves ready to interpret purposively the concept of indirect discrimination so as to lessen the reliance on statistics'. Their importance continues as shown in, for example, *Seymour-Smith*[34] in which the House of Lords gave judgment in a long-running case that had begun with the dismissal of the applicants in 1991. The House of Lords had referred the case to the ECJ for guidance, amongst other matters, on the legal test:

> *for establishing whether a measure adopted by a Member State has such a degree of disparate effect as between men and women as to amount to indirect discrimination for the purposes of Article 119 [now 141] of the EC Treaty unless shown to be based on objectively justified factors other than sex.*

The ECJ responded[35] by stating that the first question, when attempting to establish whether there was indirect discrimination, was to ask whether the

---

30 *EU Proposals to combat discrimination* (1999)
31 According to the Report the Council for Racial Equality described it as 'broader, more workable and more accessible'
32 Council Directive 97/80/EC on the burden of proof in cases of discrimination based on sex OJ L14/6, 20 January 1998
33 Article 2.2 Directive 97/80/EC
34 *R v Secretary of State for Employment, ex parte Seymour-Smith and Perez (No 2)*
35 Case C-167/97 [1999] IRLR 253 at p. 278.

measure in question had a more unfavourable impact on women than on men. After this it is a question of statistics. This means considering and comparing the respective proportions of men and women that were able to satisfy the requirement of the two-year rule. The ECJ further stated:

> it must be ascertained whether the statistics available indicate that a considerably smaller percentage of women than men is able to satisfy the condition of two years' employment required by the disputed rule. That situation would be evidence of apparent sex discrimination unless the disputed rule were justified by objective factors unrelated to any discrimination based on sex.

In this case, the House of Lords decided that the statistics did not indicate a significant difference, although it was accepted that such measures should be reviewed from time to time.[36] The Government argued, as objective justification for the measure, that it would encourage recruitment as some employers were reluctant to employ new staff because of the lack of such a rule. This argument appeared to be accepted by the court, although it is somewhat ironic that the final decision was given some time after the qualifying period was reduced to one year with little apparent affect on recruitment.

In *Rutherford v Secretary of State (No.2)* (see below for further consideration), the issue of statistics was considered in a case where a man complained that the inability to claim unfair dismissal and redundancy payments[37] after retirement age were indirectly discriminatory on the grounds of sex. His argument was that a considerably higher proportion of men worked after the age of 65 compared to women and that, therefore, these rules indirectly discriminated against men. The Court of Appeal followed the approach taken in *Seymour-Smith* by insisting that the Employment Tribunal should have primarily compared the respective proportions of men and women who could satisfy the age requirement, that is, the entire workforce between the ages of 16 and 65.[38]

A further issue arises because the definition of indirect discrimination refers to persons of 'a particular age'. Colm O'Cinneide[39] questions how this meaning relates to an 'age group' for the purposes of indirect discrimination. He gives

---

36   The need to assess provisions periodically in the light of social developments was made by the ECJ in *Commission v United Kingdom* [1984].

37   Sections 109 and 156 ERA 1996

38   The House of Lords subsequently upheld the decison of the Court of Appeal, but disagreed with the reasoning, see [2006] IRLR 551 HL.

39   O'Cinneide (2005); drawing upon information about the Irish, Dutch and Slovakian experiences

the example of a claimant alleging that a requirement that applicants possess a particular skill (for example computer skills) puts persons of his particular age at a disadvantage. In such a situation should the relevant age group be:

- all those persons of the same chronological age;

- all those of a similar age;

- all those of a similar/identical age who are potential applicants for the job;

- all those of a similar/identical age with a similar educational background;

- all those of a similar/identical age resident in a particular geographical area; or

- some other group?

These questions, of course, arise in decisions on comparisons concerning other grounds for discrimination. What makes age different is 'the fluid nature of age groups and the constantly shifting comparisons that can be made between different age groups, presenting difficulties in identifying suitable comparators'.[40]

JUSTIFICATION

Article 2.2(b)(i) provides a defence of justification. This can be where the provision, criterion or practice is 'objectively justified by a legitimate aim and the means of achieving that aim are appropriate and necessary'. This is further discussed below, but it is worth noting that the Commission, in its 1999 proposals, further explained the situation:

> The emphasis on objective justification in cases of indirect discrimination is put on two elements. Firstly, the aim of the provision, criterion or practice which establishes a difference in treatment must deserve protection and must be sufficiently substantial to justify it taking precedence over the principle of equal treatment. Secondly, the means employed to achieve this aim must be appropriate and necessary.

Thus, there can be objective justification for a difference in treatment between groups if the difference in treatment:

- deserves protection;

- is sufficiently substantial for it to take precedence over the principle of equal treatment;

---

40   Ibid.

- the means for achieving this difference in treatment are both appropriate and necessary.

It is for the employer to justify the difference in treatment, if necessary, in accordance with Article 9 of the Directive on the Burden of Proof.[41]

In the case of *Werner Mangold*,[42] the European Court of Justice considered a situation where German law allowed for the employer to conclude, without restriction, fixed-term contracts of employment with employees over the age of 52.[43] There were issues connected to the Fixed-term Workers Directive, but also with regard to the age aspects of the Framework Directive on Equal Treatment. The purpose of the German legislation, according to the national government, was to encourage the vocational integration of unemployed workers. The Court agreed that such a purpose could be 'objectively and reasonably' justified. The question then was whether this legitimate objective was 'appropriate and necessary'. The problem was that the national legislation applied to all people over the age of 53 and not just to those who were unemployed. The Court concluded:

> *In so far as such legislation takes the age of the worker concerned as the only criterion for the application of a fixed-term contract of employment, when it has not shown that fixing an age threshold, as such, regardless of any other consideration linked to the structure of the labour market in question or the personal situation of the person concerned, is objectively necessary to the attainment of the objective pursued. Observance of the principle of proportionality requires every derogation from an individual right to reconcile, so far as is possible, the requirements of the principle of equal treatment with those of the aim pursued.*

Thus, it was on the grounds of proportionality that the Court held the measure to be not in accord with Community law and it seems difficult to disagree with that conclusion. Taking away the employment protection rights from employed older workers was not appropriate and necessary when introducing a measure to help unemployed older workers. What is alarming about this case is the easy acceptance by the Court that the measure was objectively justifiable in the first place. It is possible to take away the rights to employment protection of older workers who become employed for some social objective, however laudable. It is a reflection of the fault with Article 6 of the Framework Directive

---

41 Directive 97/80/EC
42 *Mangold v Helm*
43 This is, of course, a simplification, but the purpose here is to concentrate on the aspects of the decision concerning age discrimination

which allows age discrimination when it is necessary for some other legitimate objective.

The Court also stated that the Framework Directive did not in itself lay down the principle of equal treatment in the field of employment and occupation. Its purpose was, according to Article 1, to lay down a general framework for combating discrimination on the various grounds. The source of the underlying principle was to be found in other international instruments and the 'constitutional traditions common to the Member States' and the principle of non-discrimination on the grounds of age must, thus, be regarded as a general principle of Community law.

HARASSMENT

Article 2.3 provides that harassment is another form of discrimination. Harassment has a similar meaning to the definition in the Equal Treatment Directive (76/207/EEC as amended)[44] and the Race Directive. It occurs when there is unwanted conduct which takes place for the purpose or effect of violating a person's dignity or of creating an intimidating, hostile, degrading, humiliating or offensive environment.

There is also, of course, the possibility of protection under the Protection from Harassment Act 1997. Section 7(2) states that 'references to harassing a person include alarming the person or causing the person distress'. It is clear that this needs to happen on more than one occasion.[45] *Majrowski v Guy's and St Thomas's NHS Trust* concerned an allegation that an employee was bullied, intimidated and harassed by his departmental manager. He took proceedings on the grounds that the treatment amounted to harassment under the Act and that the Trust was vicariously liable for the actions of the manager. The Court of Appeal agreed that the employer was vicariously liable but the judgment also raised another intriguing issue. The Court stated that:

> *The issue arises not only where one employee in the course of his employment, harasses another employee, but where an employee, in the course of his employment, harasses an outsider, such as a customer of his employer or some other third party with whom his work brings him into regular contact. It is thus likely to be a risk incidental to employment.*

---

44   Articles 2.2 and 2.3
45   Section 7(3) Protection from Harassment Act 1997; see also *Banks v Ablex Ltd*

It is an interesting piece of speculation to imagine a customer or supplier bringing an action for harassment against an employer because an employee has harassed them on the grounds of their age.

INSTRUCTION TO DISCRIMINATE

An instruction to discriminate against persons on the grounds of age will be deemed to be a form of direct or indirect discrimination.[46] This is intended to stop discrimination by third parties on behalf of the employer. One example might be with employment agencies used by employers to supply permanent and/or temporary staff. An express or implied instruction to only supply candidates within a particular age range will effectively discriminate against others on the grounds of age. Presumably also instructing an advertising agency only to place recruitment advertising in certain journals, which appeal to a particular age group, might also be seen as an instruction to discriminate.

FURTHER EXCEPTIONS

Article 2.5 provides that the Directive is without prejudice to 'measures laid down by law which, in a democratic society, are necessary for':

- public security

- the maintenance of public order

- the prevention of criminal offences

- the protection of health

- the protection of the rights and freedoms of others.

It is not altogether clear why this clause was included. It does not appear in the Race Directive. One can imagine, however, some parts of this being used to justify discrimination on the grounds of age. The first is with regard to 'public security and the maintenance of public order'. Age limits on membership of the armed forces, the police and the fire service might be justified, although the armed forces exception is included in Article 3.4. Whether it might be possible to only justify 'active' roles in these professions, rather than all roles, remains an issue. There are also serious issues perhaps in relation to the private sector. Will it be possible, for example, to restrict the employment of older workers in the private security sector because of the perceived need to have younger workers to deal with issues related to the 'prevention of criminal offences'?

---

46   Article 2.5

The exception that might be of greatest concern is that linked to 'the protection of health'. This can mean the protection of young workers with exceptions being made to their working hours, breaks and so on as in the Working Time Regulations 1998.[47] It might also justify discrimination against younger workers for the same reasons. Older workers might also be vulnerable as generalised employer concerns about competence and age lead to such workers being prevented from carrying out their work, thus restricting their employment opportunities.

SCOPE

The Directive applies to both the public and the private sector and has a wide scope, albeit limited to the areas of employment and vocational guidance and training. In particular it applies to:

- conditions for access to employment, self-employment or to occupation, including selection criteria and recruitment conditions;

- all types of activity and at all levels of the professional hierarchy, including promotion;

- access to all types and all levels of vocational guidance and vocational training, including practical work experience;

- employment and working conditions;

- pay;

- dismissals;

- membership of, or involvement in, workers' and employers' organisations, including any benefits provided;

- any organisation whose members carry on a profession, including any benefits provided.

The Directive also specifically excludes:

- payments of any kind made by state schemes, including social security or social protection schemes;

- the armed forces, at the Member State's discretion.

Thus, the scope is wide, but it is still limited to the fields of employment and vocational training. Age discrimination has a more limited scope than those

---

47 SI 1998/1833

measures concerned with sex and race. The Race Directive, for example, includes all the areas of application as for age, but also includes social protection, such as social security and health care, social advantage, education and access to and supply of goods and services which are available to the public, including housing.[48]

The argument as to whether age discrimination is different to other forms of discrimination, such as those concerned with gender or race, is an interesting one.

There appears to be a hierarchy of protection whereby governments rank discrimination in some order of importance. It might be possible to hypothesise that there is such a hierarchy, with race and ethnic origin perhaps being given widest reach, with disability and age amongst others being given the narrowest scope of operation, that is, in employment only.[49] Such a hierarchy might reflect the relative importance placed upon the different areas of discrimination as a result of a political imperative. One could also argue with some justification that age appears to be at the bottom of the hierarchy given that there are likely to be significant areas of exclusion even in relation to employment.

The advantage of distinguishing sub-groups is that questions about equal treatment and equal approaches between the groups can be asked and, as a result, it may be possible to justify differences of treatment. It has been argued that there are categories of discrimination grounds that are different from each other with perhaps three groups.[50] The first group is where the categories are unchangeable, such as race; the second can be referred to on some biological basis such as sex, age and some disability; the third category reflects a chosen lifestyle such as religion or sexual orientation. Whether one agrees with these categorisations or not, they do illustrate the possibility of taking a different approach to each group. Separating into groups such as this, however, may reinforce a hierarchical approach and lead to different solutions to ending discrimination with reference to particular groups which weaken any application of the principle of equal treatment.

Another answer may be that all the rules have been adopted pragmatically and individually and there is a superficial acceptance of a uniform approach with certain exceptions. Others have also argued that the formal equal treatment

48   Article 3.1 Race Directive 2000/43/EC
49   Fredman (2001)
50   Schiek (2002)

approach apparent in the Directives may be an insufficient concept to deal with more subtle forms of discrimination.[51]

If vocational training is included in the scope of the legislation, then why not health as well? A person's ability to receive adequate and continuing health protection and cure is closely linked to his or her employability. Older workers may need more curative health care and younger workers perhaps more preventative health care. To discriminate on the grounds of health against any group on the basis of their chronological age is to possibly inhibit their prospects of work and their prospects within work.

OCCUPATIONAL REQUIREMENTS AND JUSTIFICATION OF DIFFERENCES OF TREATMENT ON THE GROUNDS OF AGE[52]

Articles 4 and 6 of the Framework Directive provide for the exceptions to the principle of equal treatment as they apply to age. Article 4.1 states that Member States may provide that a difference of treatment which is based on a characteristic related to age shall not constitute discrimination where such a characteristic 'constitutes a genuine and determining occupational requirement, provided that the objective is legitimate and the requirement is proportionate'.

The House of Lords Select Committee[53] pointed out that it was strange to say that a difference of treatment based on such a characteristic did not constitute discrimination. Such a difference of treatment is discrimination, but it is permissible discrimination because it can be justified within the terms of this definition. It has been pointed out that this might benefit the protected group in some cases.[54] One example might be in the travel business where those operating 18–30 holidays would prefer their reps to be in the same age group. In the same way those operating holidays for those over the age of 50 might also prefer reps in this age group. The problem with applying this sort of logic to age is that one person's discrimination is another person's justification. Both of these age group justifications discriminate against the other group on the basis of age.

Article 6 then takes this further. It actually provides for specific exceptions to the principle of equal treatment. Firstly, it again states that differences of

51 *Critical Review of Academic Literature Relating to the EU Directives to Combat Discrimination* (2004)
52 Article 5, which is missed out here, is concerned with reasonable accommodation for persons with disabilities
53 Ninth Report
54 Whittle (2002)

treatment on the grounds of age shall not constitute discrimination under certain circumstances. The reality is that these differences of treatment do constitute age discrimination but such discrimination is to be allowed under certain circumstances. They must be:

> *objectively and reasonably justified by a legitimate aim, including legitimate employment policy, labour market and vocational training objectives.*

In addition, the means of achieving the aim must be 'appropriate and necessary'. It is not clear what 'legitimate employment policy' means. The result is that the ultimate boundaries of age discrimination legislation are to be left to the courts with, one suspects, a large amount of litigation and uncertainty whilst the courts search for the boundary definitions.

Article 6 then continues to give some specific examples of differences in treatment which could be justified. Age discrimination is the only ground of discrimination in the Framework Directive that receives this special attention of having its own specified lists of areas where discrimination is to be justified. The list is:

(a)   the setting of special conditions on access to employment and vocational training, employment and occupation (including dismissal and remuneration conditions) for young people, older workers and persons with caring responsibilities in order to promote their vocational integration or ensure their protection.

These differences in treatment could, of course, be positive as well as negative; so extra protection for young workers in terms of working hours, health and safety and so on might be justifiable here. What is perhaps most interesting, apart from the lack of definition, is the groups affected, namely young workers, older workers and those with caring responsibilities. Who is a young person? Who is an older worker? Those aged in between are not a subject of these allowable exceptions. There is no interpretive article in this directive, so it will be left to the courts to decide in each circumstance presumably, somewhat adding to future uncertainties;

(b)   the fixing of minimum conditions of age, professional experience or seniority of service for access to employment or to certain advantages linked to employment.

One wonders what the effect of removing the word age from this area of justified discrimination would be. Clearly there are some jobs which require certain levels of experience or seniority of service, but why cannot these be quantified without the use of age in the criteria. There are some jobs which might just require some 'life experience', but this needs to be justified. The inclusion of a minimum age must be wrong because it assumes that experience and knowledge is gained at a uniform rate amongst the population, which is self-evidently untrue;

(c)   the fixing of a minimum age for recruitment which takes into account the training period and the need for a reasonable period of work before the individual retires.

This difference of treatment assumes a retirement age which will limit a person's working life and therefore limit the return that an employer might receive in return. This rule might become more complex if mandatory retirement ages did not exist.

When discussing similar proposals before the House of Lords Select Committee (see above) EurolinkAge stated that this Article would 'not produce any clear benefits for older workers in Europe who currently suffer from age discriminatory practices'. The list is non-exhaustive.[55]

The Commission representative stated that this Article:

was designed to fix clear limits, to insist on the principles of objective justification, necessity and proportionality, and to give some indicative examples in order to clarify the type of exception which is envisaged, and provide certainty concerning the most widespread and clearly justified examples.

The UK Government had a similar vision. The Minister for Employment told the House of Commons European Standing Committee, reviewing the proposed Directive, that:

The Government have welcomed the proposal. It is important to establish minimum standards to combat discrimination at work throughout the whole European Community. The key to tackling discrimination, however, is not just the aspiration to end it ... It is essential to ensure workable and proportionate mechanisms that deliver redress effectively. Otherwise we risk introducing a parody of proper standards and unnecessary litigation. Such an outcome would undermine the

---

55   The list is headed by the statement 'Some differences of treatment may include, among others.'

> *confidence of the public, employers and employees, whose support is*
> *essential to the effectiveness of the measures.*

It is difficult not to interpret this as a statement of minimalist standards and that it is a result of considering age discrimination differently to the other grounds contained in the Directive and elsewhere.

Article 6.2 provides that retirement ages can be fixed for the purposes of admission to or retirement from social security and invalidity benefits, and the use of ages for actuarial purposes in such schemes.

Professor Hepple has argued for the provision of a non-exhaustive list by the British Government of specific exceptions to the principle of equal treatment. He quoted examples of a genuine occupational qualification; minimum age requirements for training or employment, maximum age limits for training.[56]

POSITIVE ACTION

Article 7.1 provides that the principle of equal treatment will not stop Member States from maintaining or adopting specific measures 'to prevent or compensate for disadvantages' linked to age.

Positive action is not positive discrimination of course. The limits for the latter have been drawn by the European Court of Justice in relation to other grounds of discrimination. A good example of this was in *Badeck*[57] where a rule, introduced by a regional authority in Germany, to ensure equal access for men and women in public sector jobs was considered. The European Court of Justice held that the Equal Treatment Directive (76/207/EC) and the principle of equal treatment did not preclude such a rule. It was acceptable to take positive action so that where male and female applicants had equal qualifications, then priority could be given to the female applicant. Positive discrimination would have, of course, enabled the employer to select female candidates with lesser qualifications than men.[58]

Positive action is a term that includes measures designed both to counter the effects of past discriminatory practices and to assist members of the protected group to compete on an equal basis with those not in the protected group. This may include, for example, the encouragement of applications from the

---

56   Hepple (2001)
57   *Application by Badeck and others*
58   See also *Marschall v Land Nordrhein-Westfalen*

disadvantaged group, through extra advertising; or the provision of special training opportunities for employees in the disadvantaged group.

This is not a positive obligation upon Member States but only a discretionary option which might be taken up in particular circumstances. It is, therefore, a weak power which may not be an important factor in tackling age discrimination. This is because, in contrast to other forms of discrimination, there is much age discrimination to be allowed, some of which may be positive discrimination by favouring one group over another.[59] In relation to age where the whole working population is the protected group, positive action for one age group may result in negative effects for other age groups. Thus, a decision to only recruit younger employees in the interest of long-term staff planning will have an effect on older applicants. This will not be a case of helping the protected group in contrast with those not in the protected group; it is a case of advantaging one part of the protected group against another part of the same group.

MINIMUM REQUIREMENTS

There are two aspects to this.[60] One is the opportunity for Member States to introduce or maintain provisions which are more favourable to the principle of equal treatment than that which is required by the Framework Directive. The other is that Member States are forbidden to use the Directive as a means of, or justification for, a reduction in the level of protection already offered in the Member State concerned.

There is little likelihood of the first happening in the United Kingdom. The Age Regulations are introduced under powers in Section 2 of the European Communities Act 1972 which do not empower the Government to go beyond that which is contained in the Directive which is being transposed. An example of the second aspect was the proposal by the Government to level out the amount of entitlement for redundancy payments to one week's pay per year of service for all age groups. On the face of it, this was a measure reducing the amount of discrimination between the different age groups, so that all received the same entitlement. In practice, of course, it reduced the amount of entitlement due to those over the age of 41 years from one and a half week's pay per year of service to one weeks' pay per year of service.[61]

---

59 The duty on employers to make adjustments for disabled employees and applicants is, of course, an exception to this and is an example of using positive action to combat historic discrimination

60 Articles 8.1 and 8.2

61 Subject to the statutory maximum for a week's pay

REMEDIES AND ENFORCEMENT

Article 8 is concerned with access to justice and ensuring that there are adequate judicial and administrative procedures to allow persons, who consider themselves affected by a failure to apply the principle of equal treatment to them, to enforce their rights under the Directive. National provisions on time limits for initiating action are not affected by this.

The Directive[62] also provides that Member States shall ensure that

> *associations, organisations or other legal entities which have, in accordance with the criteria laid down in national law, a legitimate interest in ensuring that the provisions of this Directive are complied with, may engage, either on behalf or in support of the complainant, with his or her approval, in any judicial and/or administrative procedure for the enforcement of obligations under this Directive.*

This is an expansion of the proposal in the Commission's 1999 document and provides for the possibility of organisations taking up and pursuing cases on behalf of an individual or individuals. This is important because it excludes the possibility of class actions being taken on behalf of unnamed individuals or groups. The new Human Rights Commission will be able to intervene and pursue cases, as will presumably other bodies that have a 'legitimate interest', such as trade unions. The TUC's spokesperson[63] before the House of Lords Committee[64] stated that it would be useful 'in circumstances when it was a difficult case and an individual might find it too stressful, or when it was a case that tested a particular point in law'.

Once cases have been initiated, then the burden of proof[65] is as that provided for in the approach of the Burden of Proof Directive[66], namely that the complainant need only establish facts 'from which it may be presumed that there has been direct or indirect discrimination'. It is then for the respondent to show that there has been no breach of the principle of equal treatment. The wording used is identical to that used in Article 4.1 of the Burden of Proof Directive. The same words are used in Article 8 of the Race Directive.

This is a powerful weapon when trying to show that discrimination has taken place. In *Igen Ltd v Wong* for example, the Court of Appeal stated that

---

62 Article 8.2
63 Kay Carberry
64 See above
65 See Article 10.1
66 Directive 97/80/EC, which applied to sex discrimination

Employment Tribunals were required to go through a two-stage process. The first was for the applicant to prove facts from which the Tribunal could decide, in the absence of an adequate explanation, that the respondent had committed, or is to be treated as having committed, an act of discrimination. The Employment Tribunal is being asked to make assumptions which may not subsequently turn out to be true when the second stage is reached. The fact that there is no adequate explanation is enough to shift the burden of proof to the respondent. Thus, in the second stage, the respondent needs to show that they did not commit, or are not to be treated as having committed, the unlawful act. If they fail to do this then the Tribunal will decide in the complainant's favour. There is a high standard for the respondent as in order to discharge the burden of proof, they have to show, on the balance of probabilities, that the treatment was 'in no sense whatsoever' on the grounds of sex.[67] The Court stated that 'no discrimination whatsoever' was compatible with the Burden of Proof Directive.

It is clear that a consistent approach to the burden of proof on all grounds of discrimination is to be encouraged, so it is likely that cases such as *Igen* will be used in age discrimination cases, thus placing a significant task on employers to show that their treatment was 'in no sense whatsoever' on the grounds of age. Hypothetically, this might require employers to show dramatic changes of policy as a result of the Regulations. If an employer has a long history of making employment decisions on the basis of age quite lawfully, then, unless there has been an overt change in policy, that history presumably will be a contributory factor in showing evidence that the employer has committed an unlawful act.

Victimisation of individuals as a result of making a complaint or bringing an action on the protected ground is also unlawful. Member States are required to introduce measures that ensure the protection of employees against dismissal or any 'other adverse treatment' by the employer, as a reaction to a complaint or any legal proceedings that have been concerned with enforcing compliance of the principle of equal treatment.[68] The wording in the Race Directive is not quite the same as that in the Framework Directive. Article 9 of that Directive requires the introduction of measures to ensure protection 'from any adverse treatment or adverse consequences'. This may be a result of the wider scope of the Race Directive, in that it applies to more than just employment matters. Certainly, the European Commission guide to its 1999 proposals on the Framework Directive pointed out that fear of dismissal was one of the major obstacles to employees

---

67   The Burden of Proof Directive concerned sex discrimination
68   Article 11

taking action or making a complaint, which is why it is specifically mentioned in Article 11.

Sanctions for failure to comply with the national measures are to be 'effective, proportionate and dissuasive'. These may include, according to the Framework Directive, payment of compensation to the victim.[69]

In respect of other measures, the Directive states that any laws, regulations or administrative provisions contrary to the principle of equal treatment are abolished. Also, any provisions contrary to this principle which are contained in contracts or collective agreements, or internal rules for trade unions, employers' organisations and so on are to be declared null and void.[70] The reference to contracts presumably includes contracts of employment. Thus, any provisions of a contract of employment that are contrary to the principle of equal treatment as regards to age are to be declared null and void. This is a potentially important tool for challenges against inadequate implementation of the Directive by the UK Government. A contract of employment which contains a retirement age, or a default retirement age in accordance with the UK Age Regulations, must be challengeable on the basis that it contravenes the principle of equal treatment as it allows the dismissal of employees merely because they have reached a certain chronological age (see Chapter 5).

INFORMATION AND DIALOGUE

Article 11 of the Framework Directive requires the Member States to ensure the provisions of the national rules 'are brought to the attention of the persons concerned by all appropriate means, for example at the workplace'. There is, therefore, a need to publicise and disseminate information about the Age Regulations. The Commission regards this as important because:

> The principle of equal treatment needs to be fully understood and accepted as desirable for society, ensuring that decisions are taken on an objective basis, thereby promoting stability and social coherence. The more effective the system of public information and prevention is, the less need there is for individual remedies.[71]

So it is not just about disseminating information; it is also about making sure that the principle of equal treatment is both understood and accepted. This requires a much more positive approach by Government. The benefit, according to this quote, is that this acceptance will lead to less need for individual complaints and presumably litigation because employers and employees will

---

69 Article 17, which is identical to Article 15 of the Race Directive
70 Article 16
71 Taken for the 1999 consultation on the proposed Framework Directive

accept that the principle of equal treatment applies to age as well as the other grounds in the Directive!

Somewhat unsurprisingly, the Government representatives at the House of Lords European Committee[72] objected to this and another Article[73] in the Directive which requires national governments to promote a dialogue with the social partners[74] with a view to fostering equal treatment in such matters as monitoring workplace practices, collective agreements, codes of conduct and through research. The escape clause for the British Government is that this dialogue should take place in accordance with national traditions and practice. For the United Kingdom this might mean minimal social dialogue on these issues. This attitude was exemplified by the Home Office spokesperson at the House of Lords Committee who stated that the Directives:

> *should not prescribe in so much detail in terms of how we … go about, for example, negotiation with the social partners which would cut across well-established practices that we have in this country.*

The spokesperson for the Department for Education also stated that matters concerning dissemination and information were 'best decided at the national level'.

In addition to the above, there is an obligation to encourage dialogue with appropriate non–governmental organisations which have a 'legitimate interest' in the fight against discrimination.[75]

THE MISSING ELEMENTS

The Race Directive has a requirement, in Article 13, for Member States to set up an independent body for the promotion of equal treatment with regards to racial or ethnic origin. The same is true of the Equal Treatment Directive in relation to discrimination on the grounds of sex. It is odd that the Framework Directive has no such requirement with regard to the other grounds of discrimination. This is not an issue in the United Kingdom where there is to be one body covering all the proposed grounds, but it may be an issue elsewhere in the European Union. It may be that the model of one or more independent bodies may not be correct for all Member States, but it does seem to weaken the enforcement provisions if there is not even to be an equivalent organisation.

---

72   See above
73   Article 13
74   Employers and trade unions
75   Article 14

The second element missing may be the absence of any provision to give public authorities or employers a positive duty to promote the principle of equal treatment. In the United Kingdom, there is such a duty imposed in relation to some of the grounds of discrimination, but by no means all. Why isn't there a duty on all employers and public authorities to promote equal treatment on all the grounds, including age? This would be better than the alternative approach which is concerned with an adversarial process based upon retrospective fault finding.[76]

Implementation of the age aspects of the Framework Directive has presented a particular challenge to some Member States as most did not have any existing general legislation concerning age discrimination.[77] There are two contrasting 'models or patterns' that have emerged in the way that Member States have faced up to these difficulties.[78] One pattern or model has been to directly enact the provisions of the Directive, using the same or very similar words. This has happened in Italy, Cyprus and Greece as well as Denmark, Austria, Slovakia and Slovenia. The alternative model or pattern is to indulge in elaborate debate as to how the age aspects of the Directive might be fully integrated into national law. This debate tends to be difficult and complex as in Belgium, Germany, Netherlands and the United Kingdom.

---

76   This is a point made to the House of Lords Committee by Professor Bob Hepple
77   Cormack and Bell (2005)
78   Ibid.

CHAPTER 4
Age Discrimination at Work

There are a number of features associated with age discrimination, in contrast to other grounds. These are:

- Everyone has an age, but everyone's age is different. This is not entirely true of course, because some people are born at the same time and many are born near to each other in terms of days or months so as to make no difference. What is being suggested here is that the entire population of the United Kingdom and indeed the world has an age. The Directive and the Age Regulations apply to the entire population of the United Kingdom who are in work or applying for work. There is no other ground of discrimination about which this can be said.

- Despite almost everyone being in this protected group, there are many subdivisions. Younger workers may have different experiences of discrimination in comparison to older workers. Although, therefore, it is correct to talk about age discrimination, it would perhaps be more useful to talk about the sub-groups such as:

  - young age discrimination (16–24 years)

  - middle age discrimination (25–49 years)

  - older age discrimination (50–SPA[1])

  - senior age discrimination (over SPA).

- In the majority of cases, although sadly not all, workers will not only have an age but they will at some time in their lives be a member of each of these sub-groups in turn, although never more than one at a time.

It could be argued that each of these sub-groups has certain characteristics and might equally suffer from direct or indirect discrimination or harassment at work in relation to their age. It might be that the numerous exceptions which can be objectively justified, or currently exist, can only be understood (or properly opposed) by looking at these groups in turn and trying to consider

---

1   State pension age

what age discrimination they might suffer from and what measures might be needed.[2]

YOUNG AGE DISCRIMINATION

Not so long ago I met a distinguished labour lawyer from the United States and described to him what was proposed in terms of age discrimination legislation in the United Kingdom and the European Union. He was astonished that it was proposed to include young people as part of the protected group. In the United States it is only those over the age of 40 years who are protected. My American colleague could not understand how young people could be thought of as being discriminated against in the same way as older people. The point is that the sort of discrimination suffered by young people, because of their age, may be different to that suffered by older people but it may still constitute direct or indirect discrimination and harassment. What is certainly true is that the outcomes of the discrimination may be different for young people in contrast to older ones. One analysis[3] looked at the 16–19-year-old age group and their reason for leaving their last job. The biggest reason, accounting for some 36 per cent of the group was that they resigned. Whatever the reason for the resignation, there was enough confidence amongst the age group to voluntarily leave their existing job. Whether it was to go to another job or not, this is not an option so readily available to older workers. The same analysis, when it looked at why people in their 50s left their last job, found that only 8 per cent did so through resignation. The problem for this latter group is that leaving a job often means leaving the workforce forever because of widespread age discrimination in recruitment practices. None of this is to say that young people do not suffer age discrimination, only to say that it might be different and might have different consequences to age discrimination suffered by some older age groups.

For the sake of convenience this group is identified as everyone who is over school leaving age and under 25 years. Those of working age who are in this age group are distinguishable from other young workers because many of them are in education and, as a result, a large proportion of this group work part-time.

The 2001 census revealed the population figures by age group in Table 4.1.

---

2   My inspiration for this Chapter and for taking this approach comes from a publication of the Employers Forum on Age called *Age at Work: the definitive guide to the UK's workforce* published in 2005; work done in 2004

3   See *Age at Work* (2005).

Thus, the 15–19-year-old group make up roughly 6–7 per cent of the population, with a slightly smaller number of 20–24-year-olds. The 2001 census also revealed the ageing population when for the first time there were more people over the age of 60, than there were people under the age of 16.[4]

Table 4.1   Population statistics for those aged 10–24 (2001)[5]

Age range	Total	Male	Female
10–14	3 880 557	1 987 606	1 892 951
15–19	3 663 782	1 870 508	1 793 274
20–24	3 545 984	1 765 257	1 780 727

The employment statistics from the Labour Force Survey in Table 4.2 reveal the following about young persons' employment:[6]

Table 4.2   Labour statistics for 16–24-year-olds[7]

Age range	Total employed	Employment rate (%)
16–17	632 000	40.6
18–24	3 383 000	66.3

Interestingly, there are a much larger proportion of males in the 18–24-year-old group who are at work (69.3 per cent) as compared with females (63.2 per cent). All these employment rates are lower than the age groups above them.[8] This will reflect the numbers in education and not in paid work.

Many of those that are in employment are in part-time work. If one looks at the statistics for part-time workers, this assumption is borne out: of the total of some 7 million part-time[9] workers in the United Kingdom, some 1.135 million were either students or pupils at school. It is even more pronounced when one look at the figures for each sex in Table 4.3.

---

4   21 per cent of the population were 60+, whilst 20 per cent were under 16 years
5   These figures come from the 2001 census and are available on the Government statistics website at www.statistics.gov.uk. The figures for the 10–14 year age group are included here because it is actually the 15–19 year age group in 2006
6   These figures do not fit into my classification of age groups, but I use them as an indicator; see www.statistics.gov.uk
7   These figures are for the period January to March 2005
8   80.5 per cent of those in the 25–34-year-old bracket for example
9   The exact figure for January–March 2005 was 7 113 000

Thus, over 30 per cent of males working part-time are students or pupils. Prior to the introduction of the Part-time Workers Regulations 2000,[10] the traditional remedy for part-time workers who had been discriminated against was to claim sex discrimination, on the basis that the great majority of part-time workers are female. It is interesting to speculate whether there might be an opportunity to add a claim for indirect age discrimination to a future action on discrimination against part-time workers.

Table 4.3   Young people working part-time

Category	Number
Male part-time	1589000
Male student or pupil part-timers	501000
Female part-time	5525000
Female student or pupil part-timers	634000

Teenage workers are concentrated in the hospitality and retail sectors where there appears to be more part-time and flexible work opportunities for students. Thus, 17 per cent of 16–19-year-old workers work in the hotel and restaurant sector (compared to a national average of 4 per cent) and 39 per cent work in the wholesale, retail and motor trade sector (compared to a national figure of 16 per cent).[11]

Unemployment is an important issue for these age groups also. Some 10.4 per cent of 18–24-year-olds were regarded as unemployed compared to a national average rate of 4.8 per cent.

PERCEPTIONS OF DISCRIMINATION

A survey of a limited number of young people aged between 16 and 30 years was carried out in 2001.[12] This was part of the Government's evaluation of the Code of Practice on Age Diversity in Employment.[13] It perhaps illustrates why age discrimination experienced by young workers is different to that experienced by older ones.

Respondents' perceptions, according to the report, of their treatment at work was directly related to their qualifications and experience, so those with

10 Part-time Workers (Prevention of Less Favourable Treatment) Regulations 2000 SI 2000/1551
11 *Age at Work* (2005)
12 *Ageism: Attitudes and Experiences of Young People* (2001); see Age Positive website www. agepositive.gov.uk
13 See Chapter 1

more marketable skills seemed more protected from age discrimination. It is difficult to know how seriously to take this study because it is not clear that the treatment suffered by the young people concerned was the result of age discrimination or something else. The report states, for example, that:

> *This research suggests that school leavers with few or no qualifications were more likely to experience age discrimination. In contrast, older respondents were generally more mature and confident and, having established themselves in work, were less likely to report instances of age discrimination, although some recalled such treatment in the past.*

This may suggest that the adverse treatment is not just about age, but also about relevant qualifications. Despite this, the survey does produce some useful illustrative information. If one looked at the employment cycle, as illustrated in the Code of Practice on Age Diversity, it is possible to recognise where age discrimination might take place:

- Recruitment – various job advertisements may contain minimum ages for jobs; these might be the result of occupational or statutory requirements (see below). The participants in focus groups in this analysis gave examples of employers wanting a secretary who was 'a bright young thing' which was a euphemism for wanting an employee who was a young attractive girl; others suggested that young people were recruited because they were cheaper; others suggested that euphemisms in recruitment advertisements such as 'mature personality' or needing experience were examples of discrimination against the young.

- Selection – being told that they were too young for a job was an example given of age discrimination in the selection process. This appeared to be true of the Army, for example, with a minimum age of 18 years.

- Pay – there were examples of young people being paid less than others for doing similar work and sometimes this appeared to be justified on the grounds of age.

- Training – surprisingly the analysis reports a mixed picture on training. One would have thought that this was an area in which young workers were treated more favourably than others, but some employers seemed to want employees to prove themselves and their commitment to the organisation first before investing in training.

- Promotion – there was, amongst the group, a widespread acceptance that promotion usually came with length of service and/or experience on the job; so there were few instances of young people feeling that they were not promoted because of their age. Such instances did include a statement like 'you're still young, you've got plenty of time ahead of you'. Other statements seemed to reflect insecurity amongst the participants that maybe they did not have the experience to be promoted over older workers.

- Pensions – some employers encouraged staff to join their pension scheme as soon as possible; others had an approach which took into account length of service or age.

- Redundancy and retirement – few redundancies and little interest in retirement were reported!

The report suggested that ageism could take different forms: firstly, 'pure ageism' where age was overtly the factor influencing decisions, for example on admittance to a pension scheme; secondly, 'partial ageism' where age is interrelated with other factors, such as experience needed; thirdly, 'false ageism' where age is a euphemism for something else.

The young people surveyed were aware that older people had stereotypical views of them and that they were seen as:

- less reliable and more likely to take days off;

- less committed and responsible;

- more involved in their social life than their work.

Although there were positive views held by the respondents about the benefits of working with older people, there were also views that older people could:

- talk down to younger people and treat them like children;

- pick on young, inexperienced recruits;

- doubt or belittle their abilities or capacity to do a good job;

- be a bit stuck in their ways and be reluctant to change or take advice from younger people;

- be resentful of younger people's ability to learn new tricks and specifically to be resentful of their ability with new technology.[14]

Thus, there is at least the perception of discrimination amongst young workers and undoubtedly such discrimination takes place. There are also perhaps a number of examples of occupational and statutory restrictions against young workers.

STATUTORY RESTRICTIONS

There are a number of restrictions imposed on young people at work by the Working Time Regulations 1998.[15] These derive from the European Council Directive concerning certain aspects of working time.[16] The purpose of the Directive is really summed up in Article 1.3 which states that:

> *Member States shall ensure in general that employers guarantee that young people have working conditions which suit their age.*
>
> *They shall ensure in general that young people are protected against economic exploitation and against any work likely to harm their safety, health or physical, mental, moral or social development or to jeopardise their education.*

The Directive applies to any person under the age of 18 who has a contract of employment or an employment relationship[17] and employment of those under the official school leaving age is, with some minor exceptions, effectively eliminated.[18] The Directive assumes that young people are especially vulnerable at work and special measures are needed to protect them. It then goes on to prescribe special rules concerning working time, night work, rest periods, holidays and breaks.[19] These rules are transposed into national law in the Working Time Regulations 1998, such as limitations on working hours contained in Regulation 5A and the prohibition of employing young people to work at night is contained in Regulation 6A.[20] These measures are clearly examples of measures adopted on the basis of age, but are perhaps useful examples of positive action in favour of a sub-group with perceived special needs.

---

14 This list, as with all the previous material in this section comes from *Ageism: Attitudes and Experiences of Young People* (2001)
15 SI 1998/1833
16 Directive 94/33/EC OJ L216/12
17 Article 2.1
18 Articles 1.1 and 4
19 Articles 8–13
20 In fact the prohibition is working during the 'restricted period' which is between 10 p.m. and 6 a.m. – Article 2(1)

In contrast to these statutory measures which discriminate in favour of young workers, the measures concerned with the national minimum wage certainly discriminate against them. The full rate for the national minimum wage in 2006 is £5.35 per hour. There are, however, differing rates for those under the age of 22. The development rate for those aged 18–21 years inclusive is £4.45 per hour and the rate for 16 and 17 years is just £3.00 per hour.[21] The lower rate for those under the age of 22, of course, is designed to strike a balance between helping young people into the job market and preventing exploitation. The rate for 16- and 17-year-olds was only introduced in October 2004.

The assumption of the Low Pay Commission, who were originally opposed to a minimum wage at this level, was that 16- and 17-year-olds formed a distinct segment of the market, most of whom were in training or education. By the time of their fourth report they had become concerned about the number of full-time jobs with 'extremely low rates of pay' which provided minimal training and few development prospects.[22] The result was the recommendation for a national minimum wage for 16- and 17-year-olds 'on the assumption that it is compatible with the age strand of the European Employment Directive (2000/78/EC)'.[23] The Government obviously decided that this was the case and is keeping the lower rates of pay for young people, although it is difficult to see how in some cases such a low minimum does not discriminate against young workers in comparison to others.

In contrast to keeping the measures concerning health and safety and the national minimum wage, the Government did accept that the redundancy payments system did discriminate, but not only against young workers. It also discriminated against the middle age workers (see below). Firstly, there was a two-year qualifying period[24] before an individual was entitled to a redundancy payment. This effectively meant that anyone under the age of 18 years could not qualify for a redundancy payment because they would not have served the two years necessary. The amount of payment varied also, so that we come up with a table for young workers[25] like that contained in Table 4.4.

21　Only applies to those over school leaving age as from the last Friday in June in the school year of the 16ᵗʰ birthday

22　See *Protecting Young Workers: the national minimum wage* (2004)

23　Ibid. para 12

24　Employment Rights Act 1996, section 155

25　Ibid., section 162

Of course the week's pay is subject to a statutory maximum[26] and workers of 41 years and older were entitled to a greater amount (see below). The Government initially was of the view that this was discrimination that could not be justified, so in the 2005 draft it proposed that although the maximum 20-year entitlement was kept, it was to be equalised such that all received a similar amount. In the event it was not able to come to any other solution than to justify the existing discriminatory approach and just removed the upper and lower age limits.

Table 4.4   Redundancy payments to young people

Age	Amount
16–17	Nil
18–21	½ week's pay for each year of service
22–25	1 week's pay per year of service

OCCUPATIONAL RESTRICTIONS

There are other occupational restrictions which may be the result of law or the result of convention. These tend to affect workers in the young, older and senior age groups. Examples of those affecting the young are usually concerned with minimum age restrictions, such as HGV drivers, retail staff involved in the sale of alcohol or gambling activities. There may be less direct restrictions such as higher insurance premiums for younger people employed in driving or hazardous activities.[27] A further consideration of occupational and other restrictions in a number of areas of employment are considered towards the end of this Chapter.

OBJECTIVE JUSTIFICATION

In the event of a challenge to these exceptions, the Government would have to show, in the words of the Framework Directive, that they were 'objectively and reasonably justified by a legitimate aim'. Presumably they would argue justification for the exceptions contained in the Working Time Regulations 1998 and for the difference in treatment on the national minimum wage in accordance with the first exception contained in Article 6 of the Directive, namely:

> *the setting of special conditions on access to employment and vocational training, employment and occupation (including dismissal and*

---

26   Ibid., section 227
27   *Occupational age restrictions* (2001)

remuneration conditions) for young people, older workers and persons
with caring responsibilities in order to promote their vocational
integration or ensure their protection.

The health and safety measures contained in the Working Time Regulations concern protection, whilst the lower rate of minimum wage concern their 'vocational integration' or at least are seen as an aid to securing them a place in the workforce. This is not presumably an argument that can be put with regard to redundancy payments. If this is correct, then this is a good example of the continuing discrimination allowed for by the Framework Directive. The justification for paying less, based on age, is to assist people into work, but we would never consider using this justification for helping people discriminated against on any of the other grounds. For example, according to the 2001 census Bangladeshi men had four times the unemployment rate of white men, so should we have an exception to the Race Relations Act 1976 which states that employers may pay Bangladeshi men a lower rate than white men to encourage their employment? The answer of course is no – it would breach totally the principle of equal treatment. Then one wonders why it is therefore permissible to discriminate against young people on the grounds of age to help them into employment?

MIDDLE AGE DISCRIMINATION

I use this to refer to those aged between 25 and 49. It is an absurd range really because there are, as a generalisation, large differences in the lifestyles and perhaps work styles at the two ends of the spectrum. Nevertheless, it is meaningful in terms of age discrimination, because it serves to highlight the fact that many of the issues relate to workers outside this age range. This is not for one moment to suggest that age discrimination does not take place within the middle age group. It also seems apparent that the divisions are gradual so that young age discrimination issues gradually become less important at the bottom end, whilst discrimination against older workers becomes more of an issue towards the top end of this range. It is also clear that there are gender issues within this age range with women being perceived as becoming older workers at an earlier stage than men.

The 2001 census revealed the population figures by age group shown in Table 4.5.

Table 4.5   Population statistics for those aged 25–49 (2001)[28]

Age range	Total	Male	Female
25–29	3867015	1895469	1971546
30–34	4493532	2199767	2293765
35–39	4625777	2277678	2348099
40–44	4151613	2056545	2095068
45–49	3735986	1851391	1884595

This is where the bulk of the workforce is. There are some 21 million people in these age groups. The employment rates are higher than for all the other age groups (Table 4.6).

Table 4.6   Labour statistics for 25–49-year-olds[29]

Age range	Total employed	Employment rate (%)
25–34	6280000	80.5
35–49	10798000	82.2

This is the age which is characterised by the number of people who have young children. Some 68 per cent of those in their 30s and over 80 per cent of those in their 40s have children, compared to less than 20 per cent of people in their 20s. As a result, some 41 per cent of women workers between the ages of 25 and 44 work part-time. This is compared to 4 per cent of men in the same age group who work part-time.[30] Interestingly, research done for the Equal Opportunities Commission suggests that it is the arrival of the second child which is most likely to trigger part-time working by the mother.[31] The EOC's research also shows that part-time women workers are earning some 40 per cent less per hour than men working full-time and because of discrimination against them, many women were not working at their full potential. The issues of part-time work and equal pay are essentially sex discrimination issues, but there may be a link to age discrimination for older women workers. Women continue to work part-time into their 50s and, according to EOC statistics, some 47 per cent of women workers in the 45–64 years age bracket work part-time compared to some 9 per cent of men in the same age group. As is suggested in

---

28   These figures come from the 2001 census and are available on the Government statistics website at www.statistics.gov.uk
29   These figures are for the period January to March 2005
30   *Facts about Women and Men in Great Britain* (2005)
31   *Part-time working is no crime – so why pay the penalty* (2005)

Chapter 7, it may not be correct to assume that discrimination against women workers of different ages is the same and that there is a connection between age discrimination and sex discrimination which will need to be examined closely in the future.

The analysis by the Employers' Forum on age[32] suggests that the 30s are the 'golden age' of recruitment. Indeed, the figures suggest that this can apply to those in their 40s also. Less than 6 per cent of 30–39-year-olds and some 10 per cent in the 40–49 year age group state that they have been put off applying for a job because of their age. This is lower than any other age group.

People also reach their professional peak in their 30s and 40s (see Table 4.7).

Clearly there may be individual examples of direct age discrimination within this group, but it is difficult to see where one could argue indirect discrimination issues on the basis of statistics, within this group, except perhaps at the margins. The lumping together of this wide age range is a crude attempt to simplify the analysis on my part, but it is partly as a result of the way that official statistics also put these groups together. It is not possible to identify many statutory or occupational (see below) restrictions that apply to this group. There is the issue of redundancy payments which advantages those over the age of 41 years (see above).

Table 4.7   Distribution of work amongst 30- and 40-year-olds (%)

Occupation	20s	30s	40s
Higher managerial and professional	8	14	13
Lower managerial and professional	20	26	26
Intermediate occupations	14	11	10
Small employers and own account workers	4	8	9
Lower supervisory and technical	9	10	10
Semi-routine occupations	15	13	13
Routine occupations	11	9	9
Never worked, unemployed and other	19	9	10

One conclusion is that, except perhaps for those at the younger and older age extremities, this is the group that is least likely to suffer from age discrimination,

32   *Age at Work* (2005)

except insofar as it may relate to other grounds of discrimination. Thus, discrimination against part-time workers may effectively also be discrimination against a certain age group. Similarly, there is a greater likelihood of becoming disabled the older one becomes (see Chapter 7), so there may be links to certain age groups and disabilities; for example over a quarter of people who gave up a job in their 40s did so for health reasons. This compares to 13 per cent of such people in their 30s and 8 per cent of people in their 20s.[33] The Age Discrimination in Employment Act 1967 in the United States only protects those employees over the age of 40 and one must wonder whether it is the Americans that have the right approach. Those over the age of 40 are more likely to suffer age discrimination and its debilitating effects than those under this age.

Perhaps one can argue that if the Framework Directive and the UK Age Regulations were just about tackling age discrimination, then one might accept that regulation for much of this age group is unnecessary. However, the Directive at least is about more than this: it is also about establishing the principle of equal treatment, in which case one would have to argue that it should apply to all and that this is not just a principle that can apply to some age groups and not others. The extent to which the UK Age Regulations benefit this group of workers in practice is discussed elsewhere (Chapter 8).

OLDER AGE DISCRIMINATION

This age group begins at 50 years and ends at 65 years (State Pension Age (SPA)) except for women, who still have a SPA of 60 years. For these people the age range is 50–59 years. This difference in the age of pension entitlement will of course be gradually levelled upwards, so that by 2020, all people will have an SPA of 65 years. It is of course the disappearance of large numbers of people in this age group from the workforce and from those who would claim to be economically active that was a major motivation for governments to take action on age discrimination.

The 2001 census revealed the population figures by age group shown in Table 4.8.

The total numbers of people in employment between the ages of 50 and the SPA are 6 368 000, representing an employment rate of 70.4 per cent. This compares to an employment rate of 82.2 per cent for those in the lower age group of 35–49 years.

---

33   *Age at Work* (2005)

Table 4.8   Population statistics for those aged 50–64 (2001)[34]

Age range	Total	Male	Female
50–54	4040576	2003158	2037418
55–59	3339004	1651396	1687608
60–64*	2880074	1409684	1470390

* These figures include women who will have retired and become economically inactive

There is ample evidence that discrimination takes place against this age group in relation to work. Older workers are more likely to lose their jobs through redundancy. This figure was one in ten workers in the 55–64 year age group according to one survey.[35]

Some conclusions of a DfEE report on older workers were:

- Older workers were less likely to be in paid work than younger groups and when they did work they were more likely to be working as self-employed or part-time.

- There was a greater risk of becoming economically inactive beyond the ages of 50 and 55 years.

- Taking all forms of inactivity together, the chances of men leaving inactivity for paid work were sharply reduced after the age of 50 years and 'were close to zero for those over 60'.

- For women, the chances of moving out of inactivity were much reduced after the age of 40 years and 'was particularly uncommon for those in their late 50s'.[36]

The 2003 DTI consultation provided generalised definitions but, interestingly, suggested that direct discrimination can occur when a decision is made on the basis of a person's actual or *perceived* age. Examples of age discrimination given in this Government consultation document are:

- being forced to retire after reaching a certain age;

- not being given a job they applied for because of their age;

- being told their age was a barrier to general advancement;

- assumptions being made about abilities due to age;

---

34 2001 census statistics available at www.statistics.gov.uk
35 *Age discrimination at work: Survey Report* (2001)
36 *Characteristics of Older Workers* (1998)

- being selected for redundancy because of age.

There is also some evidence that individuals in this age group deselect themselves from jobs because they assume that their age will be a hindrance in applying for jobs. Some 21 per cent of the age group claimed to have been put off from applying for jobs because of their age. This is greater than any other group apart from the 16–19-year-olds.[37]

A further survey with personal business and other advisers[38] of mostly small- and medium-sized enterprises also found that age played a significant role in the workplace. Three-quarters of business advisers said that age was a factor for employers when recruiting and most felt that employers preferred to recruit younger people. A third felt that age was important for employers when arranging training and that older workers were unable to learn new skills as a result of lacking motivation, resistance to change and inflexibility. A fifth of advisers felt that age was a consideration in promotion for organisations. As many small businesses were owner-managed, the age of the owner-manager played an important part in decision making. Generally, people preferred to recruit those younger than themselves.

This perception that age is a problem when applying for jobs is an acceptance of the reality of the situation. If one looks at the occupational restrictions described in the sector summaries below, the same perception seems to be shared by employers and the public when they are involved. It is as if there is a piece of mass self-delusion taking place based on an accepted prejudice that older people are a problem when it comes to employment. It is a piece of self-delusion that is not based on animosity but on an unfounded and unproven prejudice often resulting from a total lack of contact with older workers.

Gender is also an issue, with women more likely than men to say that their age is a problem in recruitment. As over 50 per cent of women in this age group work in the public sector, there must be parts of the private sector which have no or very few female employees over the age of 50, thus having no opportunity to move away from their stereotypical view of older workers.

Health is an increasingly important issue when workers reach this age group. One in eight over-50s is economically inactive because of long-term illness (see Chapter 7 on the relationship between age and disability). Some 33 per cent gave up work for health reasons, some 15 per cent took early retirement and

---

37 *Age at Work* (2005)
38 Advisers working for South London Training and Enterprise Council and Business Link for London; the survey report *Significance of age in the workplace* was completed in 2001

some 16 per cent were made redundant or took voluntary redundancy. This compares to some 13 per cent of people in their 30s, for example, who gave up work for health reasons and 11 per cent who were made redundant or took voluntary redundancy.

The major piece of discrimination based upon age that takes place against this age group is the event of mandatory retirement. At a certain age many employees are ejected from the workforce, purely because they have reached the stipulated age for this event to take place. This issue is important enough to have a separate chapter in this book (Chapter 5). It is worth reflecting, however, how unfortunate it is that this situation has been reached.

Trade unions and others fought long and hard for the right to retire with an adequate pension. It is doubtful whether the pension levels required were ever met, but there was a principle established that enabled workers to retire with dignity. This event has now, however, become an example of age discrimination. This is partly because there is a much longer life expectancy now, than when the first state pension was introduced by the Lloyd George Government a century ago. It is also, and more importantly, an expression of the belief that individuals should have the right to decide and not to be treated as a class to whom certain things should be done regardless of their personal circumstances or wants. It is the denial of this individualist approach that allows the UK Government to continue with a default retirement age.

SENIOR AGE DISCRIMINATION

Some people over the age of 60/65 wish to continue to work and some people under this age wish to continue working when they reach the SPA. In fact, some 34 per cent of those in their 50s in one survey stated that 'the idea of retirement doesn't make sense to me'.[39]

Total numbers in employment over the SPA fall quite considerably when compared to younger age groups. Nevertheless, there are quite significant numbers of people involved. Some 1 048 000 people are over the SPA[40] representing an employment rate of 9.8 per cent. This compares to an employment rate of over 70 per cent for the next age group down (see above). This figure indicates an increasing trend. In the autumn of 1999, for example, the employment rate for those over the SPA stood at 7.9 per cent.[41] Some 86 per cent of the age group are described as economically inactive.

---

39   *Age at Work* (2005)
40   In this case all women 60+ and all men 65+
41   *Older Workers; statistical information booklet* (2004)

Table 4.9   Population statistics for those aged over SPA (2001)[42]

Age range	Total	Male	Female
60–64	2 880 074	1 409 684	1 470 390
65–69	2 595 939	1 241 382	1 355 557
70–74	2 339 319	1 059 156	1 280 163
75–79	1 967 088	817 738	1 149 350
80+	2 437 653	792 719	1 644 934

Some 75 per cent of women who still worked after SPA were aged 60–64 and almost a quarter of these worked for organisations where the retirement age was 65 years.

The characteristics of all over the SPA, when compared to other age groups, are that they are much more likely to be self-employed and/or working part-time for lower pay (Table 4.10).

Table 4.10   Characteristics of older workers compared to other age groups[43]

% in employment who are aged:	16–24	25–49	50–SPA	SPA+
Self-employed	3.7	12.2	17.7	25.8
Part-time	34.7	21.1	24.9	69.8
In a permanent job	86.4	95.5	95.7	89.5
Average gross hourly wage (£)	6.15	11.23	10.92	8.40

The two biggest sectors in which senior workers are active are in 'distribution, hotels and restaurants' together with 'public administration, education and health'.[44] A significant number of people wish to continue working after SPA.[45] Important reasons for wishing to continue working are continuing job satisfaction and finance.

It is important, however, not to treat this group (or any of the others) as an homogenous class. There are different motivations for wishing to continue

---

42   2001 census figures, available at www.statistics.gov.uk
43   Ibid.
44   Ibid.
45   *Age discrimination at work Survey Report* (2001); about one-quarter of the survey expressed a desire to continue working beyond SPA

to work after SPA. This may be a result of cultural traditions or lifestyle or work-style adopted throughout a working life. It may be that an individual's perception of the event of retirement may depend upon that individual's approach to work and indeed the nature of the work itself. One analysis looks at groups that it calls 'workers' and 'creatives and professionals'.[46] The former consisted of the traditional working class positions such as secretaries, baker, stockman, milkman and hairdresser, although there were others who perceived themselves as being in this group. The characteristic of this group was the division between work and the rest of an individual's life. In contrast to this the 'professionals and creatives' were people who saw work as part of their identity or a vocation. Work was something that they would continue to do. Often such people could not envisage not working. 'Workers' on the other hand looked at their working life as a means to an end, as a way of supporting themselves and their families. This is an over-simplified version of the analysis, but it illustrates how it is possible for different groups to have a totally different approach to retirement. For 'workers' it was a natural event, often welcomed. For the others it might represent something that has to be got round in order to carry on doing the things that are occupying one's life. The first might be characterised by a worker continuing to work in the employment they had before reaching retirement age. For the latter group it might mean developing activities on a self-employed basis. These are crude generalisations[47] but they do indicate the need not to assume that all people who reach retirement age have the same means or motivations. Clearly the amount of choice that people have depends upon a large number of financial, cultural and working life factors.

The extent to which attitudes to retirement are shaped by societal influences can be judged by surveys about the anticipated retirement age. One survey showed that many people regarded the SPA as the natural age to retire. Some 40 per cent of those working were expected to retire at the SPA. The report[48] suggested that there were two main elements to creating this expectation. The first was the SPA itself being a set age defined by Government. The second was that, at this age, a second source of income became available, thus assisting with the financial means to retire. The same report suggested that there was no hard evidence that employers' fixed retirement age had a widespread influence on whether people retired before SPA, but that there was evidence to such that fixed retirement ages may stop some people from working beyond retirement age (see Chapter 5).

---

46 *Changing Priorities, Transformed Opportunities?* (2005)
47 These are my crude generalisations and in no way intended to reflect upon the interesting work done by Jane Parry and Rebecca Taylor in *Changing Priorities*
48 *Factors affecting the labour market participation of older workers* (2003)

Not entirely surprising is the statistic that almost 20 per cent of people in their 60s are dreading retirement and almost the same number of people have been put off applying for work because of their age.[49]

SURVEY OF RETIRED TRADE UNION MEMBERS

In 2003 a survey was conducted of the retired membership of two trade unions in the public sector, NATFHE and PCS.[50] The respondents were asked if they thought that they had been discriminated against in their career on the basis of age.[51] A significant proportion (31.7 per cent) claimed that they had been.

The two most significant areas were:

- in applying for jobs 14.9 per cent;

- in respect of promotion 14.2 per cent.

The two other major areas were in respect of training opportunities (5.5 per cent) and on the grounds of redundancy (5.2 per cent).

The next question asked whether respondents had suffered from harassment at work on the basis of their age. The questionnaire provided the definition of harassment put forward by the Government in the consultation exercise (see Chapter 3). Some 8.6 per cent responded by saying yes.

Respondents were asked whether age discrimination should be made unlawful in all circumstances, some circumstances or not at all. The majority felt that this should be the case in all circumstances (56.2 per cent) with a substantial minority (40.9 per cent) stating that it should be made unlawful in some circumstances. Relatively few respondents preferred the not at all option (3.0 per cent).

The questionnaire then posed a number of scenarios in order to test the respondents' resolve in making such discrimination unlawful. The questions were posed in such a way as to be supportive of the Government's proposed approach to allowing exceptions to the general rule of non-discrimination.

---

49 See *Age at Work* (2005)

50 National Association of Teachers in Further and Higher Education and the Public and Civil Service Union; the survey was carried out by Malcolm Sargeant at Middlesex University

51 In all 1 363 forms were sent out. A total of 648 responses were received. This represented a 47.5 per cent return. Not all questions were answered by all respondents. Percentages given are percentages of actual replies.

Scenario 1

Young people should continue to receive a lower rate of national minimum wage than those over 21 years of age.

Views were divided with some 43 per cent agreeing with this statement and some 47.4 per cent disagreeing.

Scenario 2

At present older people receive a higher rate of redundancy pay than younger workers. This should be ended and all receive the same rate.

Interestingly a large majority (56 per cent) disagreed with this statement, with only 34.8 per cent agreeing. A much greater proportion of male respondents (38 per cent) than female respondents agreed (23.6 per cent).

Scenario 3

Employers should be able to stipulate the age at which workers are recruited, in order to make sure that they have a balanced and age diverse workforce.

Perhaps reflecting the numbers that thought that they had been discriminated against in applying for jobs, there was a majority who disagreed with this statement (56.4 per cent).

Female respondents were much less likely to agree (18.9 per cent) than male ones (35.8 per cent).

Scenario 4

There are some circumstances where the employer should be able to discriminate on the grounds of age on whether to give employee training.

A clear majority disagreed with this proposition (57.8 per cent), although again, more men were willing to agree (39.9 per cent) than women (22.4 per cent).

Scenario 5

There are some jobs, such as in modelling or those concerned with public safety such as airline pilots, where it is right that age should be one of the selection criteria for both recruitment and retirement, regardless of a person's capacity.

A majority agreed with the statement (57.2 per cent), although there were substantial numbers who disagreed (36.3 per cent). Significantly more men agreed (62 per cent) than women (40.6 per cent).

Scenario 6

Some benefits, such as longer holidays or extra privileges associated with seniority, can be justified on the basis of rewarding service, even though they inevitably mean that older workers receive more benefits than younger ones.

A large majority agreed with this statement (70.7 per cent). This was the case for female respondents (64.2 per cent) and male respondents (67.6 per cent).

Almost one-third claimed to have suffered age discrimination and one in twelve claimed to have been harassed for a reason connected to their chronological age. Generally they were opposed to age discrimination and universal mandatory retirement ages (see Chapter 5), but there seemed to be a tendency to approve of exception that might benefit the older worker, such as those associated with length of service.

OCCUPATIONAL AGE RESTRICTIONS[52]

Below is a summary of four sector reports about occupational age restrictions. They illustrate the fact that discrimination is likely to take place on the basis of people's perceptions that are related to age. This is not only about employers' perceptions, but also about how employees see themselves and often about how the public perceive them. Thus, age restrictions occur in the retail and finance sector because employers perceive that the public require certain ages for certain functions, for example young people for fashion and beauty and older people for financial advice. Working practices also play a part; for example in law, where there is a tradition, especially amongst big City law firms, of working long and unsociable hours. These, it is suggested by others, effectively discriminate against older workers or those of a certain age who have dependants to look after. There is also an element of tradition about age in certain workforces which affects the way employers operate and perhaps the type of applicant who applies. Few of these restrictions are the result of law. Rather they are the result of informal work practices based upon ageist assumptions.

---

52 All the information here comes from a series of sector reviews carried out for the report *Occupational Age Restrictions* (2001)

It is interesting to look at the different age group responses in answering the question as to whether they have been put off applying for work because of the problems they perceive arise out of being their age (Table 4.11).[53]

Table 4.11   People put off applying for a job because of age

Age	Number (%)
Teens	25
20s	17
30s	6
40s	n/a*
50s	21
60s	18

* No figure available and one must conjecture that it increases with age. It is probably the under-25s and the over-50s who are most likely to suffer from age discrimination.

RETAIL SECTOR

Partly because of the large number of part-time and casual retail positions, many of which are occupied by students, the age group for this sector is skewed towards the young. Thus, some 24 per cent of employees were aged between 16 and 24 (compared to 14 per cent nationally); 52 per cent were aged between 25 and 49 (62 per cent nationally); and 22 per cent were aged over 50 (24 per cent nationally). Some examples given of occupational restrictions were:

- There were some formal restrictions related to betting and the sale of alcohol by under-18-year-olds.

- Many graduate schemes had an upper age limit of 24. Many companies, however, provided less training for the young, less-skilled workers because they perceived younger workers as being disloyal and unreliable.

- There is a tendency for retailers to recruit the age group that they perceive will help sell their products; thus 'younger, attractive people' are more likely to be recruited into the fashion and beauty industry; school leavers are unlikely to be recruited in a mother and child store. One representative organisation is quoted as saying: 'You are most likely to find yourself being sold a washing machine

53   *Age at Work* (2005)

by a woman in her early 30s and a hi-fi or mobile phone by a man in his late teens or early 20s.'

- There were few people over 50 years on British Retail Institute training courses, perhaps because of an unwillingness to train people of this age.

The sector report concluded with examples of unjustified age discrimination:

- employers' deliberate or informal age restrictions, particularly in recruitment and training;

- customer perceptions and stereotyping of age groups, so that some employers recruit in line with these stereotypes;

- sector-wide traditions, which have created an image and practices that are not attractive to particular age groups.

LAW SECTOR

As a result of the way in which people qualify to become a solicitor or a barrister, there is effectively a minimum recruitment age of 23–24 years. Figures indicate that few people enter the profession in their late 30s or above and most late entries are people who have qualified through the lengthy legal executive route. The average age for those entering the profession as solicitors was:

- 27.8 years for those who have a qualifying law degree;

- 29.9 years for those who have completed a non-law degree;

- 33.9 years for those qualifying through the legal executive route.

Examples of possible discrimination are:

- There is a culture of long and unsociable hours, which may limit, in practice or by perception, the recruitment of older workers and also the retention of female solicitors in their 30s, or other ages with young children. There is also a problem for those groups with dependants with the small amount of part-time work available.

- One study[54] found that older students were 15 per cent less likely to be employed following training than younger students.

- Another study[55] found that 25 per cent of newly qualified solicitors were discriminated against because of their age and that the two

54 *Entry in the legal professions* (2000) cited in *Occupational age restrictions sector review: Law* (2001)
55 *Part-time working is no crime – so why pay the penalty* (2005)

most common forms of age discrimination were 'hostility from colleagues or employment on less favourable terms'.

FINANCE SECTOR

The age profile for the finance sector[56] showed that it is younger than that of the UK average age for the workforce. There are significantly more employees (about one-third) in the 25–34 age group and the majority of employees are in the 25–49 years group (over two-thirds of the workforce). The study did not find evidence of formal age restrictions within the sector and concluded that it was:

> An industry traditionally characterised by age restrictive practices, but with many companies now adopting age diverse policies ... but ... the culture change has not reached all parts of the sector.

There were some age limitations, however, although they were held not to be 'endemic across the sector'. These related mainly to a reluctance to recruit new entrants past a certain age. Other limitations included the perception held by potential employees about the fact that the sector only recruited young graduates.

Some occupations, however, were more interested in mature entrants. These tended to be those concerned with giving advice in building societies or in relation to insurance needs. Despite this, there was anecdotal evidence from employees in the industry which suggested that there were age limitations for older workers. Indeed, one chief executive of an insurance company is quoted as saying:

> Most large insurance companies claim that they look at people's skills, abilities and competence rather than their age. In reality, ageism slips into the recruitment process.

There were though examples given of good practice by employers who had adopted age diverse policies.

TRANSPORT SECTOR

There are about 1.7 million people employed in the transport sector. The age profile is older than the UK workforce average, although there were variations between different parts of the sector; for example some 57 per cent of road

---

56 Defined here as high street and investment banks, building societies, accountancy and insurance

transport operatives were over 40 years of age, compared to some 37 per cent for the 'inside people' such as the storekeepers and despatch clerks.

The report covers a number of areas, but only the road haulage part is considered here. The important legal restriction concerning age is that licences to drive large vehicles are restricted to those over the age of 21. Most companies expressed a preference for employing those over the age of 25 as drivers. This was partly because of the higher cost of insurance for the under-25s and a perception that younger people take more risks and are, therefore, less safe on the roads.

There is also an effective upper age limit of 45, which is related to health. After this age drivers needed a regular health check, which apparently deterred many individuals from continuing. The result is a narrow band of employment of between 25 and 45 years.[57]

---

57 There are also sector reports on food manufacture, local authorities, animal care, medical and IT

CHAPTER 5

Retirement

Retirement means 'cessation of service as an employee of the employer in question'. It does not mean or include a 'change in the nature of service as an employee of the employer in question'.[1] It is, therefore, the leaving of the particular workforce by the employee.

There have traditionally, perhaps, been a number of types of retirement age. These are the pensionable retirement age, the contractual retirement age and the actual or normal retirement age. These may all take place at the same time, or they may occur at different times.

Pensionable retirement age is that established by the pension scheme to which an individual belongs. This may range from 55 years upwards, but may be lower for particular occupations, where there may be objective justification. The state pension retirement age is being equalised so that by 2020 it will be the same for men and for women. In order to eliminate the contractual retirement age, the link between it and the pensionable retirement age needs to be broken.

The link between contractual and normal retirement age has been considered in a number of cases. In effect it is the difference between what the contract states and what the normal practice in the organisation is. Often this has been an argument in favour of extending the retirement age, but not always. *Cross v British Airways*, for example, concerned the pilots and crew of an airline called British Caledonian Airways (BCal) which was taken over by British Airways in 1988. The BCal staff had a contractual retirement age of 60 in contrast to that of British Airways which was at the lower age of 55. The case was mostly about whether a relevant transfer had taken place within the meaning of the TUPE Regulations,[2] as well as a sex discrimination issue. It did, however, also discuss contractual and normal retirement ages. Some 13 years later the BCal staff were arguing that a TUPE transfer had taken place, so that their contracts of employment containing the 60-year retirement age had transferred intact. The Employment Appeal Tribunal had no doubt that, notwithstanding this argument, the normal retirement age for BA was 55 and that the BCal staff

---

1   *Venebles v Hornby*
2   Then the Transfer of Undertakings (Protection of Employment) Regulations 1981 SI 1981/1784

had become 'fully integrated with the other pilots and cabin crew'. Mr Justice Burton stated in his judgment:

> It [the 55 year retirement age] was ratified and applied constantly over the thirteen-year period; by the imposition and acceptance of BA's policy by its (mistaken) incorporation into the terms and conditions of employment, by the discussion about possible changes to such policy and a decision to leave it unchanged, by numerous people retiring in accordance with it, including, as is common ground, a substantial number, probably in three figures, of former BCal employees (and indeed no-one retiring on any other basis).

Thus, the reality of the normal retirement age – the age at which people actually retired in practice – outweighed any contractual considerations. This is a well-established view. In *Waite v GCHQ*,[3] the House of Lords held that normal retiring age 'is the age at which employees in a group can reasonably expect to be compelled to retire unless there is a special reason in a particular case for a different age to apply'. Thus, the test was one of reasonable expectation. The Court further held:

> The contractual retiring age does not conclusively fix the normal retiring age. Where there is a contractual retiring age applicable to all, or nearly all, the relevant employees, there is a presumption that contractual retiring age is the normal retiring age for the group.

This presumption, however, can be challenged by evidence that in practice a different retiring age is used, insofar as it has created a reasonable expectation that the non contractual age is the one that will be used. 'Normal' is not necessarily the same as 'usual'. This would imply a statistical approach which might be unsatisfactory. One needs to consider whether there were special reasons for some people to have been given a different retirement age.

It may be that as a result of the Age Regulations 2006 the concept of the normal retirement age may disappear. Actual retirement ages will be subject to individual ratification and the concept of what the normal retirement age is may become a subject of academic study, unless it forms, of course, part of the evidence of discrimination on the grounds of age.

Prior to the Age Regulations 2006 there had not been any law that required an employer to set a mandatory retirement date in their contracts of employment, although there is an obligation to inform employees of any

---

3   *Waite v Government Communications Headquarters*

terms and conditions relating to pension schemes.[4] There were, however, legal consequences in terms of employment protection and this was the problem facing Colonel Waite in this case. Employees who continued in employment beyond the contractual retirement age (provided that this is the same as the normal retirement age) lost their right to protection against unfair dismissal[5] and their right to redundancy payments.[6] It is questionable how much the Age Regulations have changed this in practice. Indeed, it is argued elsewhere in this book (see Chapter 8) that the introduction of a default retirement age combined with the removal of the age limit for claiming unfair dismissal in the 2006 Regulations might result in it being more likely that employees would be dismissed for reasons of retirement.

Many individuals do not retire at the contractual retirement age and many employers do, in some form or other, permit employees to work beyond normal retirement age. One DTI survey suggested that as many as one in four employers allowed this to happen, although it was less likely to occur in larger organisations.[7] The retirement age in organisations has always seemed to be a cut-off at which the employee loses their important employment rights to the employer. *Taylor v Secretary of State for Scotland*[8] concerned a Mr George Taylor who was a prison officer in the Scottish Prison Service. The service had a minimum retirement age of 55, but at its discretion the employer could allow the employee to continue working until a maximum age of 60. Mr Taylor was allowed to continue to work after 55 as long as he carried out the full range of duties and provided he maintained an acceptable attendance record and satisfactory performance. Three years later, after a review, the employer decided to give notice to all those over the age of 55 in order to recruit a younger workforce. The Employment Tribunal found that 'the change in the retiring arrangements was part of a policy to bring about the loss of 1000 staff for the purposes of bringing in younger employees with different skills who could be paid less'. This large-scale piece of age discrimination was carried out by a Government Agency in 1994; just a few years before the, admittedly new, Government in 1997 launched its Code of Practice on Age Diversity in Employment (see Chapter 2).

Some two years earlier, the employer, the Scottish Prison Service, had issued an equal opportunities policy which included age. The policy stated that 'no one in the service should be discriminated against on the grounds of gender,

---

4   Employment Rights Act 1996, section 1(4)(d)(iii)
5   Ibid., section 109
6   Ibid., section 156
7   Carried out for the DTI report on the Code of Practice on Age Diversity
8   [2000] IRLR 503

race, religion, sexual preference, disability or age'. Mr Taylor claimed the dismissal amounted to a breach of contract as the equal opportunities policy was incorporated into his contract of employment. The Employment Tribunal agreed with this, but Mr Taylor lost at the Employment Appeal Tribunal[9], the Court of Session[10] and the House of Lords.[11] What emerged really was a view that the employer's discretion, after the minimum retirement age had been reached, was unaffected by the equal opportunities policy, which said nothing about conditions for retirement. Indeed, the Court of Session said that it was impossible to have a retirement policy which was not discriminatory as it would inevitably lead to the employment of younger people who might be paid less.

Others have argued that having a retirement age amounted to sex discrimination. *Rutherford and another v Secretary of State for Trade and Industry*[12] concerned a Mr John Rutherford who had worked for a company called Harvest Town Circle Ltd. He was 67 years old when he was dismissed for redundancy. The Employment Rights Act appeared to stop him from pursuing a claim for unfair dismissal because of his age. He argued that the upper age limit amounted to indirect sex discrimination against men. The Employment Tribunal agreed because the proportion of men who were economically active after the age of 65 was 8 per cent in 1998 (the year of dismissal) compared to 3 per cent of women. The employers argued that there were social policy considerations for limiting claims after the age of 65, but the Employment Tribunal said no evidence of this had been produced. The Employment Appeal Tribunal[13] allowed the appeal because it stated that there were serious flaws in the approach adopted by the lower court.

In a joined case Mr Samuel Bentley was dismissed from his employment at the age of 73 when the firm appointed receivers. He brought proceedings for a redundancy payment, which also seemed denied to him because of his age. In this case, the Employment Tribunal[14] focused on age bands 55–64 and 65–74. It concluded that in 1998 and 2001 the legislative measures adversely affected a substantially higher number of males than females and rejected the Secretary of State's argument that the correct pool was the whole workforce between 16 and 79 years who had one year's service (98.88 per cent of men and 99.01 per cent of women in 2001). As a result, the Employment Tribunal held that there was no

9   [1997] IRLR 608
10   [1999] IRLR 363
11   [2000] IRLR 502
12   [2004] IRLR 892; see also *Nash v Mash/Roe Group Ltd* [1998] IRLR 168
13   [2001] IRLR 599
14   [2002] IRLR 768

objective justification for the discriminatory legislation denying a redundancy payment to a man over retirement age.

The Employment Appeal Tribunal[15] allowed the appeal stating that the Tribunal should have taken the figures for the whole workforce, so then no disparate impact could be shown. In the joined appeals the Court of Appeal agreed.[16] There was a need to follow the approach in *Seymour-Smith*[17] when dealing with cases of disparate impact. The Court held that:

> The employment tribunal erred in regarding as irrelevant to its consideration the figures relied upon by the Secretary of State relating to those in the workforce who could comply with the age requirement. If the correct approach is taken, the statistics in evidence clearly establish that the difference in the working population between the proportion of men aged under 65 who can comply and the proportion of women aged under 65 who can comply is very small indeed. The disparities are certainly not 'considerable' in the sense required by Seymour-Smith.

The Court was obviously right in its judgment because it was looking at a sex discrimination claim. One wonders whether the different approach of the Employment Tribunal was because they were looking at the matter more from an age discrimination perspective. Clearly the differential treatment of different age groups was not an issue for the appeal courts in considering the differing potential impact of the measures on different sexes.[18]

WHY HAVE A RETIREMENT AGE?

It is projected that there will be one million fewer working-age people under the age of 50 and three million more aged over 50 by 2022.[19] Older workers will play an increasingly important part in the economy, so it does seem strange that the Government still insists on allowing the practice of compulsory retirement by employers which means ending the contribution of many millions of workers to the economy. There is now enough evidence to show that for many, the leaving of the workforce means entering poverty. In fact, Government policy appears contradictory. On the one hand, employers are to be protected from any claims provided they dismiss employees at the default retirement age (see Chapter 8).

---

15   [2003] IRLR 858

16   [2004] IRLR 893

17   *R v Secretary of State for Employment ex parte Seymour-Smith* [2000] IRLR 263 HL

18   The House of Lords subsequently disagreed with this statistical approach but held that one sex was not disadvantages as compared to another, see *Rutherford v Secretary of State* [2006] IRLR 551 HL

19   Whiting (2005); the figures come from projections by the Government Actuary's Department

On the other hand, the Government introduced in 2005 a scheme to allow people to defer their state pension as an incentive for them to continue working.

This is not to say that employers should conduct an age-neutral policy in the workplace and assume that age is not an issue for workers of different ages. Workers in their 50s and 60s may experience a wide range of personal circumstances which are not necessarily experienced by younger workers and a failure to take these other factors into account may end up amounting to age discrimination at work. One study suggests that there are a number of issues that can play a major part in work decisions of older workers, especially with regard to when they might decide to retire:[20]

- Health and fitness issues – many people may live and work longer, but for a substantial minority health issues will have an important effect on their working lives, for example the large numbers of people who retire for reasons of sickness and disability.

- Having caring responsibilities – about one in five people in their 50s has responsibility for care in relation to older relatives and to grandchildren.

- People's views and outlook may change as they get older – work may become less important than roles in the family or the community, especially, for example in relation to partners who may retire or have health or other problems. The conduct of a sensible policy requires an appreciation of this rather than a strictly neutral policy which tries to ignore age altogether.

There are over one million economically active people over state pension age. This is made up of 362 000 men and 711 000 women. This represents an economic activity rate of about 10 per cent in total: 9 per cent for men and 10.5 per cent for women.[21] Both men and women who continue to work are more likely to be self-employed and/or working part-time than other groups. Thus, some 37.4 per cent of all workers in work over the age of 65 years are self-employed (46 per cent of men and 23.1 per cent of women) compared to the 50–54 age group which had 15.1 per cent who were self-employed. Some 73.9 per cent of over-65s, in work, are part-timers (66.6 per cent of men and 86.2 per cent of women) compared to the 50–54 age group where 23 per cent worked part-time.[22]

---

20   Hirsch (2003)
21   Figures from the *Labour Force Survey* at June 2005, Office for National Statistics
22   Whiting (2005)

These figures do not necessarily suggest that there is anything wrong with working part-time or being self-employed, but are perhaps a reflection of the wish for flexible forms of working for this age group. It is interesting that the research also suggests that the older a person was when leaving full-time employment the less likely they were to make the transition to retirement through flexible employment, or 'bridge employment':[23]

> *In some cases bridge employment represents a positive choice, giving older workers the opportunity to undertake new and challenging work on their own terms; in other situations it is merely a downgrading of people's previous working conditions.*[24]

Research suggests that about one-third of all those who begin to draw their pensions are aged 54 years or less and about two-thirds are aged 59 years or under.[25] A DTI survey showed that only 43 per cent of the male respondents and 40 per cent of the female ones expected to retire at the state pension age, although one in three would like to retire earlier.[26] According to the Government Green Paper *Working and Saving for Retirement,* the mean age for men retiring in the United Kingdom is 62.6 years and for women 61.1 years. Amongst those already retired and who had retired early, the survey found that 33 per cent had retired because of illness or disability, 16 per cent were made redundant and 17 per cent had their workplace closed or changed. Perhaps not surprisingly, given these figures, some three-quarters of all firms have no employees over the age of 60.[27]

What is clear is that many people retire early out of choice. It would be wrong to argue that a compulsory retirement system which may breach individual human rights is not welcomed by many. Retirement offers many opportunities for people and for many it must be an exciting and challenging new chapter in their lives. It is seen as a reward for a lifetime of work. It is a strange concept, however, that says that we should all have the same retirement age regardless of our wishes or needs. Surely the only sustainable argument in favour of retirement must be an argument in favour of a variable and flexible retirement age. Otherwise it becomes coercive and unwelcome to many.

There are a number of traditional reasons for having a fixed retirement age: firstly, that occupational pensions have a normal retirement date; secondly, that there is a correlation between state pension age and normal retirement date;

---

23   Ibid. drawing upon research by Lissenburgh and Smeaton (2003)
24   Ibid.
25   *Early retirement schemes still the norm in final salary schemes* (2002)
26   See DTI report on the Code of Practice
27   Grattan (2002)

thirdly, that it is a means of older workers make way for younger ones; and finally, it was said that younger workers have a higher level of productivity.[28]

OCCUPATIONAL PENSIONS

The importance of occupational pension schemes is that they all have a normal retirement age. This retirement age is often the contractual retirement age. In a major retirement survey of people with a fixed retirement age, it emerged that some 87 per cent of the men and 61 per cent of the women were members of an occupational pension scheme.[29] Having a fixed retirement age is a characteristic of defined benefit schemes and is needed for the purpose of actuarial calculations of the potential liabilities of the schemes. Any move away from this, as typified by the numbers of such schemes being closed to new members, means that the fixed age is less important. The development of individual and more mobile schemes based upon contributions means that an individual can decide on their retirement age, depending upon the size of the fund that they have accumulated during their career.

Defined benefit schemes have of course a strong presence in the public sector. Even here they have a limited effect upon actual retirement ages. Retirement for reasons of health is, for example, a major reason for leaving work early. Table 5.1 shows retirement levels in the English and Welsh Prison Service[30] between 1998 and 2001 as an example. Some jobs in this service must be regarded as stressful and likely perhaps to lead to higher than normal levels of retirement through sickness. The figures show overall a high rate of retirement for health reasons. They also show that only a minority of retirements take place at the normal retirement age (raised from 55 years to 60 years in 1987).

Table 5.1   Prison service retirements – all staff

Year	Total	Age+	Age norm	Early	Health
1998	933	360	172	49	352
1999	1 002	435	178	71	318
2000	936	455	131	69	281
2001	1137	506	224	174	233
1998–2001	4008	1756	705	363	1184

(Age + = retirement after normal retirement age; Age norm = retirement at normal retirement age; Early = retirement (e.g. for structural reasons) before normal retirement age; Health is retirement for health reasons.)

28   *Retirement ages in the UK: a review of the literature* (2003)
29   Ibid; the original source was *The Dynamics of Retirement* (1997)
30   Figures kindly supplied by the Prison Service

The table shows that, over the four years in question, almost 30 per cent of retirements in the Prison Service were for reasons of health. In fact, over the period, less than 18 per cent of employees retired at the contractual retirement age. In what one would imagine to be the most stressful parts of the Service, amongst prison officers and senior prison officers, the figures (Table 5.2) show that about 37 per cent of retirements were for reasons of health, whilst only about 15 per cent retired at the contractual retirement date.

Table 5.2   Prison service retirements – prison officers and senior prison officers

Year	Total	Age+	Age norm	Early	Health
1998	408	143	53	9	203
1999	449	177	74	18	180
2000	398	180	51	16	151
2001	554	229	86	101	138
1998- 2001	1809	729	264	144	672

Part of the explanation for the high proportion of individuals working beyond normal retirement age is the practice of prison officers moving to other operational grades, rather than continuing in their front line role.

A similar story emerges from retirement statistics for teachers (Table 5.3).[31]

Table 5.3   School teacher retirements

Year	Total	Age	Early	Health	Other
1998/99	10901	5266	2917	2718	-
1999/00	11709	5858	3140	2711	-
2000/01	13107	6084	3139	3023	861
2001/02	13654	6291	2561	2689	2113

In the period 1998 to 2002, approximately 49 per cent of teachers retired at their contractual retirement age. All the rest retired early, including about 23 per cent of the total who retired for health reasons.

---

31   Statistics and information from Teachers' Superannuation Working Party 2002

STATE PENSION AGE

The state pension age is another major influence on the retirement age in contracts of employment. More than three-quarters of men have a retirement age which is the same as the state retirement age. Prior to 1989, retirement was a prerequisite of receiving the state pension, but this is no longer so. 'Many people see state pension age as the point at which society as a whole regards it as reasonable that they should stop working.'[32]

MAKING WAY FOR YOUNGER WORKERS

Retiring older workers to make way for new workers entering the workforce has always been an argument by both employers and trade unions in favour of making people retire at a certain age. On a global scale this approach assumes that there are a finite number of jobs available and if older workers did not leave the workforce, then there would be few jobs for young people eager to enter the workforce. On a smaller level, it provides a simple means for employers to carry out workforce planning as older (and more senior) workers retire they can be replaced by suitably trained and promoted or recruited younger employees.

The global argument has a simplistic charm but is clearly nonsense. It assumes a static society and a static economy. It is termed the 'lump of labour fallacy.'[33]

> The lump of labour fallacy ignores the fact that, in a flexible labour market, wages can and do adjust. More people competing for jobs means that people are less keen to demand wage increases. This reduces inflationary pressures and allows interest rates (and higher non-inflationary growth) than would otherwise be the case.

A large number of new jobs are created in the UK economy each year. These are not jobs held by older workers denying a place to younger ones. There is no evidence that a lack of a mandatory retirement age would stop younger people entering the job market, as there is no evidence that the existence of a contractual retirement age would do so either.

The employer argument is seen as a means of enabling employers to plan their workforce, so that perhaps they can recruit, retain and train younger people to take over the positions of those that leave through retirement. This may be the effect in some organisations, but again it assumes a static workforce and an ordered procession in and out of organisations. Most HRM people will

32 *Retirement ages in the UK: a review of the literature* (2003)
33 See *Winning the Generation Game* (2000)

know that this is not the reality within organisations. Even the contractual retirement age cannot be relied upon to make this model of workforce planning happen. As has already been shown, most people retire at a different time to the expected retirement date, sometimes through ill health and sometimes for other reasons. It is difficult to see how this helps workforce planning.

YOUNGER WORKERS ARE MORE PRODUCTIVE

This last statement is, of course, not true except in a limited number of cases:

> *There is no evidence to support the view that older workers are inherently*
> *less productive than younger workers, except in a limited range of jobs*
> *requiring rapid reactions or physical strength, and people tend to move*
> *out of these as they become harder for them. Only where older workers*
> *do not receive the same level of training as younger workers doing the*
> *same kind of work does their performance show differences.*[34]

There are two aspects to this reason for keeping a mandatory retirement age. Firstly, there is the one dealt with in this quotation which is really about having stereotypical views about older and younger workers: older workers are slower, more resistant to change and so on. Hopefully, by the time you get to this part of the book you will have seen enough evidence to show that such generalisations should be unacceptable. The second factor is an important one: it is the likelihood that older workers, or those nearing retirement, earn more than younger workers for apparently doing the same or similar jobs. If one measures productivity as a return on costs, then it might be possible to argue the productivity point based on the lower wages of younger workers. An example of this in action is the *Taylor v Secretary of State for Scotland* case discussed above, where some 1000 prison officers were retired in a deliberate policy to recruit younger and less expensive workers. This is a reflection perhaps of having long salary scales which of course employers and trade unions have argued in favour of being retained. The longer scales are a combination of reward for service and a reflection of extra skills and knowledge attained by older workers.

Regardless of whether there is truth to the argument, however, the outcome is that older and more expensive employees can be removed because of their age and replaced by younger, cheaper employees, giving the employer a gain financially and perhaps managerially. This situation is not changed by the Age Regulations 2006, where the employer will be able to continue to do this.

---

34 *Retirement ages in the UK: a review of the literature* (2003)

EARLY RETIREMENT

Early retirement policies have been a means of encouraging older workers to exit the workforce. It is a contributory cause for there being almost three million people aged between 50 and state retirement age who are outside the labour market. The change in the workforce after the age of 50 years is quite staggering. The Cabinet office report *Winning the Generation Game* (2000) stated that at age 50, over 90 per cent of men are in the labour force in France and almost 90 per cent in the United States, Sweden and the United Kingdom. By the age of 60 years this had fallen to:

France	40 per cent
USA	67 per cent
Sweden	70 per cent
UK	48 per cent

Interestingly, in the United Kingdom, only one in ten of the 50–65 year age group were looking for work, but only 18 per cent classified themselves as retired. The same report tried to categorise these 'missing people' into five groups:

1.   Early retired, affluent professionals – some 12 per cent of the total; they have retired voluntarily and have good occupational pensions and savings, as well as being homeowners.

2.   Occupational pensioners with changed expectations – homeowners with low mortgages who took early retirement because there was little alternative to this; having to adjust lifestyle to new income level.

3.   Displaced workers on invalidity benefit – former skilled manual workers who had been in a previous job for over ten years; made redundant due to company closure with small occupational income; have tried to get work again but have been unsuccessful; now de-motivated and health has suffered, so are now on invalidity benefit; wary of taking work now because of the effect on state income.

4.   Family carers – some 85 per cent of these are women; not looking for work and supported by low-paid partner; not been in full-time employment for some time and now caring for elderly relative and maybe grandchildren.

5.   Job seekers – unskilled men with few educational qualifications; have some temporary jobs but money is tight and health beginning to fail.

It is possible to argue that early retirement is a voluntary process and that, often, workers will volunteer for early retirement. It is also possible to argue that early retirement policies are a manifestation of how age discrimination had become an acceptable method of reducing the size of a workforce. It is older workers who qualify for early retirement and who, often with the agreement of the trade unions, are selected for exiting purely because of their chronological age. It is an example of indirect discrimination, which has its major impact on older workers.

One report claimed:[35]

> Trade unions often appear to condone these practices, on the basis that redundancy and unemployment is more acceptable for older than for younger workers. In the UK, for example, trade unions sometimes campaign for 'voluntary' redundancy measures, in practice targeted at older workers, in order to avoid compulsory redundancies spread across all age groups.

It is not possible to say how many of these 'voluntary' schemes are really voluntary (although the European Commission estimated that some 40 per cent of early retirees felt that there was an element of coercion in their decision[36]) or what proportion of affected workers feel under pressure to accept enhanced benefits, which might not be available in a situation of compulsory redundancies. The practice is seen as an acceptable way of dismissing older workers in order to avoid dismissing workers in other age groups.

The relationship between voluntary and involuntary redundancy and early retirement was considered in *Agco Ltd v Massey Ferguson Works Pension Trust Ltd*. This concerned a situation where a large number of people (1090) were made compulsorily redundant and a much smaller number (20) took voluntary redundancy. The pension scheme provided retirement benefits for any member over the age of 50 years who 'retires from service at the request of the employer'. The issue was whether voluntary or compulsory redundancy meant retiring at the request of the employer. Did the term 'request of the employer' mean that the employee should have a choice or could it apply to situations where request meant no choice, as in a compulsory redundancy situation?

The Court recognised that even in voluntary situations there could exist the threat of the 'sword of Damocles', where if there were insufficient volunteers,

---

35   Drury (1993)
36   *Towards a Europe for all Ages* (1999)

then there might be compulsory redundancies on less favourable terms. Retirement, however, was an entirely consensual event. Rix LJ stated:

> It might be regretted when it comes, but in employment terms it is an entirely consensual event, the event of retirement, and it comes about by effluxion of time and the expiry of the contract of employment. It seems to me that the concept of dismissal by the employer is very far from the kernel of meaning.

Compulsory redundancies and most other forms of dismissal are not consensual events and could not be said to be events when the employee retires at the request of the employer. These were not events that took place as a result of the exercise of the employee's own free will. Voluntary redundancy, however, despite 'the theoretical existence of an element of pressure or coercion', is to be seen as a consensual event and, therefore, those that took voluntary redundancy were entitled to claim that they had taken retirement at the request of the employer.

In the past, UK Governments have encouraged policies of early retirement, although the Job Release Scheme was halted in 1988. Insufficient is known about the effects on individuals who are 'early-retired', although one French study suggested:[37]

> After an explosion of initial optimism, early retirees are quickly faced with a change in the reality of their lives, in a society which has not yet developed honourable alternative roles which could be taken on by young, active and healthy retirees.

The study suggested that many such people refuse to join organisations for older people or find an alternative role for themselves outside work. They are also likely to find it more difficult to return to work and, in the words of the French study, 'their standard of living will also fall'.

Early retirement on enhanced packages was an attractive way for employers to reduce the size of their workforces, not least because such schemes could often be funded by the pension scheme rather than by the employer. The enhanced packages are now less common, but there remains pressure on older employees to consider such retirement. NATFHE (1995) stated its position as:

> Providing attractive redundancy packages to encourage early retirement as a means of reducing staff numbers perpetuates negative stereotypes of older workers abilities and worth. Older workers may be subjected

---

37   Gaullier (1988)

to moral pressure to leave both from management and from younger colleagues who may see older staff as standing in the way of their own advancement. Psychological bullying and devaluing older workers in an attempt to produce mass early retirements is universal.

One problem is that most people do most of their saving for retirement after the age of 50. People who are not in work are less able to save which may result in poverty and ill health in old age.

REPLACING THE MANDATORY RETIREMENT AGE

It has been suggested that retirement is 'both the leading form of age discrimination and the driving force behind the wider development of ageism in modern societies'.[38]

Despite the views of the Court in *Agco* (see above) it is difficult to see how retirement can be generalised as a consensual event. The age of retirement may be in the contract of employment and, of course, that will make it part of the agreed terms between employer and employee. Taking the view that the employment contract, 'as a voluntary consensual relationship sanctioned by the civil law, is suffused with an individualism that ignores the economic reality behind the bargain'[39], one might argue that the reality is that people have just accepted the term without ever really considering it or agreeing to it.

The contractual retirement age, and now the default retirement age contained in the Age Regulations 2006, is an event where an employee is treated less favourably than other employees because of their chronological age. At this age, the employee is dismissed from their employment. To describe it as a contract that terminates through the 'effluxion of time' as was stated in *Agco* is to misunderstand the event. It cannot be equated with the ending of a fixed-term contract which does run out at the appointed time, although even this can amount to a dismissal. It is a point where the employer will be protected from claims of age discrimination or unfair dismissal. Provided in future an employer follows the correct procedure, a person will lose all their protection against losing their job and ending their working life.

In the Age Regulations 2006 (see Chapter 8) the Government has taken the retirement age issue from the contract of employment and enshrined it in statute.

---

38   See Walker (1990)
39   Wedderburn (1986), p. 142

According to the 2005 Consultation document, the Framework Directive 'allows age discrimination if it can be objectively justified'.[40] The Government obviously is convinced that the proposed national default retirement age can be so justified. It will be difficult to argue that the allowing of compulsory retirement does not amount to less favourable treatment. It must, therefore, be able to objectively justify the introduction of this new concept of a national default retirement age. The difference between this and a national retirement age seems to be the element of choice. Employers and employees can agree about retirement and then the default retirement age need not apply, although compulsory retirement before the age of 65 is to become unlawful.[41]

The Framework Directive does not say a great deal about retirement ages. Paragraph 14 of the preamble states that the Directive shall be 'without prejudice to national provisions laying down retirement ages'. Article 6.2 allows for the fixing of ages for invalidity and retirement schemes, and the use of ages for actuarial calculations, without it constituting age discrimination. Article 8.2 provides that any measures implementing the Directive shall not lessen the protection against discrimination that already exists in the Member State.

Unfortunately for the United Kingdom Government, there have been no national provisions laying down a retirement age. Most retirement ages are a matter of contract and are ostensibly a matter for negotiation between the employer and the employee or the employee's representative. A significant minority of people do not, however, have such a term in their contract of employment. It is difficult to see how a national default retirement age can be introduced without it being seen as a worsening of the position of those people without one prior to the Age Regulations.

Perversely, the Government may be relying on paragraph 14, as well as paragraph 15, and Article 6.2 to justify the introduction of a default age. Paragraph 15 of the preamble 15 states that:

> the appreciation of the facts from which it may be inferred that there has been direct or indirect discrimination is a matter for national judicial or other competent bodies, in accordance with rules of national law or practice.

Thus, one would need to argue that, in accordance with Article 6.2, the United Kingdom does fix the age for the payment of retirement benefit and that this is an age set by many pension schemes, so that the normal retirement

---

40   Para 6.1.3
41   Sargeant (2006), *ILJ* (forthcoming)

age for individuals coincides with the pensionable retirement age. In effect therefore, there are national provisions laying down retirement ages and it would be open to the British courts to confirm whether there are facts from which they could infer that there has been discrimination.

In adopting the policy of introducing a default retirement age the Government has entirely adopted an employers/business agenda. There is no pretence that it is anything else. The 2005 Consultation document states that:

> In setting the default age, we have taken careful note of a number of representations we received in the course of consultations, which made it clear that significant numbers of employers use a set retirement age as a necessary part of their workforce planning. Whilst an increasing number of employers are able to organise their business around the best practice of having no set retirement age for all or particular groups of their workforce, some nevertheless still rely on it heavily. This is our primary reason for setting the default retirement age [emphasis added].[42]

It will be interesting to see how the Government argues that employers' lack of best practice amounts to objective justification for introducing the national default retirement age in any future challenge at the European Court of Justice. The fact that this employers' agenda has been adopted can be seen in the responses to the 2003 Consultation. Most of the employer responses supported the introduction of the default retirement age and all the trade unions who responded opposed it. The employers were concerned with how to end people's careers with dignity, rather than through disciplinary procedures. There was a general assumption that older workers would decline in competence and capability as they aged, but would nevertheless wait to be dismissed or retired rather than leave voluntarily. Thus, the British Hospitality Association stated that there were bound to be circumstances where employees wished to continue working and the employer wished them to retire. Having to go through the formal disciplinary procedure on competence grounds may be much more distressing than having to retire at a certain age. British Energy stated that:

> We would not want to resort to using our capability/competence procedure for long-serving loyal employees who chose to stay on to a point where it affects their ability to do the job effectively. The effect would be very negative on staff morale generally if this were to happen in organisations.

---

42   Para 6.1.14

The Food and Drink Federation was also concerned that employees kept on at the moment until retirement would lose out. They stated that:

> We think that the abolition of the mandatory retirement age would send entirely the wrong signal. We believe that the focus of this legislation should be ensuring fair treatment for older employees in their employment.

In contrast to this the TGWU stated that:

> The T & G has grave concerns that allowing a default mandatory retirement age of 70 [which was proposed at the time] will have the effect of creating a legislative justification for age discrimination. We are unclear why the government proposes to allow discrimination against 70 year olds when it is outlawing it for workers in their 60s, and we believe that the government's approach should instead emphasise choice for older workers, and a flexible period of retirement for people aged 50+. We want to encourage collective agreements in this area; failing competency is a completely different issue from ageing and the two should be clearly separated.

RETIREMENT PENSIONS

One of the consistent themes of responses to Government consultation on age discrimination has been that of the trade unions which have been concerned that an abolition of the mandatory retirement age, or any change to the retirement age, should not be at the expense of an individual's right to a decent retirement pension. There has been a suspicion that measures affecting the retirement age are really intended to reduce the current pension entitlement of workers at a certain age. One trade union, Amicus, for example, declared that it was against setting a default retirement age at 70[43] because this would encourage employers to reduce pension benefits currently available at state pension age. Creating an opportunity for the minority who wish to carry on working must not be at the expense of others. One way for employers to reduce costs is for there to be a later retirement age with reduced benefits for those who retire earlier; Amicus believed that 'the government should seek to protect the current right of those employees who are contractually entitled to retire on full pension not later than 65'.[44]

---

43   This was a proposal in 2003 consultation
44   Amicus response to the 2003 DTI consultation exercise, published in 2005

Britain's trade unions have been campaigning firstly, for a retirement pension and secondly, for a reasonable level of income, since the latter part of the nineteenth century. The first significant step towards this took place in 1908 with the adoption of the Old Age Pensions Act. This was introduced by David Lloyd George who was then Chancellor of the Exchequer in the Liberal Government. The Act introduced, from 1 January 1909, a general non-contributory pension of five shillings (25p) per week from the age of 70, for those with an income of less than £26 per annum. This is not a great amount as five shillings in 1909 is probably worth about £16 today. It was also means tested. In 1925 the pension age was reduced to 65 years for both men and women. The 1925 Act introduced contributory flat rate benefits for insured workers and wives and gave rights to pensions to married women when their spouses reached retirement age. It also provided some pensions for older women.[45] The pension age for women was further reduced to 60 years in 1940 and means tested supplementary pensions for people over pension age and for widows were introduced.[46] In 1948, the post-Second World War Labour Government, following the Beveridge Report, adopted the National Insurance Act which introduced a compulsory and comprehensive contributory state scheme for all. It also allowed married women to opt out and rely on their husbands' contributions and receive a reduced rate of 60 per cent of the full state pension (this was abolished in the Social Security Act 1975). At the beginning, pension levels were set at £1 and 6 shillings (£1.30) for a single person and £2 and 2 shillings (£2.10) for a married couple. It was paid from the age of 65 for men and 60 for women.[47] The achievement of these pensions has not been followed by achievements in the setting of amounts that provide for a comfortable retirement on their own. It is the fear of trade unions that any measures to change the retirement age might lead to even a lessening of what is provided now.

The assumption behind the trade union campaigns has, of course, been that those who retire at the end of their working life are entitled to a reasonable income in their retirement. This may be the approach in some other EU Member States but has not been the case in the United Kingdom. The purpose of the state pension seems to be to prevent poverty only. The Pensions Commission in its first report summed this position up:

> *Among the rich developed countries the UK is therefore in a specific group with Ireland, New Zealand and Canada, where the state pension is primarily designed to prevent poverty rather than to provide income*

---

45 Widows, Orphans and Old Age Contributory Pensions Act 1925
46 Old Age and Widows Pensions Act 1940
47 It also allowed working married women to opt out and rely on their husband's insurance for pension income. This option was eventually abolished by the Social Security Act 1975

replacement. In these systems, replacement rates for those on half average earnings during working life are not far below continental levels but they are much lower for the average earner.[48]

Given this situation it seems rather strange to force people to give up work and enter into near poverty. Many people have some alternative income to add to the State Pension, but many do not. Some 59 per cent of employees work for a firm with a fixed retirement age – 68 per cent men and 48 per cent women.[49] More than twice as many professional men (76 per cent) are members of an occupational pensions scheme compared to unskilled workers (34 per cent); for women the figures are 71 per cent and 27 per cent. One particular group at a disadvantage are part-time women employees, 28 per cent of whom are in occupational pension schemes compared to 55 per cent of full-timers.

An acceptance that state pension provision in the United Kingdom is actually about the alleviation of poverty, rather than about replacement of income from work, might effect the argument about the mandatory retirement age, contained in so many contracts of employment, and the so-called default retirement age. If the reality is that for many pensioners the objective of the state pension is the alleviation of poverty, then it does not seem sensible to argue for a mandatory retirement age. The logic of the argument for the stipulation of this age is that it is intended to drive many into poverty and then give them the minimum financial help contained in the state retirement pension. One argument for retaining flexibility is to enable some people to work their way out of poverty. The second report of the Turner Commission on pensions argued for more flexibility around retirement. It said, of the state pension system, that:

Given demographic trends, either the average generosity of this system (relative to national earnings) or pensionable ages must rise, or the tax/ national insurance contributions devoted to pensions must rise as a percentage of GDP.[50]

Not only was the old system unfair it was also unsustainable given the change in the demographic make-up of the population.

Most other unions supported this call for flexibility, such as the GMB which stated that some members look forward to a fixed retirement age and others wanted more flexibility:

---

48 *Pensions: Challenges and Choices The First Report of the Pensions Commission* (2004)
49 *Ageing and employment policies UK* (2004)
50 *A New Pension Settlement for the Twenty-First Century: The Second Report of the Pensions Commission* (2005)

The GMB wants to see a framework which enables employers and trade unions to come together to develop a flexible approach to retirement. This would enable older workers to scale down their activity gradually by working part-time.

Thus, we are to have a default retirement age of 65. Retirement below the age of 65 will need to be objectively justified and presumably this will be entirely possible and proper in some cases. The proposals are that Section 98 of the Employment Rights Act 1996 is amended to add another fair reason for dismissal which will be 'retirement of the employee'. There is, however, no requirement to go through any statutory dismissal procedure. This is replaced by a statutory retirement procedure as outlined in new Sections 98ZA to 98ZE of the Employment Rights Act.

For retirement to be taken as the only reason for dismissal, it must take place on the default retirement age, or another date which can be objectively justifiable. There is still the opportunity for the employee to claim that the real reason for dismissal was some other reason and that the planned retirement would not have taken place but for this other reason, or if the dismissal amounts to unlawful discrimination under the Regulations. This will not be easy and the 2005 Consultation states that there will be a heavy burden of proof on the employee. The planned retirement date is 65 years unless there is an alternative date which is the normal retirement age, in which case it is that date.[51] Having established that the reason for dismissal is retirement on the planned date is fair, there is then a procedure in which the employer and employee must participate. Failure on the employer's part in this regard may render the dismissal unfair.

The statutory retirement procedure comprises a duty on the employer to consider a request from the employee to work beyond retirement.[52] There is a duty upon the employer to inform the employee of the intended retirement date and the employee's right to make a request. There is then a statutory right for the employee to request that he or she be not retired on the intended retirement date. The employer then has a duty to consider this request. This is done by holding a meeting with the employee, unless not reasonably practicable. The TUC, in its response to the 2005 consultation, thought this procedure weak, especially as there is no obligation upon the employer to give reasons for refusals. The CBI was concerned that the decision reached as a result of the

---

51   Sections 98ZA-98ZC Employment Rights Act 1996 as amended
52   Age Regulations, Schedule 7

duty to consider procedure should not be challengeable at an Employment Tribunal.

There is also an appeal procedure for the employee if turned down and timescales for meetings and decisions. Most notably there is an absence of criteria to be used by the employer in their consideration of the employee's request. Their only duty is to follow the procedure and consider it.

Thus the situation will be that where there is no consensual retirement, the employer may dismiss the employee and this dismissal will be a 'fair' dismissal provided it takes place on the planned retirement date and the employer follows the statutory retirement procedure for consideration of any request from the employee not to retire. The Government's 2005 Consultation document states that:

> We want to encourage employers and employees to extend working life beyond the national default retirement age.

It is difficult to comprehend this measure achieving this objective, given the employers' enthusiasm for a default retirement age in response to the Government's 2003 Consultation. The Government also proposes to review in 2011 the necessity of keeping the default retirement age. Unfortunately, the result of this procrastination in decision making is that a large number of people will be compulsory retired during this period and exited from the work force in contravention of the Government's intended outcome.

The likely outcome of any decision by the employer not to require the employee to retire at the planned retirement date is for the employer to agree a new date. In effect, this will allow the employee to continue on a fixed-term contract. This will be important for the employer because the Government plans to repeal Section 109 of the Employment Rights Act 1996, so that employees over the normal retirement age or 65 will continue to receive protection against unfair dismissal, unlike the period prior to the Regulations.[53]

In this sense, older workers – those over 65 or the normal retirement date – will continue to be discriminated against. This will be as a result of the Age Regulations which were, perhaps idealistically speaking, intended to stop age discrimination. Older workers will have no security, knowing that their employer can legitimately dismiss them at each new planned retirement date, provided a procedure of information and consideration is followed. This continuing discrimination against this age group is emphasised by the fact

---

53   Age Regulations, Schedule 6

that those over 65 years will also not have protection against discrimination in recruitment. One of the most difficult issues for older workers is finding work. According to the Age Regulations employers will be able legitimately to discriminate against the over-65s in recruitment and selection.[54]

The Government suggests that the concept of retirement needs to be challenged.[55] A traditional pattern of a lifelong job followed by retirement at the end of working life is an increasingly inaccurate description of the reality today. The reality, however, is that often the actual or normal retirement age is linked, where there is a choice, to the receipt of financial support from the state benefit system, the state retirement pension and any occupational pension scheme available. Merely abolishing the contractual retirement age is likely to achieve little on its own. It is the manipulation and availability of financial benefits, such as enhanced pension benefits on early retirement, that are likely to alter perceptions of when people should or could retire. Much also, however, depends upon how successful the Government is in changing attitudes of employers and employees to the justifiability of age discrimination, so that employers, for example, are not able to say that all persons of a certain age are too old to employ.

54   Age Regulations, Regulation 7(4)
55   *Winning the Generation Game* (2000)

CHAPTER 6
Experiences in Other Countries

The purpose of this Chapter is to examine the operation of age discrimination legislation in a number of other States.[1] It is not intended to be a comprehensive analysis, but seeks to highlight some of the issues that have resulted from the introduction of legislation and the resulting litigation in other countries.[2]

AUSTRALIA

In 2004, the Federal Government adopted the Age Discrimination Act (ADA). As an illustration of the similarity of concerns with the United Kingdom experience, the explanatory memorandum accompanying the Australian legislation stated that:

> *The proposed new age discrimination bill will be an integral part of a wide range of key Government policy priorities to respond to the ageing workforce and population.... Age discrimination is clearly a problem for both younger and older Australians. In relation to older Australians, in particular, many recent reports have emphasised the negative consequences of age discrimination on the wellbeing of older Australians and the broader consequences for the community. There is also evidence that the ageing of Australia's population will lead to an increase in the problem of age discrimination if Government action is not taken to address this issue. Government action is needed to address the generally unfounded negative stereotypes that employers and policy makers may have about both younger and older Australians, which limit their contribution to the community and the economy.*

Indeed, by 2051 over 25 per cent of Australians will be aged 65 years plus.

The key features of anti-discrimination laws in Australia are summed up as follows:[3]

---

1   I would like to thank Niduk Wijayasingha of Middlesex University for her research help with this Chapter
2   See also Hornstein (2001)
3   Taken from the Explanatory Memorandum accompanying the Commonwealth Age Discrimination Bill 2003, p. 3; now the Age Discrimination Act 2004

- such protection derives from Commonwealth, State and Territory statute;

- both direct and indirect discrimination are covered;

- discrimination on certain grounds, such as sex, race, disability and age, are prohibited in 'key areas of public life' such as work, access to goods, services and facilities, access to premises, places and transport, and education;

- provides for a range of exceptions to allow for legitimate distinctions;

- public awareness and education are important elements in overcoming discrimination;

- creates various institutions to consider infringements.

STATE LEVEL

It is at State level, rather than at the Commonwealth level, that measures against age discrimination were initiated. The first legislation making it unlawful was adopted by the State of South Australia by an amendment in 1990 to the Equal Opportunity Act 1984. Queensland followed suit in 1992, Western Australia in 1993 and New South Wales in 1994. Other States followed with the last one being Tasmania in 1999.

The Equal Opportunity Act in South Australia covered discrimination on sex, race, disability, sexuality, pregnancy and sexual harassment. The amendment concerning age came into effect in June 1991. The Act follows the UK Sex Discrimination Act and Race Relations Act to include provisions relating to direct and indirect discrimination. Discrimination in the areas of recruitment and selection, terms and conditions offered, training, promotion and transfer opportunities, and subjecting the employee to dismissal or some other detriment are all forbidden.[4] There was also an exception for a genuine occupational requirement as well as for retirement ages.[5] Specific exceptions, apart from the genuine occupational requirement, are employment in a private household and where a person may not be able to perform adequately, given as a person is not being able:

---

4   Section 85b
5   Section 85f

- to perform adequately, and without endangering himself or herself or other persons, the work genuinely and reasonably required for the employment or position in question; or

- to respond adequately to situations of emergency that should reasonably be anticipated in connection with the employment or position in question.

The mandatory retirement age also came within the provisions of the Act when it was effectively abolished from 1 January 1994.

FEDERAL ACTION

The Workplace Relations Act 1996 contains some provisions concerning discrimination in employment, including discrimination on the grounds of age. Section 3j of the Act states that its principal objective is:

respecting and valuing diversity in the workforce by helping to prevent and eliminate discrimination on the basis of race, colour, sex, sexual preference, age, physical or mental disability, marital status, family responsibilities, pregnancy, religion, political opinion, national extraction or social origin.

Complaints about discrimination in employment can be made to the Human Rights and Equal Opportunity Commission (HREOC). Complaints included:

- age requirements in agency job vacancies;

- age requirements for vacancies in the defence forces;

- complaints from those over 65 refused employment;

- age discrimination and trade union membership;

- older people being treated less well in redundancy packages.

A precursor of the 2004 Federal legislation was a major report by the HREOC called *Age Matters; a report on age discrimination.* This report was presented in May 2000. It considered issues of age discrimination where 'an opportunity is denied to a person solely because of his or her chronological age and age is irrelevant to the person's ability to take advantage of that opportunity'.

The report is not dissimilar in its scope to the UK Government's consultations on the Age Discrimination Regulations. This included the question of job-related exceptions to the anti-discrimination legislation. One such is a part of the Workplace Relations Act 1996 which provides an exemption when the age distinction is based on the inherent requirements of the job. The HREOC had received complaints about age distinctions in the Australian defence forces. In one case cited, *Bradley's Case*, the complainant claimed that he was discriminated against when he was denied access to the Specialist Service Officer Scheme. Entry was limited to the age range of 19 to 28. Mr Bradley was 37 years old. The army argued that older officers would not have the required level of fitness nor would they be able to cope with the stress. The HREOC did not accept that there was a direct correlation between the applicant's age and the ability to meet the entrance criteria, so it was held to be discriminatory.

The report found evidence of continuing age discrimination, such as a Drake Personnel survey of the top 500 Australian employers, which indicated that none would choose to employ managers or executives in their 50s and 65 per cent said that this group would be the first to go in the event of redundancies.[6]

Amongst its recommendations it concluded:[7]

> *All Australian States and Territories now have legislation making age discrimination unlawful, although the scope of the legislation differs significantly in some respects such as compulsory retirement. Federal law is now the weakest and most inadequate. It does not make age discrimination unlawful. It deals only with employment and then very narrowly and ineffectively.*
>
> *More effectively, the Commonwealth could enact a broader Age Discrimination Act comparable in its scope and application to the existing federal anti-discrimination Acts.*

The Age Discrimination Act 2004 covers more than just work. It also applies to access to goods, services and facilities; access to premises and transport; Federal laws and programmes; education; accommodation and land. Its objects are contained in Section 3, some of which are in stark contrast to the UK Age Regulations. These objects of the Act include:

- to eliminate, as far as possible, discrimination against persons on the grounds of age in the areas of work, education, access to premises, the provision of goods, services and facilities ...;

- to ensure, as far as practicable, that everyone has the same right to equality before the law, regardless of age, as the rest of the community;

---

6   Page 12
7   Pages 116–117

- to allow appropriate benefits and other assistance to be given to people of a certain age, particularly younger and older persons, in recognition of their particular circumstances;

- to promote recognition and acceptance within the community of the principle that people of all ages have the same fundamental rights;

- to respond to demographic change by removing barriers to older people particularly in the workforce and changing negative stereotypes about older people.

There are a number of exceptions of course. One of these is contained in Section 6 of the Act and stops claims for both age discrimination and disability discrimination. It is recognised that there is a significant overlap between these two and, somewhat distressingly, the answer for the Australian legislature is to make sure that claims cannot be made on the two grounds, unless, of course, the cause of complaint is distinguishable. Other exemptions are the inherent requirements of the job[8] (see below); youth wages[9]; superannuation, insurance and credit[10]; and positive discrimination[11] (this is to be permitted to allow measures for the benefit of a particular age group, or to prevent or reduce a disadvantage that might be suffered by a particular age group).

DEFINITIONS

The ADA provides that direct discrimination occurs where, because of a person's age, the discriminator treats the aggrieved person less favourably than they would a person of a different age and the discriminator does so because of:

- the age of the aggrieved person; or

- a characteristic that appertains generally to persons of the age of the aggrieved person; or

- a characteristic that is generally imputed to persons of the age of the aggrieved person.[12]

Indirect discrimination occurs where a person:

---

8   ADA 2004 , section 18(4)
9   Ibid., section 25
10   Ibid., section 37; Superannuation relates to the accumulation of retirement savings and life assurance calculations. Insurance and credit relate to non-employment law issues, but it is interesting to speculate how we in the United Kingdom would deal with these issues if age discrimination legislation were to spread to other fields. The Australian proposals will exempt actuarial calculations used to work out insurance risk and credit ratings.
11   Ibid., section 33
12   Ibid., section 14

- imposes, or proposes to impose, a condition, requirement or practice; and

- the condition, requirement or practice is not reasonable in the circumstances; and

- the condition, requirement or practice has, or is likely to have, the effect of disadvantaging persons of the same age as the aggrieved person.[13]

The burden of proof that the condition, requirement or practice is reasonable in the circumstances rests with the discriminator.[14] A further important feature is that the legislation applies to a much wider framework than just employment.

In employment terms the Act specifically makes unlawful age discrimination in relation to:[15]

- the arrangements made for the purpose of determining who should be offered employment;

- in determining who should be offered employment;

- in the terms and conditions offered and made available;

- denying or limiting access to opportunities for promotion, transfer or training;

- dismissals;

- subjecting the employee to any other detriment.

The ADA 2004 also provides an exemption for positive discrimination.[16] Provided the act is consistent with the purposes of the ADA, then positive discrimination is permitted in relation to acts which:

- provide a bona fide benefit to persons of a particular age. An example of this might be a hairdresser giving a discount to senior citizens;[17]

- are intended to meet a need that arises out of the age of the persons of a particular age, such as the provision of extra welfare services for the young such as helping with homelessness;

---

13 Ibid., section 15
14 Ibid., section 15(3)
15 Ibid., section 18
16 ADA 2004, section 33
17 The examples are taken from the explanatory memorandum to the Act

- are intended to reduce a disadvantage experienced by persons of a particular age, the provision of additional notice entitlements for older workers.

As in the United Kingdom, there is also an exemption for youth wages, in this case for those under the age of 21. This is designed to aid the recruitment of young people.

Attitudinal change is an objective of the Australian legislation so that 'people are judged on their actual capacity, rather than age being used as a blunt proxy for capacity'.[18] This Act is part of that process and has the specific objective of reducing the incidence of age discrimination.

INHERENT REQUIREMENTS OF THE JOB

There is an exemption in the ADA 2004 which allows an employer to discriminate on the grounds of age if the person 'is unable to carry out the inherent requirements of the particular employment because of his or her age'. This reflects the State and Territory laws on this subject. The term seems to be a general catch-all for jobs which require people of a certain age to perform the duties of a particular job.

Quantas Airways Ltd v Christie concerned an airline pilot who worked for Quantas Airways. His employment had ended when he reached the age of 60. He claimed that his employment had been terminated in breach of Section 170DF(1)f of the Industrial Relations Act 1988[19], which prohibited termination of an employee's employment on the grounds of age. Section 170DF(2) provided for an exception to this rule:

> *(2) Subsection (1) does not prevent a matter referred to in paragraph (1)(f) from being a reason for terminating employment if the reason is based on the inherent requirements of the particular post.*

The Court observed that just because an employer requires employment to come to an end when an employee reaches a certain age, this does not necessarily mean that one should automatically conclude that the termination of employment at that age is by reason of age. This issue was also considered in *Stanley Edward Griffin v Australian Postal Corporation.*[20] Mr Griffin was retired at the age of 65 against his will. He wished to continue working and claimed that he had been terminated on the grounds of his age and that this amounted to age

---

18 See Guide to the Employment Bill 2003 page 10
19 Now the Workplace Relations Act 1996
20 Industrial Relations Court of Australia 980001 September 15 1998

discrimination contrary to the New South Wales Anti Discrimination Act 1977. The issue for the Court was whether it had jurisdiction. The *Australian Post* argued that it did not terminate Mr Griffin's employment, but rather it came to an end as a result of an agreement or the operation of law. In other words, the term of the contract of employment had expired. This is an interesting concept which suggests that everyone who has a contract of employment which stipulates a retirement age is really on a fixed-term contract and that there is no such concept of permanent employment in these circumstances.

Quantas argued that it did not terminate Mr Christie's appointment. It argued that his employment also came to an end by 'the effluxion of time'. This was because there was a term in his contract, or a condition of his employment relationship, that his employment would terminate not later than his 60th birthday.[21] The only argument in favour of its retirement policy put forward by Quantas when this case reached the High Court was the 'Rule of 60', incorporated into the Convention on International Civil Aviation, which allows States to exclude from its airspace any aircraft flown by a pilot over the age of 60 years. This would severely limit the number of flights that Mr Christie could operate.[22] The earlier Court had, as a result of this, concluded that being under the age of 60 was an inherent requirement of the job as an airline captain. The Court had adopted the definition of 'inherent requirements' as meaning that:

> There must be a clear and definite relationship between the inherent or intrinsic characteristics of the employment and the disability in question, the very nature of which disqualifies the person from being able to perform the characteristic tasks or skills required in the specific performance.[23]

The problem in this case was that Mr Christie could perform the 'characteristic tasks or skills required', but was unable to do so because of the international nature of the job. The argument was whether, therefore, the 'inherent requirement' rule should be interpreted narrowly or widely.

The High Court did not favour the narrow interpretation and suggested that a practical method of deciding whether there was an inherent requirement was to ask whether the position would be essentially the same if that requirement was dispensed with. In this case the issue was whether he could continue to do the job without flying the international routes and that this would not have

---

21 The retirement issue was covered by an agreement between the employers and the Australian Federation of Airline Pilots which seemed to have been incorporated into the contract of employment

22 The Court stated that this left just flights to New Zealand, Denpasar (Indonesia) and Fiji

23 *X v Department of Defense*

been possible without creating a special position for him vis-à-vis the way that work for pilots was organised.

The issue was also considered in the Federal Court in *Commonwealth of Australia v Human Rights and Equal Opportunity Commission* (the HREOC). This concerned an application for judicial review of a finding by the HREOC that the Australian Defence Force had discriminated against Mr Bradley on the grounds of age (see above) when they refused to consider his application for appointment to a helicopter pilot training scheme on the grounds of his age.

The army argued that the age range was a result of the inherent requirements of the job which included medical fitness, physical performance, training failures (of other mature pilots), peer-group integration and obtaining a sufficient return on their investment. In an obvious stereotypical argument the army stated that:

> *Experience in Australian and overseas armed forces has shown that mature aged qualified pilots encounter a high incidence of difficulty in 'unlearning' acquired habits and skills to adapt to the unique requirements of military aviation. Also the physical, psychological and social stresses encountered during training are such that an older entrant would be a very high risk of failure.*

The HREOC had concluded that the rule was discriminatory and that the selected age range was not an inherent requirement of the job. The army's concerns could have been met by the other criteria, including medical fitness. It was the connection between these inherent requirements and the age range that was the problem. As Tamberlin J stated:

> *The consequences of using a broad criterion such as age to correlate with the inherent requirements of the job is that the broader the criterion, the greater will be the number of cases in which discrimination is allowed to occur.*

CANADA

Canada, like Australia, has a federal system of government. Age discrimination measures are provided by the human rights legislation at both federal level and within the ten provinces. Generally speaking, this protection is part of a wider protection against discrimination in a number of different areas apart from employment.[24] In this human rights sense the purpose of anti-discrimination

---

24   See Gunderson (2003), pp. 318–328; also Gunderson (2001)

laws 'is to prevent the violation of human dignity and freedom through the imposition of disadvantage, stereotyping, or political or social prejudice'.[25]

The Canadian Charter of Rights and Freedoms was adopted in 1982 and is an important factor in the regulation of discrimination issues. Section 15(1) states:

> *Every individual is equal before and under the law and has the right to the equal protection and equal benefit of the law without discrimination and, in particular, without discrimination based on race, national or ethnic origin, colour, religion, sex, age or mental or physical disability.*

These rights are limited by Article 1, which states:

> *The Canadian Charter of Rights and Freedoms guarantees the rights and freedoms set out in it subject only to such reasonable limits prescribed by law as can be demonstrably justified in a free and democratic society.*

Thus the freedom from discrimination in Article 15 is subject to reasonable limitation as set out in Article 1. This has had an effect on the Canadian approach to protection from age discrimination, especially with respect to the rules on mandatory retirement. These rules are limited in two different ways by the different Provincial Governments.[26] The first is to have a maximum age at which the legislation ceases to apply (British Columbia, Saskatchewan, Ontario and Newfoundland). This has the effect of allowing mandatory retirement past this age of, normally, 65. The second approach is to exclude pension and retirement plans from age discrimination legislation, thus allowing mandatory retirement in these circumstances (Federal Government, Alberta, Quebec, New Brunswick, Nova Scotia, Prince Edward Island).

The approach to the Article 1 restriction is set out in *McKinney v University of Guelph*. The Court held that were a number of steps:

- an assessment of the objectives of the law to determine whether they are sufficiently important to warrant the limitation;

- the challenged law is then subject to a proportionality test to balance the objectives against the nature of the right, the extent of its infringement, and the degree to which the limitation furthers other rights or policies of importance.

---

25 *Policy on discrimination against older persons because of age* (2002); see www.ohrc.on.ca
26 See Gunderson (2003)

McKinney concerned a number of academics who objected to being retired and based their claim upon Article 15. LaForest J was, however, quite clear that mandatory retirement was justifiable in this situation and was a reasonable limitation on Charter rights:

> *Mandatory retirement ... ensures continuing faculty renewal, a necessary process to enable universities to be centres of excellence. Universities need to be on the cutting edge of new discoveries and ideas, and this requires a continuing infusion of new people. In a closed system with limited resources, this can only be achieved by departures of other people. Mandatory retirement achieves this in an orderly way that permits long-term planning both by universities and the individual.*

This is a somewhat dated approach and might be difficult to prove. The case was somewhat limited by *GVRD Employees' Union v GVRD*[27], which suggested that the approach in *McKinney* and similar cases did not imply that mandatory retirement was always justified and that it had to be considered on a case-by-case basis. In this case the individual concerned was offered a position which was then withdrawn when it was discovered that he was over 65 years of age. The British Columbia Court of Appeal suggested that in the 11 years since *McKinney* 'the demographies of the workplace have changed considerably' and 'the social and legislative facts now available may well cast doubt on the extent to which the courts should defer to legislative decisions made over a decade ago'.

ONTARIO

Ontario is used here as an example of the activities at Provincial level. The Ontario Human Rights Commission (OHRC)[28] was established in 1961 to administer the Ontario Human Rights Code. The OHRC's role is to:

- investigate complaints of discrimination and harassment;

- try to settle complaints between parties;

- prevent discrimination through public education and public policy;

- investigate situations where discriminatory behaviour exists.

The Code has been updated on a number of occasions, most recently in 2002. It is concerned with freedom from discrimination in a number of areas

---

27   *Greater Vancouver Regional District Employees' Union v Greater Vancouver Regional District*
28   www.ohrc.on.ca

including services, accommodation and contracts as well as employment. Section 5(1) records that:

> *Every person has a right to equal treatment with respect to employment without discrimination because of race, ancestry, place of origin, colour, ethnic origin, citizenship, creed, age, record of offences, marital status, same-sex partnership status, family status or disability.*

Age means being between 18 and 65 years (see above). The right to equal treatment in employment includes discrimination that takes place in applying for posts and applies to employment agencies. There are certain exceptions with regard to bona fide qualifications because of the nature of the employment and those attending to the personal or medical needs of an individual, a child, spouse or same-sex partner.

Most of the complaints on the grounds of age are related to employment, although they were only a small proportion of the total. Some 69.03 per cent of all complaints received related to employment matters (Table 6.1).[29]

The average settlement for all complaints amounted to $6,147.11, but the average settlement for age complaints was $8,854.57.

MANDATORY RETIREMENT

In 2004, the Ontario Government held a consultation exercise on whether to end the mandatory retirement age. The OHRC, as part of that consultation, submitted that mandatory retirement is a:

> *form of age discrimination because it involves making an employment decision solely on the basis of age, and not the person's ability to do the job; it undermines older Ontarians' independence, participation, and ability to make choices, which is contrary to the values of the Code; and, it can have serious financial impacts on certain groups, such as women, recent immigrants, racialized communities and persons with disabilities.*

In 2005, the Ontario Government introduced legislation to amend the definition of age in the Ontario Human Rights Code. The Code defined age as meaning ages between 18 and 65. The new legislation has the effect of removing the upper limit, so as to effectively make many mandatory retirement ages unlawful.

---

29   *Ontario Human Rights Commission Year-End Results 2002–2003*

Table 6.1   New employment complaints to the OHRC 2004–2005

Type	Number
Age	184
Ancestry	143
Citizenship	28
Creed	105
Disability	1 342
Ethnic origin	314
Family status	107
Marital status	53
Race and colour	735
Sex and pregnancy	668
Sexual harassment	209
Sexual orientation	86

There is still to be a bona fide occupational requirement which may justify the retention of some compulsory retirement ages. In such cases the employer must show that:

- an age-based job requirement or qualification is a bona fide occupational requirement;

- the employee does not meet the job requirement or qualification; and

- the employee could not be accommodated without causing undue hardship to the employer.

The Minister of Labour at the time stated:

> *Ending mandatory retirement would allow workers to retire based on lifestyle, circumstances and priorities. We listened to the needs and concerns of business, labour and others who have consulted with us and are doing this in a way that protects existing rights to pension, early retirement and benefit plans.*

This is a refreshing attitude which the British Government might consider emulating, rather than introducing a national mandatory retirement age through the concept of the 'default retirement age' (see Chapter 5). The likely impact in terms of numbers, according to the Ontario Government is likely to be small with only about 4000 people, out of a workforce of 6.6 million, taking advantage of the change.[30]

IRELAND

The Equality Authority in Ireland produced a report in conjunction with older people's groups which distinguished between biological ageing and social ageing:[31]

> *Biological ageing is a continuous process. However, societal attitudes, assumptions and barriers create social ageing, which is the subject of much of this report. For instance, the link between chronological age and what is and is not expected of a person at that age is socially conditioned. These social constructs can be taken as the received wisdom by people generally because they have not been examined reflectively or critically or remain unchallenged. In this kind of setting it may be very hard for individuals to see how their actions are in fact ageist rather than 'plain common sense'. Where people cannot see that there is something ageist in their assumptions and principles it may be hard to bring about change in behaviour or practice.*

The Employment Equality Act 1998, as amended by the Equality Act 2004, includes age discrimination in employment within its scope. The Equal Status Act 2000 covers certain other areas apart from employment. Section 6(1) of the 1998 Act provides that discrimination shall be taken to occur where:

> *A person is treated less favourably than another person is, had been or would be treated in a comparable situation on any of the grounds specified in subsection (2)*

Subsection 6(2) then refers to a number of discriminatory grounds, as between any two persons, including 'that they are of different ages'. The lower age limit is the statutory school leaving age (16 years), although employers may set a minimum recruitment age of 18 if they so wish.[32]

A number of specific areas are contained in the Act[33] which provides protection against discrimination in relation to:

- access to employment

---

30 For more information see the Ontario Ministry of Labour website at www.labour.gov.on.ca
31 *Implementing Equality for Older People* (2004)
32 Employment Equality Act 1998, section 6(3)
33 Ibid., section 8

- conditions of employment

- training or experience for or in relation to employment

- promotion or re-grading

- classification of posts.

A non-discriminatory equality clause is implied into every contract of employment (excluding pensions), unless the employer can show that there are non-discriminatory reasons for the differences.[34] The Act also provides protection from indirect discrimination[35] and harassment in the workplace[36].

A number of exceptions to the principle of non-discrimination are permitted:

- a provision that permits the setting of different retirement ages, whether voluntarily or compulsorily, of employees or any group of employees;[37]

- a provision that permits the setting of a maximum recruitment age when taking into account the period of time involved in training and the need for a reasonable period of time prior to retirement age when the recruit will be effective in the job;

- the setting of different rates of remuneration or different terms and conditions if the difference is based on relative seniority or length of service in a particular post.[38]

The retirement age in the public sector for people who joined before 1 April 2004 is 65. Some occupations such as the police, firefighters and the armed forces have provisions for earlier retirement. The minimum retirement age is now 65 for people who joined the public sector after 1 April 2004. This means that new entrants to the public sector will not have to retire at 65 but can continue working, subject to suitability and health requirements.

Section 38 of the Act also provided for the continuation of the previously existing Employment Equality Agency and renamed it as the Equality Authority. The Authority has four main functions:

---

34 Ibid., section 30
35 Ibid., section 31
36 Ibid., section 14A
37 According to ibid., section 6(3)(c), the offering of a fixed-term contract to a person over the compulsory retirement age shall not be taken as constituting discrimination on the age ground
38 Ibid., section 34(3)–(5)

- to work towards the elimination of discrimination in relation to employment;

- to promote equality of opportunity in relation to matters to which the Act applies;

- to provide information to the public and keep under review the relevant Acts;

- to keep under review the working of the Pensions Act 1990 as regards the principle of equal treatment.

The Authority's annual report for 2004 showed the range of complaints referred to it (Table 6.2).[39]

Table 6.2 Equality Authority Statistics 2004

Grounds	Casework activity
Gender	88
Age	42
Disability	60
Race	118
Traveller community	7
Marital status	4
Family status	5
Sexual orientation	5
Religion	4
Multiple grounds	37
Total	370

If there is sufficient information to infer discrimination on the basis of age, then the burden of proof is with the employer to show that the action complained of was for a non-discriminatory reason.

Ireland, of course, is the nearest jurisdiction to the United Kingdom, which has had age discrimination legislation for some years. Some of the issues raised are those connected with the following.

---

39   See the Equality Tribunal website at www.equalitytribunal.ie

PROMOTION

In *Gillen v Department of Health and Children*,[40] Mr Gillen claimed that he had been discriminated against on the grounds of age during two competitions for promotion within the Department. He was 54 years old. In the first competition there were six successful candidates chosen from 23 applicants. There were five other applicants who were also over the age of 50 and none of them were selected. In the second competition there were 20 applicants, including seven who were aged 50 or more. The successful candidate was 35 years old. Mr Gillen claimed to have more appropriate experience than the successful candidates. He had also been told on a number of occasions that he was suitable for promotion. Two other internal competitions also resulted in no one of 50 or above being appointed. The Equality Officer, who was investigating, secured information about the respondent's promotion statistics since 1998 and was also influenced by the fact that no records of the interviews were kept. The outcome was a finding that the employee had established a prima facie case of age discrimination and that the employer had failed to rebut it. Apart from recommendations to reform its selection processes, the Department was ordered to pay the complainant €40000 as compensation for the consequences of discrimination.

Carroll v Monaghan Vocational Guidance Education Committee also concerned a complaint of age discrimination in a public body's promotion process. Mrs Mary Carroll applied for one of six Special Duties Teacher Posts in the College for which she worked. There were 12 applicants and all the successful candidates were younger than her. The employer should have followed Department of Education and Science advice about the weight to be given to experience and service. It purported to do so, but it was clear that teachers with less experience had been awarded higher scores against these criteria than Mrs Carroll. In fact, the candidates with the longest experience received the lowest marks. Again, there were no interview notes available so the employer was unable to back up its assertion that appointments had been made on a meritorious basis on the day of the interviews. The employer was not, therefore, able to rebut the prima facie case established by the complainant and was ordered to pay her back pay (she had subsequently been promoted) and give her €10000 as compensation for distress suffered.

---

40   Equality Officer's decision DEC-E2003-035

EARLY RETIREMENT[41]

Mr McLoughlin worked for Bus Éireann as a bus driver for 23 years. He successfully applied for a voluntary severance package which was on offer from the employer. Before he left he asked to be considered for any part-time work vacancies that might occur. After he had left he again applied, but was told that it was not company policy to re-employ people who had taken early retirement. Statistics, subsequently requested by the Equality Authority, showed that over 96 per cent of those who took advantage of the voluntary severance scheme were over the age of 50. The Equality Officer found that the claimant had been indirectly discriminated against on the ground of age and awarded him €3000 as compensation. She also ordered the employer to treat any future application from Mr McLoughlin in the same manner as any other candidate.

RECRUITMENT

Hughes v Aer Lingus concerned a 53-year-old applicant for a cabin crew position. She was experienced in the job, having worked for another airline for some years. Aer Lingus held preliminary walk-in interviews in which the claimant participated. She received a favourable report and progressed to the second interview stage where she was questioned about how she would cope with younger people being in charge and how, being older, she would feel about starting again on the bottom rung of the ladder. She was subsequently turned down and complained that she had been turned down because of her age. The employer responded by rejecting this and said that it was because she had so much experience that the interviewers had concluded that she would have difficulties taking a much more junior post than she was used to. In the event the employer was able to show that it had employed three people over the age of 50 in the recruitment exercise, albeit out of 150 successful applicants. The Equality Officer accepted that there was not a blanket policy on not considering older applicants for cabin crew positions and concluded that she had failed to establish a prima facie case that she was not recruited because of her age. However, the Equality Officer then went on to conclude that the claimant was subject to a discriminatory line of questioning in the second interview. As a result, the company was held to have discriminated on the grounds of age. It was obliged to pay €3000 as compensation and to give the claimant a further interview by a different interview board within 12 weeks if it had not offered her a post within the same time period.

One further example, cited in the Equality Authority Annual Report 2004 was about a claimant who went for an interview for a position as a legal

---

41   *Brian McLoughlin v Bus Éireann*

secretary with a firm of solicitors. During the interview she was asked her age and whether she was married. She responded by saying that the first question was not relevant and that she did not think it correct to ask the second. At that point the potential employer terminated the interview and subsequently agreed to mediation. The result was that the firm of solicitors apologised to the claimant and paid her compensation.

ADVERTISING

Ryanair published an advertisement in the *Irish Times* for a Director of Regulatory Affairs.[42] In the advertisement the company stated that it needed 'a young and dynamic professional' and also that 'the ideal candidate will be young, dynamic ...'. The complaint was that this was in breach of Section 10(1) of the Employment Equality Act which provides that a person must not publish, or cause to be published, as advertisement, relating to employment, which indicates an intention to discriminate or might reasonably be understood as indication such an intention. The respondent claimed that it was not in contravention of the Act because it did not advertise a particular age or age range and that the word young was always used in conjunction with the word dynamic. It stated that it wanted to attract not only experienced candidates but also those who might have less experience. In the event the respondent said that 30 candidates had applied and, of those that gave the information, their ages were between 25 and 38. The successful candidate was 32. The Equality Officer found the complaint to be justified and stated:

> In my view many people who are older rightly regard themselves as young or young at heart. However, most people in that situation recognise that others may not, necessarily, regard them in the same light. In my opinion, people in such a situation seeking employment would feel rejected and excluded when they see an advertisement which specifies 'young' as a requirement for a job.

The Equality Officer awarded £8000 in compensation and also that the respondent carry out a full review of its equal opportunities policies to ensure compliance with the Act.

Other cases concerning advertising were also summarised in the 2004 Equality Authority's annual report:

> A newspaper published a recruitment agency advertisement for 'young and dynamic' people for jobs in telesales. Subsequently the newspaper and the Agency apologised for the mistake and agreed to re-advertise the

---

42 *Equality Authority v Ryanair*

jobs as well as reviewing their own policies with regard to proof reading of advertisements.

An advertisement appeared in a newspaper in 2004 stating, 'My client is seeking an enthusiastic young person looking to springboard their career.' The Equality Authority requested the re-advertisement of the position and that no appointment should be made as a result of the original advertisement.

UNITED STATES OF AMERICA

One report for the US Government defined age discrimination as the rejection of an older worker because of assumptions about the effect of age on the worker's ability to perform, regardless of whether there was any factual basis for the assumptions.[43]

During the debate on what was to become the Civil Rights Act of 1964, the US Congress rejected attempts to amend the Bill[44] by adding age discrimination to the others being considered at the time, such as race, colour, sex and religion. Instead it directed the Secretary of Labor to investigate the issue and make recommendations for future action.[45] The result of this investigation was a report to Congress entitled *The Older American Worker-Age Discrimination in Employment* in June 1965. It stated that:

> *Collectively, the leading studies on various aspects of the effects of aging document the conclusion that chronological age is a poor indicator of working ability. Health, mental and physical capacities, work attitudes, and job performance are individual traits at any age. Indeed, measures of traits in different age groups usually show many of the older workers to be superior to the average for the younger group and many of the younger ones inferior to the average for the older group.[46]*

The report concluded that many employers adopted specific age limits and that these limits had a marked effect on the employment of older workers. This arbitrary age discrimination caused harm by firstly depriving the economy of the productive labour of millions as well as adding substantially increased social security costs and secondly it inflicted economic and psychological injury on those affected. It stated that age discrimination was rarely based on

---

43   Gregory (2001)
44   See Eglit (1999)
45   The House of Representatives rejected the amendment by 123-94 and the Senate by 63-28.
46   Page 81

the rationale that motivated racial discrimination, but that it was still based on stereotypes which had no basis in fact. The report stated that:

> We find no significant evidence of ... the kind of dislike or intolerance that sometimes exists in the case of race, color, religion, or national origin, and which is based on considerations entirely unrelated to ability to perform a job.

It did go on to say, however, that:

> We do find substantial evidence of ... discrimination based on unsupported general assumptions about the effect of age on ability ... in hiring practices that take the form of specific age limits applied to older workers as a group.[47]

There had been a history of legislation at State level to outlaw age discrimination in employment. Indeed, in 1965, there were 20 States that already had such legislation, including Colorado which had introduced such a law as far back as 1903. The majority of these laws outlawed discrimination against older workers (those between 40 and 65 years), although Colorado, Idaho, Louisiana, New Jersey and Oregon had either lower minimum ages or none at all.

In 1964 also, the President[48] issued an Executive Order[49] establishing a policy against age discrimination in employment by Federal contractors and sub-contractors. The Order provided that contractors and sub-contractors could not discriminate on the basis of age in hiring, promotion, termination or terms and conditions of employment. It also barred age limits in recruitment advertising.

The outcome of these measures and this debate was the Age Discrimination in Employment Act 1967 (the ADEA).

AGE DISCRIMINATION IN EMPLOYMENT ACT 1967

The ADEA is only concerned with older workers, in contrast to the UK Regulations which cover all ages. It applies to workers who are least 40 years of age.[50] The Act also only applies to those employers who had at least 20 employees for 20 or more calendar weeks in the preceding year.[51] The ADEA:

47 See Eglit (1999)
48 Lyndon B. Johnson
49 Order No 11141, February 12 1964
50 ADEA, section 12(a)
51 ADEA, section 11(b)

requires the employer to ignore an employee's age (absent a statutory exemption or defense); it does not specify further characteristics that an employer must ignore.[52]

The Act itself has been amended on a number of occasions. Most notably this included the Age Discrimination in Employment Act Amendments of 1978 which increased the upper age limit (from 65 years imposed when the Act was originally adopted) to 70 years for non-federal employees and removed it altogether for federal employees. It also stopped mandatory retirement prior to the age of 70. In 1986 this was further amended so that the upper age limit of 70 for protection was effectively removed for all workers. There were also further substantial amendments brought about by the Older Workers Benefit Protection Act of 1990 and the Civil Rights Act of 1991.

The purpose of the ADEA is described in Section 2(b) as threefold:

- to promote employment of older persons based on their ability rather than age;

- to prohibit arbitrary age discrimination in employment;

- to help employers and workers find ways of meeting problems arising from the impact of age on employment.

The Act applies to labour organisations and employment agencies as well as to employers in general.

Section 4(a) states that:

It shall be unlawful for an employer—

(1) to fail or refuse to hire or to discharge any individual or otherwise discriminate against any individual with respect to his compensation, terms, conditions, or privileges of employment, because of such individual's age;

(2) to limit, segregate, or classify his employees in any way which would deprive or tend to deprive any individual of employment opportunities or otherwise adversely affect his status as an employee, because of such an individual's age;

---

52 *Hazen Paper Co v Biggins*

(3) to reduce the wage rate of any employee in order to comply with this chapter.[53]

Thus, discrimination on the grounds of age is unlawful in hiring and firing; compensation, assignment, or classification of employees; transfer, promotion, layoff, or recall; job advertisements; recruitment; testing; use of company facilities; training and apprenticeship programs; fringe benefits; pay, retirement plans, and disability leave; or other terms and conditions of employment.[54]

The ADEA does not stop all actions against all workers over the age of 40; the law allows for dismissals 'for just cause' and employers have no special responsibilities towards older workers. 'Just cause' is, of course, very different from that in the United Kingdom. In *Loeb v Textron Inc* the Court stated that the employer is entitled to make their own policy and business judgements and may fire an adequate employee if the reason is to hire a new employee who will be even better. This is provided that this is not a pretext for discrimination. The jury needs to focus on the motivation of the employer and 'not on its business judgement'.

There are, however, two general exceptions to the protection offered. The first is where 'the differentiation is based on reasonable factors other than age' and the second is for a bona fide occupational qualification (BFOQ) reasonably necessary to the normal operation of the particular business.[55]

There are a number of specific exceptions where it will not be unlawful for an employer, employment agency or labour organisation to take action that might otherwise be prohibited.[56] These are to take any action:

- to observe the terms of a bona fide seniority system that is not intended to evade the purpose of the legislation;

- to observe the terms of a bona fide employee benefits plan;

- to discharge or otherwise discipline an individual for good cause.

There is also a specific exception for 'highly compensated people'.[57] Similarly, there is an exception to the retirement provisions of the higher paid. Section 12(c)(1) states that:

---

53 ADEA, sections 4(b) and 4(c) apply similar provisions to employment agencies and labour organisations
54 List taken from EEOC's website (see below) at www.eeoc.gov
55 ADEA, section 4(f)(1)
56 ADEA, section 4(f)
57 ADEA, section 4(5); highly compensated employee within the meaning of section 414(q) of title 26 – the Internal Revenue Code of 1986

Nothing in this chapter shall be construed to prohibit compulsory retirement of any employee who has attained age of 65 years ... and for 2 years prior has been a bona fide executive or in a high policy making position and can receive a pension of at least $44 000 per annum.

ESTABLISHING AGE DISCRIMINATION

An individual claiming unlawful age discrimination will need to show disparate treatment. Disparate treatment requires it to be shown that the employer intentionally treated an individual less favourably because of their age. The onus is first on the plaintiff to establish a prima facie case of discriminatory intent. The employer is then able to argue a permissible non-discriminatory justification, then leaving the plaintiff with the opportunity to argue that this non age-based justification is false.

In *Woroski v Nashau Corporation*,[58] the Court accepted that a prima facie case had been indicated when two plaintiffs complained of age discrimination after losing their jobs in a 'reduction in force' exercise. The employers, however, were able to show a proper business motivation for large-scale downsizing and that there was a lack of evidence that the operation was 'infected by age bias'. In order to establish a prima facie case of age discrimination a plaintiff needed to show that:

- they were in the protected age group;

- they were qualified for the position;

- they were adversely affected;

- the discharge occurred under circumstances giving rise to an inference of age discrimination.

Disparate impact, on the other hand, would require an apparently neutral employment policy that in fact has an adverse impact on older workers, but cannot be justified by any sort of business necessity justification. Traditionally this had not been possible under the ADEA, but in March 2005 the US Supreme Court handed down a judgment stating that age discrimination may be shown using the disparate impact approach.

Smith v City of Jackson, Mississipi concerned a group of older police officers. The City had pay increases to all its police officers, but had given more to those with less than five years' service, in order to make their pay more competitive.

---

58   *Woroski v Nashau Corp* citing *Spence v Maryland Casualty Co; McDonnell Douglas Corp v Green*

As older officers tended to have more service, they claimed that this policy had an adverse impact upon them because of their age. A majority of the Court held that the ADEA allowed disparate impact claims, although not all for the same reason. The application of disparate impact to age was limited by the Court, for example if the employer were able to show that the prohibited practice was based on reasonable factors other than age (see below), such as seniority. Unfortunately for the plaintiffs, although the Court had made this important judgment, it also concluded that the police officers had not shown a specific practice which resulted in the alleged effect.

Unlike in the United Kingdom, where all are covered by the legislation, the United States has a protected class – those aged 40 and over. This may aid the judgment as to whether there has been discrimination on the basis of age. Discrimination against someone in the protected class in favour of someone from the unprotected class might infer age discrimination. This is not conclusive, however, as discrimination can take place between two persons within the protected class.

> *Because the ADEA prohibits discrimination on the basis of age and not class membership, the fact that a replacement is substantially younger than the plaintiff is a far more reliable indicator of age discrimination than is the fact that the plaintiff was replaced by someone outside the protected class.*[59]

REASONABLE FACTORS OTHER THAN AGE

An employer may be permitted to take actions against an older worker for reasons other than age,[60] and seems to be considered on a case-by-case basis. The employer, however, cannot rely on stereotypical images of a decline in abilities with age. On the other hand:

> *Congress made it plain that the age statute was not meant to prohibit employment decisions based on factors that sometimes accompany advancing age, such as declining health or diminished vigor and competence.*[61]

One issue is how to distinguish between discrimination on the basis of age and treatment resulting from certain characteristics that come with age. In the United Kingdom there will clearly be an important overlap with the Disability

---

59 *O/Connor v Consolidated Coin Caterers Corp* at 313; see also *Metz v Transit Mix Inc.* which concerned the dismissal of an older worker with 27 years' service in favour of a much younger worker who would be paid considerably less. See also Weber (1998)
60 See generally Mitchell (2001)
61 *Holley v Sanyo Manufacturing Inc.* quoted in *Beith v Nitrogen Products Inc.*

Discrimination Act 1995. Dismissals for capability in such circumstances may end up being tested both under the Age Discrimination Regulations and under the Disability Discrimination Act.

In *Beith v Nitrogen Products Inc,* an employer dismissed a 55-year-old employee because of back problems. He had been taken on as a temporary operator pending a physical examination. Mr Beith's examination revealed that he had some degenerative disc disease and some osteoarthritis. As a result it was recommended that he did not lift, regularly, weights over 20 lbs. On the basis of the report his employers decided that he was at high risk of being injured and claiming compensation. His employment was, therefore, terminated.

Mr Beith also happened to be the oldest employee in his Department. He obtained a second medical opinion stating that there was no reason why he should not continue working as his medical condition was normal for a man of his age. He lost his appeal because, firstly, according to the Court, he did not manage to show that he had been replaced by a younger person. This is also an issue in the United Kingdom. The US legislation has a protected class of all those of 40 years and over and it is therefore possible to look at treatment of those in the protected class and compare them with treatment of those outside the class (those under the age of 40 years) in order to try to establish a prima facie case of age discrimination. When everybody is protected such a comparison is much more difficult. Secondly, the Court also rejected Mr Beith's argument that because his back condition was an ordinary and natural consequence of ageing, then, by inference, he was really dismissed because of his age. Because such back conditions are more common in older persons, it did not follow that a dismissal because of the back condition was an age-based decision.

One commonly accepted pretext for turning down older candidates for positions is that they are overqualified. Because an older person may have a curriculum vitae which shows longer experience and perhaps more qualifications than younger candidates, employers may be able to cite 'overqualification' as a reason for turning down an application for employment. This may, at times, be a genuine reason of course, but there will also be occasions when this is just a pretext for turning down an application from someone who is, in the employer's eyes, too old to be considered. This was the claim in *E.E.O.C. v Insurance Co. of North America.* The employer placed an advertisement in a Phoenix newspaper for a 'loss control representative'. The advertisement described the ideal candidate as someone with a degree, or equivalent professional experience, two years' loss control experience, verbal and communication skills, the ability to travel and who is a self-motivated professional. Mr Pugh, who had over 30 years' relevant experience, applied. He did not obtain an interview, all the short-listed candidates were younger than him and, in the event, a 28-year-old, with no loss control experience, was recruited. During the EEOC's (see below) investigation of the recruitment process it was stated on a number of occasions that Mr Pugh was held to be overqualified.

There were other reasons given for not shortlisting him. These included the unprofessional nature of his application (handwriting on his CV and no covering letter) and the fact that he might consume too much working time in investigating uncomplicated accounts as a result of all his experience. The Court did not find that the phrase 'overqualified' in this case was a pretext for age discrimination. Indeed, if the employer's rejection was based on a genuine belief that he was overqualified, that belief did not violate the ADEA. Other courts had shown scepticism about the use of the term 'over qualified'[62], but in this case the evidence was that the assertion that Mr Pugh was overqualified was not a mask for age discrimination. This case perhaps illustrates some difficulties with proving discrimination at the application stage. At what stage does the experience that an individual candidate has become too much for the job in question? Maybe an experienced older worker applies for positions that are at a lower level than that at which they have been operating just in order to get back into the workforce. Does an employer's rejection of an older candidate on these grounds amount to age discrimination in employment? Is it valid to argue that a less-experienced person will be more suited to the role?

BONA FIDE OCCUPATIONAL QUALIFICATION

In *Western Airlines Inc. v Criswell*, it was held that an employer can show age as a BFOQ by proving that some members of the age-defined group cannot perform the job safely and efficiently and that they cannot be identified by any means other than age. The Airline operated a policy of retiring its pilots at the age of 60 and such pilots were denied reassignment as flight engineers because such posts also had a mandatory retirement age of 60. In theory. a flight engineer could be called upon to fly an aircraft if both the pilot and the co-pilot were incapacitated. The issue was whether the retirement age of 60 for flight engineers could be a genuine BFOQ.

---

62 *Taggart v Time Inc* was cited

The Airline argued that the retirement age was a BFOQ 'reasonably necessary' to the safe operation of the Airline, or the essence of the Airline's business. The essence of the Airline's business was the safe transportation of its passengers and that it could show that it was highly impractical for them to deal with each flight engineer over the age of 60 on an individual basis to decide if that particular engineer could perform the job safely. In addition, the Airline asserted that some flight engineers over the age of 60 would possess psychological and physical traits which would affect the safe performance of their duties, and that these traits could not be ascertained other than by knowing their age.

There is a two-stage approach:

1.   the employer must establish that there is a potential for unacceptable risk to the employer or third parties that older workers are more likely to pose;

2.   the employer must prove that it is impracticable to perform individual evaluations that could identify which of these older workers pose that risk.

The Court considered that:

> Throughout the legislative history of the ADEA, one empirical fact is repeatedly emphasised: the process of psychological and physiological degeneration caused by ageing varies with each individual.

It is not enough to make generalised assumptions and the BFOQ exception is construed narrowly. The safety of passengers is a priority that may justify the use of age-discriminatory measures such as a mandatory retirement age. Here, the essence of the employer's business was the safe transportation of passengers. The employer then has two options: it can establish that there is an unacceptable risk associated with all employees over a certain age, or alternatively, that it was impossible or impracticable to deal with older employees on an individual basis.[63]

Similar arguments were raised in *Mahoney v Trabucco*. This case concerned a mandatory retirement age for all state uniformed police officers in Massachusetts. The plaintiff was a uniformed police officer but was normally employed in a desk-bound capacity as a communications person. In emergencies, however, he might be called upon to take up more strenuous conventional duties carried

---

63   The case used to illustrate this was *Usery v Tamiami Trail Tours Inc*. This concerned a company which had a policy of not hiring anyone over the age of 40 as inter-city bus drivers.

out by other police officers. The issue, therefore, was whether a generalised retirement age applying to all police officers, regardless of their individual duties, could be a genuine BFOQ. The Court held that the State had failed to justify this generalised treatment:

> *To evaluate the state's BFOQ defense against the more demanding requirements of the typical member of the uniformed branch would only serve to perpetuate the stereotyping and labelling that the ADEA was designed to prohibit, and would ignore the Act's instruction to treat older Americans on the basis of individual ability.*[64]

EQUAL EMPLOYMENT OPPORTUNITY COMMISSION (EEOC)

In 1978 the ADEA was amended to transfer responsibility for conciliation, investigation and record keeping to the EEOC. The EEOC is an independent federal agency originally set up in 1964 to enforce Title VII of the Civil Rights Act of that year. It is composed of five commissioners and general counsel in addition to a chair and vice-chair appointed by the President. There are some 50 area offices situated throughout the country. It has responsibilities that cover discrimination on the basis of race, sex, national origin, religion, disability and equal pay, as well as age.

Any charges under the ADEA must first be filed with the EEOC, subject to a time limit of between 180 and 300 days after the event complained of. The EEOC will inform the employer and may then carry out an investigation and also attempt conciliation between the parties, unless it dismisses the charge. If at any time the EEOC decides that the charges will not reveal a violation of Federal law, then it will be dismissed. When a charge is dismissed, this will be explained and a notice is issued which gives the complainant 90 days in which to file a lawsuit. If the investigation establishes that discrimination has occurred, both parties will be informed and the EEOC will make a further attempt at conciliation, mediation or some form of settlement. If the EEOC fails in this then it has 90 days in which to bring the matter to court. If it decides not to sue, then it will issue a notice to the complainant giving him or her 90 days in which to file charges themselves.

The remedies available include back pay, hiring, promotion, re-instatement, other pay lost as a result of the discrimination plus legal fees. Compensatory and punitive damages are available.

---

64   At 961

The EEOC handles a significant number of age discrimination complaints each year, the majority of which are held to have no reasonable cause. The figures for 1999 to 2004 are shown in Table 6.3.

Table 6.3   EEOC statistics

Year	2000	2001	2002	2003	2004	2005
Charge receipts filed	16008	17405	19921	19124	17837	16585
No reasonable cause	8517	8388	9725	11976	9563	8866
Reasonable cause	1207	1247	801	557	515	583
Monetary benefit* ($ millions)	45.2	53.7	55.7	48.9	69.0	77.7

* Not obtained through litigation.
The balance is made up of various withdrawals, conciliations and so on.

In the fiscal year 2005, the EEOC received 16585 charges of age discrimination and resolved 14076 age discrimination charges in recovering some $77.7 million in monetary benefits for charging parties and other aggrieved individuals (not including monetary benefits obtained through litigation). The numbers are significant. The only categories in which the EEOC received more complaints, in 2004 for example, were for discrimination on the grounds of race (27696) and sex (24249).[65] There is no reason to suppose that there will be less activity in this field for those concerned with conciliation and litigation in the United Kingdom.

---

65 All these figures can be found on the EEOC's website at www.eeoc.gov

CHAPTER 7

Multiple Discrimination

There are now a growing number of anti-discrimination measures. The primary ones are:

- The Equal Pay Act 1970

- The Sex Discrimination Act 1975

- The Race Relations Act 1976

- The Disability Discrimination Act 1995[1]

- The Employment Equality (Religion or Belief) Regulations 2003[2]

- The Employment Equality (Sexual Orientation) Regulations 2003[3]

- The Equality Act 2006

- The Employment Equality (Age) Regulations 2006.

In addition, there are other measures which might, in certain circumstances, give rise to claims of indirect discrimination, such as the Part-time Workers (Prevention of Less Favourable Treatment) Regulations 2000.[4] There are also currently three statutory bodies which oversee some of these statutes, namely the Equal Opportunities Commission, the Commission for Racial Equality and the Disability Rights Commission, although it is planned to incorporate these into a single commission.

One issue here is that each of these measures deals with a different aspect of discrimination. Thus, it is possible to bring complaints about sex discrimination or race discrimination or disability discrimination individually under different statutes. It is not possible to bring complaints of multiple discrimination under one statute. They need to be addressed as separate complaints using the different pieces of statute. This is despite the fact that it is clear that there is a substantial overlap in some cases, for example between racial and religious discrimination and between discrimination on the grounds of sex and sexual orientation. The second issue is that there is no opportunity for other forms of discrimination,

---

1   Also the Disability Rights Commission Act 1999
2   SI 2003/1660
3   SI 2003/1661
4   SI 2000/1551

or multiple discrimination, to be identified. The potential grounds are those contained within the legislation or regulation. All other grounds are excluded by omission. This, of course, is a reflection of the approach of the EU, which also has Directives concerned with gender, race and a variety of other grounds contained within the Framework Directive. According to a review of the European Network of Legal Experts, there are a number of countries within the EU that do have a non-exhaustive list and allow for the possibility of other grounds.[5]

It is clear, however, that with the growing number of grounds for complaint that there are more likely to be a growing number of complaints that do not fit neatly into one or other of the categories in the individual statutes or regulations. This will be even more so when the Age Regulations are taken into account. As one report for Age Concern England stated:[6]

> *Many older people experience disadvantage and discrimination not just because of their age, but for other reasons as well – because they are black or disabled or from a religious, cultural or linguistic minority, for example.*

The same report also points out that many people suffer from discrimination throughout their lives, for example on the grounds of sex or race, and that becoming an older worker adds to the level of discrimination suffered.

ADDITIVE AND INTERSECTIONAL DISCRIMINATION

Two types of multiple discrimination have been suggested.[7] The first is 'additive discrimination', which consists of a situation where the person complaining of discrimination belongs to two separate groups, both of which are affected by discrimination legislation, for example a lesbian woman or a disabled black man. This is where a person may be able to justify individual claims under different statutes and they are essentially additive in nature. The second type consists of intersectional discrimination where the multiple discrimination cannot usefully or effectively be broken down into its component parts. It is where the sum of the parts is something more than the constituent elements. Thus, a young black woman may suffer discrimination in a way that an older black woman does not. The grounds for complaint should be that she is young and black and a woman, not necessarily three different complaints under

---

5   *European anti-discrimination law review no 2* (2005); it also contains a piece by Sandra Fredman titled 'Double trouble: multiple discrimination and the law', which makes this point

6   *Age and...multiple discrimination and older people* (2005)

7   See, for example, Hannett (2003)

firstly age regulations, then racial discrimination and then sex discrimination. Intersectional discrimination is where the different forms of discrimination meet but result in a form of discrimination that is not covered by any of the individual statutes or regulations.

An example of this occurred in *Burton v De Vere Hotels*.[8] Two young Afro-Caribbean women were amongst the casual staff waiting at tables during a dinner attended by 400 men. There was an after dinner speaker, described as a 'blue comedian', who was a guest at the dinner. During his after dinner performance the two waitresses were clearing the tables. When spotted by the speaker, he made sexually and racially offensive remarks. The two waitresses brought a complaint against the hotel that employed them under the Race Relations Act 1995. They complained that they had been unlawfully discriminated against on the grounds of their race by their employers. The reason that this unpleasant experience is related here is that these two waitresses were actually picked on because they were young, black and female, yet they brought a claim for racial discrimination. In a different legal system, which recognised intersectional discrimination, they perhaps should have been able to bring a complaint of being discriminated against because they were young black women and not just because they were black.

This may be an argument in favour of a rights-based approach to discrimination. Rather than focusing on the difference which has resulted in the discrimination, it might be more worthwhile to focus on the fact that an individual has a right not to be discriminated against. The right comes not from some category of discrimination such as race, sex or age but from a recognition that irrational discrimination breaches a fundamental human right.

The issue has been recognised in other jurisdictions. Madam Justice L'Heureux-Dubé stated in the Canadian Supreme Court:

> *categorising such discrimination as primarily racially orientated, or primarily gender orientated, misconceives the reality of discrimination as it is experienced by individuals. Discrimination may be experienced on many grounds, and where this is the case, it is not really meaningful to assert that it is one or the other. It may be more realistic to recognise that both forms of discrimination may be present and intersect.[9]*

8   The decision in this case was held, by the House of Lords, to have been wrongly decided in *MacDonald v Advocate General for Scotland; Pearce v Governing Body of Mayfield School* it is the facts of the case that are used here for illustrative purposes

9   *An intersectional approach to discrimination addressing multiple grounds in human rights claims* (2004); *Canada (A.G.) v Mossop*

Canada (see Chapter 6) has an anti-discrimination programme that is human rights-based and it might be easier to do:

> *a contextual analysis, focusing on society's response to the individual and its construction of identity, that includes examination of historical disadvantage, social, political and cultural context and socio-economic issue.*[10]

It may be that when the United Kingdom has a single equality body, that these issues will also be tackled.

There seems to be a strong likelihood that age will have a correlation with a number of other types of discrimination. In one analysis, in a jurisdiction where age discrimination is unlawful, some 56 per cent of age complaints between April 1997 and December 2000 included other grounds.[11] A report for the Ontario Human Rights Commission (OHRC) stated:[12]

> *Persons with disabilities may experience particular barriers when they identify by other grounds. For example, during the Commission's consultations on age discrimination, the Commission was told that for persons with disabilities, ageing can result in a disproportionate impact or unique experiences of discrimination.*

The OHRC has also produced a report which includes age and intersectionality.[13] This included issues related to age and gender, age and disability, and age and sexual orientation. The strongest argument for a human rights approach to age is so that it can be combined with other areas of discrimination with which it overlaps. An example of where this happens is Ontario in Canada.

AGE AND GENDER

One report for the Equality Authority in Ireland stated:

> *Older people's experiences have been acquired through living within a particular set of social, economic and cultural circumstances. So, the experience of an older professional man can be quite different from the*

---

10   Ibid.
11   In the period between April 1997 and December 2000 there were 868 complaints to the Ontario Human Rights Commission with regard to age discrimination. Of these some 56 per cent (488) included other grounds of complaint. The largest overlap was with race discrimination with 190 complaints, followed by disability with 134 complaints and sex discrimination with 131 complaints. Ontario Human Rights Commission; there is much useful information available on their web site at www.ohrc.on.ca
12   Ibid.
13   *Time for Action: Advancing Human Rights for Older Ontarians* (2004)

experience of an older woman in the home. Within the group of older people, there are people who suffer and/or have suffered discrimination on other grounds. The discrimination problems faced by the current generation of older women largely arise from past discrimination on the grounds of gender, in particular exclusion from the labour market, arising from the 'marriage bar' and caring responsibilities, and the consequent exclusion from independent pension arrangements.[14]

Older women suffer from disadvantages compared to older men. This is because: they tend to live longer, although the gap between the sexes has narrowed in recent years. There were 28 per cent more women than men over the age of 50 in 1961. This difference had narrowed to 18 per cent in 2002. Projections suggest a further narrowing with the difference in numbers being reduced to 14 per cent by 2031.[15]

Older women are often poorer because of this relative longevity and for a number of other reasons, which may include:

(i)   Women on average receive a much lower occupational pension income partly because they were dependent upon male pension holding partners

Some indication of this is shown on an EU-wide basis in Table 7.1, where there is a clear pattern of large numbers of women who do not take up paid employment once they are married and are therefore reliant on their male partner's income.

The result of this is that, on average, women's income during their lifetime is some £250 000 less than men's, with an income in retirement that is 57 per cent of men's.[16]

(ii)   Older women will have a broken work history as a result of the traditional caring role adopted by women

In 1984, for instance, when today's 65-year-old pensioner was aged 41, the employment rate for 35–49 year-old women was 65 per cent versus 88 per cent for men, and 55 per cent of these women were employed as part-timers compared to 1 per cent of men. Lower overall employment meant fewer opportunities to accrue pension rights; and part-time employment, until the early 1990s, very rarely involved pension scheme membership.[17]

---

14   *Implementing Equality for Older People* (2004)
15   *Focus on Older People* (2004)
16   *Age and...multiple discrimination and older people* (2005)
17   *Pensions: Challenges and Choices* (2004), p. 262

Table 7.1   Activity rates of married people by age in the EU[18]

Age	Females	Males
15–24	55.4	88.0
25–29	67.0	95.5
30–34	69.3	97.1
35–39	70.8	97.3
40–44	72.8	96.5
45–49	69.6	95.0
50–64	41.3	66.6

In the European Union (pre-2004 expansion) it was estimated that more than 50 per cent of working age women over the age of 50 did not have paid work.[19] Other figures show that the activity rate of women between the ages of 55 and 64 amounted to 32.9 per cent, in contrast to men who had an activity rate of 53.8 per cent.[20]

Women in the United Kingdom have suffered from the inequalities of pensions because of this. The pensions credit system is designed to improve the lot of low-income pensioners. According to Government figures, since 1997 some 1.9 million people in retirement have been lifted above the absolute poverty level, but two-thirds of this total have been women. Altogether, some 3.3 million people have received pensions credit of which some 2.18 million have been women. There are historical reasons for this, of course. At the time of the Beveridge Report at the end of the Second World War there was an assumption that women would not normally work and that they would be dependent upon their husbands as the breadwinner. This, of course, is changing. The employment rate for women in 2005 was 70 per cent, compared to 55 per cent in 1983.[21]

In the United Kingdom research has also shown that, taking all forms of inactivity together, the chances of men leaving inactivity for paid work were sharply reduced after the age of 50 'and were close to zero for those over 60'. For women, the chances of moving out of inactivity were much reduced after

---

18 These figures only refer to the legal status of marriage in 2001 and does not include co-habitation; source *Advancing women in the workplace: statistical analysis* (2004); original source *European Labour Force Survey 2001*

19 *Towards a Europe for all ages* (1999)

20 *Employment in Europe 2004*

21 *Women and pensions the evidence* (2005)

the age of 40 and 'was particularly uncommon for those older than their late 50s.'[22]

(iii)   Older women are more likely not to be in paid employment

In March 2000, the EU Council of Ministers agreed at the Lisbon Spring Council Meeting to adopt a strategy aimed at raising the rate of growth of employment. There was a particular concern about the poor performance of the EU economy compared to the USA as well as a concern with the emerging economies of Asia. By 2005 some progress had been made. According to a report by the High Level Group chaired by Wim Kok [23], Member States had stepped up their active labour market policies. The total employment rate had risen from 62.5 per cent in 1999 to 64.3 per cent in 2003. Seven Member States had met the interim target of 67 per cent by 2005. The EU as a whole, however, was still unlikely to reach the 2010 targets. The employment rate of older workers in 2003, for the whole EU, was 40.2 per cent and the employment rate for women was 55 per cent.[24]

It is interesting that the two groups who need to have their employment rate increased in order to meet the Lisbon targets are older workers and women. How much more difficult is it then if the individual is both a woman and an older worker?

The higher the level of education, the more likely it is that a person will be economically active. This applies to both men and women, but is especially marked amongst women. Amongst those with the highest level of education (tertiary level) the economic activity rate was 86.4 per cent compared to those with the lowest level who had an activity rate of 52 per cent. This might adversely affect older women who suffered discrimination in education at an earlier age.[25]

In the United Kingdom some 27 per cent of all women between 16 and state pension age are economically inactive, compared to 17 per cent of men. This gap is at its widest between the ages of 25 and 49 when some 40 per cent of such women are economically inactive, compared to just 8 per cent of men.[26] If one also looks at the reasons for inactivity amongst those over 50, then the caring role of women becomes clear. Just over 4 per cent of

---

22 *Characteristics of Older Workers* (1998)

23 *Facing the challenge: the Lisbon Strategy for growth and employment* (2004)

24 There were, of course, large variations between Member States, e.g. the employment rate for older workers in Slovenia was just under 24 per cent, compared to 69 per cent in Sweden

25 *Facing the challenge: the Lisbon Strategy for growth and employment* (2004)

26 *Women and Pensions: the evidence* (2005)

men between the ages of 50 and 64 gave 'looking after family/home' as the reason for their inactivity. This contrasts with some 26.8 per cent of women in this age group.

(iv)   Older women are more likely to work part-time and, as a result, have lower average earnings

Figures published by the European Commission show that this is a pattern of employment that is continuing. In 2003, some 30.5 per cent of employed women in the EU worked part-time, in comparison to just 6.6 per cent of male workers.[27] These figures, however, hide differences related to age and gender. One report concluded:[28]

> There is a clear gender distinction in the occurrence of part-time work by age. In general, men are most likely to be in part-time employment during their youth, while for women it is during the latter stages of their working lives. Furthermore, while the share of part-time employment for men decreases sharply from youth to prime age, for women the share remains roughly the same across these age categories.

Women are more likely to be carers of the young and the elderly than male workers, thus affecting their ability to earn pay and pensions.

In the United Kingdom the figures between the two sexes are just as pronounced. Table 7.2 shows, in the over-50s age group, how a much greater proportion of working women do so part-time compared to working men, even continuing into the over-65 age group, although the gap does narrow at this point.

Around 90 per cent of all lone parents are women and 24 per cent of all children living in Great Britain live in lone parent families.[29] It is clear that the caring duties of women are limited by the lack of available flexible work practices and that many women end up in low paid part-time jobs because these are the only ones which allow them to combine work and family commitments.[30]

---

27   *Employment in Europe 2004*
28   Ibid.
29   *Women and Pensions: the evidence* (2005)
30   Ibid.

Table 7.2   Proportion of people who work full-time and part-time by age and sex in the UK[31]

Age	Men		Women	
	FT	PT	FT	PT
50–54	94.3	5.7	58.0	42.0
55–59	88.2	11.8	48.8	51.2
60–64	76.9	23.1	29.9	70.1
65+	33.4	66.6	13.8	86.2

(v)   Women are more likely to suffer age discrimination at a younger age than men

Women are perceived as being 'older' at a much younger age than men and a greater proportion are likely, therefore, to suffer from age discrimination related to their sex. One survey showed a respondent employer stating that women who returned to work in their mid-thirties after a career break to raise children were regarded as older workers.[32] Another survey concluded that 'the disadvantage incurred in being "too young" or "too old" was found to impact more on women than men, suggesting that in these age ranges at least, being female acted to intensify age prejudice'.[33]

There have also been surveys about the effects of physical attractiveness on decisions concerning recruitment and promotion and one study did show that there was a relationship between physical attractiveness[34] and promotion. There has been also research showing that women are perceived to decline in attractiveness as they age far more than men. Thus, women are more likely than men to suffer from these prejudices as they age.[35]

SEX DISCRIMINATION CASES

It is through the use of sex discrimination legislation in the United Kingdom that the limited judicial attempts to consider age discrimination have taken place. In *Rutherford*,[36] an individual was dismissed on the grounds of redundancy at

31 Whiting (2005)
32 *Older workers: Employers' attitudes and practices* (1990)
33 Duncan and Loretto (2004)
34 This is a difficult issue because of course there is no absolute standard of what is meant by physical beauty. What is meant here I think can be better described as youthful beauty; or maybe just a male stereotype of such a thing
35 Hurley and Giannantonio (1999); see also Ashiagbor (2000)
36 *Rutherford v Secretary of State for Trade and Industry (no 2)*

the age of 67. The original Employment Tribunal agreed with him on the not unreasonable basis that significantly more men than women were economically active after the age of 65.[37] Unfortunately, the Employment Appeal Tribunal and the Court of Appeal disagreed. The latter stated that the correct population that was to be considered was not the 55–74-year-old population considered by the Tribunal but the whole workforce of 16–65 years. If one looks at this latter group, then there is very little difference between the proportions of men and women in terms of disparate impact. Thus, rather than just examining the affected workforce, the Court of Appeal decided that the correct basis was the whole population, most of whom would not wish to work beyond the age of 65. This unfortunate decision finally meant that it was not possible to use the Sex Discrimination Act 1975 to defeat age-discriminatory legislation, despite the fact that there is a close link between age and sex discrimination. Women (and men in certain circumstances) are more likely to be discriminated against on the grounds of age, but the legislation and judicial decisions did not recognise this.

AGE AND ETHNICITY

Unemployment rates generally for black and minority ethnic groups tend to be higher than for the white population. According to one report by the House of Lords Select Committee on Economic Affairs this problem is exacerbated by age:[38]

> However, this disadvantage appears to be compounded by age. In the late 1990s, the unemployment rate for whites was 5 per cent for both 35–44 year olds and for people aged between 45 and state pension age. For blacks it was 12 per cent among 35–44 year olds, and 16 per cent among those aged between 45 and state pension age, and for members of the Pakistani/Bangladeshi communities it was 13 per cent among the 35–44 age group, but 26 per cent among persons aged between 45 and state pension age.

A Commission for Racial Equality representative, speaking to the Select Committee,[39] stated that it appeared that many black and minority ethnic persons aged between 45 and state pension age suffered both an 'ethnic penalty' and an 'age penalty' in the labour market. The Select Committee noted that the Government's initiatives in this field appeared to be directed at young people

---

37   8 per cent of men compared to 3 per cent of women
38   Aspects of the Economics of an Ageing Population, para 4.29
39   Ms Maureen Fraser, para 4.30

and new entrants to the labour market[40] and recommended that more attention should be given to those over the age of 50.

The comparison of employment rates between various ethnic minorities and the white population are revealing (Table 7.3). It appears that with some groups such as the Black or Black British group, discrimination takes place against both young people and older workers.

Table 7.3   Employment rates by ethnicity and age (%)[41]

Ethnic group	16–24	25–44	45–59/64	All ages
Asian or Asian British	42	69	55	59
Black or Black British	35	69	63	60
White	67	83	74	77

This is illustrative of the fact that there may be a particular issue with younger people and race discrimination. Whilst all ages have much lower employment rates than the white population, the gap is greater with older people and younger ones, notably amongst the black or black British group. Older people from ethnic minority groups are more likely to be living in poverty than pensioners in general.[42] This may be a reflection of the discrimination in employment that they have faced during their lifetime.

It is really interesting when one looks at the breakdown of statistics for those over the age of 65. There are much greater numbers of over-65s in the white population in Great Britain than in the ethnic minority population. Thus, 14.9 per cent of white British people and 22.9 per cent of white Irish people are aged between 65 and 84 years. This contrasts with a figure of 5 per cent for all Asian or Asian British people; 6.2 per cent of all black or black British people and 4.8 per cent of Chinese ethnic people in Great Britain.[43] The reasons for this are probably too complex to be discussed here, but it may indicate that a different priority needs to be given in relation to age and ethnic minorities. It may be that discrimination against young people is proportionately more of an issue than that against the old.

---

40   *Ethnic Minorities and the Labour Market* (2003)
41   Taken from the CRE website www.cre.gov.uk; original source Labour Force Survey
42   *Age and...multiple discrimination and older people* (2005)
43   *Focus on older people* (2004)

AGE AND SEXUAL ORIENTATION

Between 5 and 7 per cent of older people are likely to be gay, lesbian or bi-sexual.[44] Older gay, lesbian and bi-sexual people have lived most of their lives under laws and attitudes which did not tolerate their sexual orientation. Whereas the laws have changed and attitudes have changed somewhat, it would still be difficult for many older people to 'come out'. The social facilities available to younger gay and lesbian people may not be suitable for older people. Unfortunately, little specific research has been done in respect of the link between age and sexual orientation. There are also issues related to older transgender people which require research.

AGE AND DISABILITY

The likelihood of disabilities and chronic conditions increases with age.[45] Older workers with disabilities are more likely to lose their jobs in workplace reorganisations as a result of fewer opportunities to train and upgrade their skills. Age and disability are a barrier when trying to get a job, according to the OHRC.[46] The number of people aged over 50 who are long-term sick or disabled has been increasing. This is somewhat paradoxical because there has also been a continuing increase in life expectancy and in the health position of older people.[47] There is a concentration in sickness-related benefit claims in areas of declining industry. It was suggested to the House of Lords Select Committee that this was because:

> As the structure of the economy has changed some workers, from old industrial sectors have seen themselves as unfit for different types of jobs in the service sector, and employers have also seen them as unsuitable.[48]

Thus, an individual's perception of their health status may have more effect than any objective medical opinion. The answer for the Select Committee was for the Government to disseminate best practice with regard to job and workplace design to facilitate the employment of older workers who might have health problems which limit their employment.

---

44   *Age and…multiple discrimination and older people* (2005), relying on estimates by Stonewall
45   See Sargeant (2005b)
46   See www.ohrc.on.ca
47   *Aspects of the economics of an ageing population* (2003), para. 5.3
48   This point was made by Mr David Coates of the TUC

In the EU some 16.4 per cent of the population state that they have a long-standing health problem or disability (LSHPD). The proportion varies amongst Member States (Table 7.4).[49]

Table 7.4   Percentage of the working population[50] with LSHPD

Country	%
EU15	*16.4*
Belgium	18.4
Denmark	19.9
Germany	11.2
Greece	10.3
Spain	8.7
France	24.6
Ireland	11.0
Italy	6.6
Luxembourg	11.7
Netherlands	25.4
Austria	12.8
Portugal	20.1
Finland	32.2
Sweden	19.9
UK	27.2

If one translates this into age ranges there is a clear pattern suggesting that the older a person becomes the more likely it is that a person will have a long-term health problem or be disabled (Table 7.5).[51] This is true of all countries in the EU.

These figures are perhaps reflected in the employment rate for older workers. If one looks at the figures for all countries in the EU, there are only five out of the 25 Member Sates where the majority of people in the

---

49   Eurostat News Release 142/2003, 5 December 2003; the figures were provided for the closing ceremony of the European Year of People with Disabilities 2003
50   Those aged 16–64 years
51   *Disability and social participation in Europe* (2001). These are different figures to Table 7.4 and are not meant to match, but are merely used to illustrate the point that older people are more likely to be disabled than younger people

Table 7.5   Age-specific percentages of people reporting disability

	Germany	France	Italy	Spain	UK	EU
16–19	7.0	7.6	3.3	2.6	12.4	6.6
20–24	8.5	7.5	1.9	1.9	8.7	6.1
25–29	8.6	8.1	2.4	3.2	11.1	7.2
30–34	8.0	9.6	3.4	4.8	13.8	8.3
35–39	11.1	12.7	3.9	6.1	15.2	10.5
40–44	12.9	13.3	6.1	8.2	15.5	12.1
45–49	16.8	17.5	7.1	9.6	20	15.5
50–54	25.4	20.9	13.0	15.7	24.9	21.1
55–59	33.5	31.1	15.6	24.5	35.7	28.9
60–64	35.1	34.3	22.5	32.2	32.6	31.7

55 to 64 years age band are in employment. These are Denmark (60.2 per cent), Estonia (52.3 per cent), Portugal (51.1 per cent), Sweden (68.6 per cent) and the United Kingdom (55.5 per cent). The lowest figures are for Slovenia (23.5 per cent), Slovakia (24.6 per cent), Poland (26.9 per cent) and Belgium (28.1 per cent).[52]

One paper by the European expert group on employment for disabled people reported that:[53]

> Disability is much more prevalent among older people: 63 per cent of people with disabilities are older than 45. For non-disabled people the corresponding percentage is only 34 per cent. So the disabled population is relatively old. This is particularly so in Germany, Greece, Italy and Spain.

> This pattern is mainly due to individuals' health condition deteriorating with age. Furthermore, many impairments leading to disability are acquired during a person's life. There may, in addition, be a 'generation factor', in so far as younger age groups experience better health and working conditions in their early working life and better health care and rehabilitation provisions, than their predecessors in older generations.

---

52   Eurostat News Release 142/2003, 5 December 2003
53   *The employment situation of people with disabilities in the European Union* (2001)

United Kingdom figures reflect a similar pattern. According to figures from the Disability Rights Commission[54] (DRC) some 19 per cent of the labour market population are long-term disabled (6860000 people) compared to 81 per cent not disabled (29342000). Of the disabled work population only some 49 per cent (3389000) are in work, compared to 81 per cent of the not disabled (23847000).

The prevalence of disability also increases with age (Table 7.6), so that some 10.3 per cent of working age men in the 20–24 years age band, for example, are disabled compared with 33.9 per cent of men in the 50–64 years age group, suggesting a high correlation between age and disability.[55]

Table 7.6   People of working age with disabilities (%)

Age	Disabled
16–24	9.4
25–34	13.2
35–49	33.8
50–59/64	43.6

In the case of disability generally it is suggested that factors affecting a disabled individual's ability or willingness to work are likely to include the severity of the disability, access to and within a potential workplace, beliefs on the likelihood of facing discrimination or the availability of suitable jobs and the trade-off between employment income and benefit receipt.[56]

Disability and age are two areas of discrimination that are closely linked and stand apart from the other grounds because perhaps there is sometimes a need to positively facilitate equal participation. There is a close correlation between age and disability and it can be argued that, because of this, age discrimination should be treated in a similar way to disability discrimination rather than, as proposed, adopting a similar approach to sex and race discrimination. This is because at a certain point there is a very high probability that disability and age merge or intersect and the discrimination takes place against an older worker who is, or is likely to become, disabled.

---

54 Disability Briefing – January 2004; figures available from the DRC's website www.drc-gb.org; the figures are based on the DRC's estimates from the summer 2003 Labour Force Survey for Great Britain
55 Smith and Twomey (2002), 415–427
56 Ibid.

It is true that the older a worker becomes the more likely it is that the individual will be disabled. The employers' response is to have a default age at which an employee can be removed from the workforce without any of the related problems (for the employer) of any potential unfair dismissal claims, discrimination claims and so on. The alternative approach posited here and elsewhere in this book is that it would be more appropriate to extend to older workers the duty of employers to make reasonable adjustments. Thus, if a person has a genuine impairment to their health, mental or physical, then the employer should be required to treat them in the same way as a disabled employee. If a worker does not have a mental or physical impairment, then the only reason for adopting the CBI approach is to dismiss them because they are likely to have such an impairment in the future. This in itself, it could be argued, may be enough to justify further protection for older workers.

THE AGEING PROCESS[57]

Reading about getting older or old can be a depressing experience. With age comes an increasing likelihood of both physical and mental ill health. Consider some of the possibilities:[58]

- Vision

Blindness and impaired vision become more common as we get older. In the United Kingdom 42 per cent of people over 75 will develop cataracts, almost 50 per cent will have age-related macular degeneration and 7 per cent will be affected by the most common form of glaucoma. Significant numbers of people will suffer from more than one condition.

- Hearing

More than half of people over 60 have a hearing loss and 30 per cent of them have to use a hearing aid. The most common cause of age-related hearing loss is through disease or damage to the hearing organ in the inner ear, or the nerve which carries hearing information to the brain.

- Dementia, depression and mental health

Up to 700 000 people are estimated to be suffering from dementia in the United Kingdom. It becomes much more common as we get older, with

57   First discussed in Sargeant (2005b)
58   I took this list and the data in Table 7.7 from the website of the national medical research charity 'Research into Ageing' www.ageing.org

nearly one in every 20 people over the age of 65 being affected. Depression affects about one person in 8 over 65.

- Osteoporosis and bone disease

Osteoporosis is a condition characterised by a thinning of the bones. As a result of hormonal changes after the menopause, the majority of women will develop osteoporosis to some extent and 50 to 70 per cent of women will suffer an osteoporotic fracture at some time. One in twelve men will also suffer significant bone loss. Thin bones are more likely to fracture, with the spine, hip, thigh, wrist and forearm being most at risk.

- Stroke and heart disease

Cardiovascular and circulatory problems, such as stroke, blood pressure problems and heart attacks, are the commonest causes of death and disability for older people. There are over 100 000 first strokes every year in the United Kingdom, 90 per cent of these affect people over 65 years.

This is not the happiest of lists and, of course, is not a comprehensive one. The word disability covers a wide range of impairments and the employment rates vary for those with different disabilities (Table 7.7). Those with a mental illness or with learning difficulties have a much lower employment rate than others.

AGE-RELATED RETIREMENT

It is around issues concerned with retirement that the link between age and disability can be seen most clearly. Those who advocate the keeping of a compulsory retirement age, for example, argue that it is a good way of allowing people to leave the workforce with dignity, rather than perhaps having to be removed because they lack capability or competence. The problem with this assertion is that the cure, mandatory retirement, also unfairly affects all those who are not suffering from a loss of competence or capability. The effects of the ageing process are not uniform and affect different people to different degrees and in different ways.

One conclusion that might be drawn from the close relationship between age and disability is that there is a distinct group who are not well protected by the present and proposed statute and regulations on disability and age. This group is the older worker, say 50+ years of age. The older worker is different from the younger or even the 'middle aged' worker, although it has to be recognised that

Table 7.7   Employment rate by type of disability (%)

Musculo-skeletal problems	**45.6**
Difficulty in seeing	44.3
Difficulty in hearing	68.1
Skin condition, allergies	69.3
Chest, breathing problems	64.0
Heart, blood pressure, circulation	50.3
Stomach, liver, kidney, digestion	52.0
Diabetes	65.1
Epilepsy	44.0
Mental illness	18.4
Depression, bad nerves	22.2
Mental illness, phobia, panics	10.4
Learning difficulties	21.4
All disabled	47.9

there is a progression from one stage to another. The older worker group has a closer relationship with disability than any of the other aged groups.

This group has a high proportion of its membership, at least one-third, who are disabled (conversely, of course, the majority of disabled workers are in this age group). It is a group with a membership that is probably more likely to become disabled in the future or at least to suffer from some degree of mental or physical impairment. The solution for employers with regard to this latter group is that there should be a mandatory retirement age. This will save the dignity of individuals in decline and save employers from having to make judgements about when an employee is no longer capable of carrying out their work competently.

If the distinctive group of older worker is not to be treated as a separate group with distinctive issues relating to discrimination at work, then at least there should be a recognition of the relevance of disability issues and that there is a likelihood of multiple discrimination. In fact in using age as the reason to retire an individual, the employer is using age as a substitute for another reason such as a desire not to have to deal with the expected decline in competence as workers become older.

It can be argued that older workers should receive similar protection to disabled workers, both in respect of any current disabilities or in respect of the likely path to disability or health impairment. In practical terms this means the extension of the duty on the employer to make adjustments in relation to access to work, the organisation of that work and, if necessary, a requirement to find alternative work. This approach is more in tune with a human rights motivated one which focuses on the rights and dignity of the individual. The preambles to all of the Directives mentioned refer to the right of all persons to equality before the law and protection against discrimination being recognised by various United Nations and/or international declarations such as the Universal Declaration of Human Rights.[59] The common thread that links them all is this human rights justification. A good approach is to say that 'the central aim of equality should be to facilitate equal participation of all in society, based on equal concern and respect for the dignity of each individual'.[60] A comparison of issues concerning older workers and disabled workers suggests that in order to facilitate equal participation there should be comparable treatment.

59 Preamble 4 of Directive 2000/78/EC, preamble 3 of Directive 2000/43/EC and preamble 2 of Directive 2002/73/EC
60 Fredman and Spencer (2003)

CHAPTER 8

Employment Equality (Age) Regulations 2006

The Age Regulations 2006, which were effective from 1 October 2006, will undoubtedly continue to require employers to examine their procedures and policies in order to ensure compliance. Prior to the Regulations being adopted, most employers had equal opportunities policies. In one survey some three-quarters of employers had equal opportunities policies, nearly all of which covered gender, ethnicity and disability/health. Only just over half (56 per cent), however, had such policies which included age.[1]

The number of employees covered was higher than these figures would suggest, because large employers were more likely to have such policies. Thus, some 84 per cent of employees worked for organisations which had an equal opportunities policy including gender; the same number for ethnicity and only a slightly smaller figure for disability (83 per cent). The figure for age was 67 per cent, making it have the least coverage. Considering that this was the one area that was not covered by legislation, this figure seems understandable. Larger organisations were, therefore, more likely to have an equal opportunities policy and more likely to have one that included age.[2] Public sector and the voluntary sector were also more likely to have policies (93 per cent each) when compared to the private sector (64 per cent).

It is likely that monitoring the workforce profile and HR practices will also be important in ensuring compliance with the Age Regulations. The same report revealed that in its survey about one-third of employers were monitoring in relation to their workforce profile, recruitment and pay. It also reported that only 5 per cent of all establishments had monitored and subsequently taken action as a result of that monitoring.

---

1   *Survey of employers' policies, practices and preferences relating to age* (2006)
2   Ibid. for all these figures; the correlation with size is marked with just 53 per cent of establishments with under 50 employees having a policy, but 98 per cent of those with 10 000 or more employees.

PART 1   GENERAL

Regulation 1 cites the title of the Regulations and the commencement date. The United Kingdom was one of a number of countries that were able to delay the implementation of the Framework Directive for up to three years. The final date for implementation was therefore December 2006, but the Government has a commitment, where possible, to only introduce new employment regulations twice a year. October 1 was the latest date that the Regulations could take effect to be in compliance both with the Directive and with its own policy on the introduction of new regulations.

Regulation 2(1) states that references to discrimination are to mean discrimination on the grounds of age (Regulation 3) and discrimination by way of victimisation (Regulation 4) and instructions to discriminate (Regulation 5) and to harassment (Regulation 6).

Regulation 2(2) defines certain terms which will be referred to in the text. Most notable here are the definitions of, firstly, the employer in relation to a job applicant. The definition of an employer is to include one that has no employees at the time. Thus, a potential employer who is seeking to recruit is also included in the definition even though they have no employees. Secondly, the definition of employment is the wider definition of someone working under a contract of services or a contract to personally do any work. This definition of worker means that some self-employed workers will also be protected by the Regulations.[3]

DIRECT DISCRIMINATION

Regulation 3(1)(a) states that a person A discriminates against a person B if, on the grounds of B's age, A treats B less favourably than he or she treats or would treat others.

The obvious example of direct discrimination with regard to age is the placing of age limits in job advertisements. Stipulating that a person must be of a certain age or within a certain age range is likely to be direct discrimination against those of other ages, except for those nearing retirement age (see below). Less obvious examples of discrimination in recruitment might be the stipulation of a certain length of experience or of the requirement for certain qualifications are potentially discriminatory if such requirements cannot be justified. The use of advertising media which only appeals, or is accessed by, a certain age group

---

3   See Employment Rights Act 1996, section 230(1)–(3)

might also infer discrimination. In the survey[4] only 6 per cent of respondents which had recruited in the previous five years had specified an age range in the advertisements for their largest occupational group, but 46 per cent had used years of experience and 62 per cent had specified qualifications in their advertised criteria. This common practice is something that employers will need to be aware of to be in conformity with the Regulations.

Of course direct discrimination is unlikely to be as obvious as this and the problem to be tackled might be an unwritten policy within an organisation, not to recruit outside a certain age range.[5] Nevertheless, the question with regard to direct discrimination is likely to be whether the complainant would have received the same treatment *but for* his or her age, to misuse the test stipulated in a sex discrimination case, *James v Eastleigh Borough Council*. Lord Goff stated in that case that:

> *This simple test possesses the double virtue that, on the one hand, it embraces both the case where the treatment derives from the application of a gender-based (age-based) criterion, and the case where it derives from the selection of the complainant because of his or her sex (age) and on the other hand it avoids, in most cases at least, complicated questions relating to concepts such as intention, motive, reason or purpose..*

With age discrimination the motive or intention is also irrelevant unless it is part of the objective justification (see below).

This is also a narrower definition of direct discrimination in the Age Regulations than that found in the Race Relations Act 1976 or the Regulations concerning sexual orientation[6] or religion or belief[7] adopted in 2003. In the Race Relations Act, a person A discriminates against a person B if, on racial grounds, A treats B less favourably. Similarly, the Regulations refer to the grounds of sexual orientation or the grounds of religion or belief. The Age Regulations, in contrast, follow the Sex Discrimination Act 1975 which refers to discrimination 'on the grounds of her sex'. In the age case discrimination is on the 'grounds of his age'. The result is that the discrimination is limited to the individual and may exclude discrimination on the basis of someone else's age. One situation might be where an applicant for a job has a much older partner and an employer decides that this might limit the person's commitment to the job, because of a

---

4   See *Survey of employers' policies, practices and preferences relating to age* (2006)
5   *Equality and Diversity: Coming of Age* (2005). This consultation accompanied the draft Regulations published in 2005 and contains many examples throughout, some of which are relied upon here
6   SI 2003/1661
7   SI 2003/1660

stereotypical view of age. The employer may take the view that the applicant will be less mobile or less committed to change because of the older partner's influence. In such a case the discrimination may not be on the grounds of the applicant's age, but on the grounds of the partner's age and, therefore, not covered by the Regulations.

A second major issue here is also that it is possible to objectively justify direct age discrimination. There is a proviso in Regulation 3(1) which allows A to show that the less favourable treatment is a 'proportionate means of achieving a legitimate aim'. The meaning of this is discussed below, but discrimination on the grounds of age is the only ground for which it is possible to justify direct discrimination apart from the limited possibility of a genuine occupational requirement.

Thirdly, Regulation 3(3)(b) provides that the reference to B's age includes B's apparent age. This is an important inclusion because it will include all those who appear to be a different age than they actually are. It is also important because, in a way, it is a step towards stopping discrimination because of a person's appearance. Mention has already been made in this book (Chapter 7) of discrimination concerned with appearance which may particularly affect women who suffer from a male-dominated concept of youthful good looks and who may suffer extra discrimination related to this as they become older. It is not entirely clear why this concept should only apply to direct discrimination and not to indirect discrimination.

INDIRECT DISCRIMINATION

Section 3(1)(b) provides that discrimination takes place when A applies to B a provision, criterion or practice which he or she applies or would apply equally to persons not of the same age group as B, but which puts or would put persons of the same age group as B at a disadvantage when compared with other persons and which also puts B at that disadvantage.

This, of course, is generally now a standard definition of indirect discrimination. An example given in the Government consultation is that of a business which requires applicants for a courier job to have held a driving licence for five years. The requirement does not mention age, but it is likely that a higher proportion of workers over the age, say, of 40 will meet the requirement than those aged, say, 25.

One of the issues for the Age Regulations and future judicial decisions will be deciding who is to be compared to whom, although Regulation 3(2) provides that a comparison of B's case with that of another person must be that the 'relevant circumstances in the one case are the same, or not materially different, in the other'.

In order to establish indirect discrimination the complainant will need to show that the treatment caused him or her a disadvantage as well as the age group to which the complainant belongs, but will also have to show that it did not cause the disadvantage for the comparator pool.[8] This makes comparisons potentially complicated. When can it be said that one age group is treated less favourably than another age group. Are 30-year-olds to be compared to 29-year-olds as different age groups? Regulation 3(3)(a) states that an age group means a group of persons 'defined by reference to age, whether by reference to a particular age or a range of ages'. This rather suggests that an age group could consist of a group of 29-year-olds or it could consist of a group consisting of under-30s, say. Such decisions are likely to be difficult ones, especially with complaints concerning discrimination in comparison with people who are not many years different in age. A case that is illustrative of this problem is one that appeared before the Labour Court in Ireland, *Superquinn v Barbara Freeman*. This case concerned a complaint that an employee, Barbara Freeman, had been unsuccessful in an application for a more senior position. Ms Freeman was 31 years of age and the successful candidate was 28 years of age. She complained that she had been discriminated against on a number of grounds, including age. She claimed that there was enough evidence to establish a prima facie case that discrimination had taken place and that the onus was now upon the employer to show that this was not the case. The Labour Court held that:

> *The existence of a difference on the grounds of age, marital status or family status between the two candidates does not of itself establish a prima facie case of discrimination. The difference in age of three years, the complainant being 31 years old and the successful candidate being 28 years old, is not in the Court's view significant enough to establish a presumption of discrimination, in the absence of other facts.*

This is not meant to be illustrative of the current state of Irish law, but illustrative of one of the problems that employment tribunals will need to deal with, that is, the meaning of an age group and what gap there might need to be to formulate an assumption of age discrimination.

Insofar as getting the right group for comparison purposes with regard to indirect discrimination, the decision of the Court of Appeal in *Rutherford*[9] is

---

8   The comparator can be real or hypothetical
9   *Rutherford v Secretary of State for Trade and Industry (No 2)*

illustrative of the problems faced. This case is discussed elsewhere in this book, but it concerned a man who was dismissed after the age of 65 and who made a claim for indirect discrimination on the basis that many more men worked beyond the age of 65 than women. Thus, a law[10] which removed rights to claim unfair dismissal and a redundancy payment after the age of 65 amounted to indirect discrimination against men. The Court of Appeal used the whole workforce of 16 to 65 years for comparison purposes, rather than, in age discrimination terms, those over the age of 65 and denied the claim. This might suggest that a different approach will be required when looking at comparators for age discrimination cases rather than sex discrimination ones, although perhaps the question of how to determine the relevant pool remains.[11]

OBJECTIVE JUSTIFICATION

One of the areas that considerably weakens the impact of the Age Regulations is the wide scope for justifying exceptions to the principle of equal treatment. The tests for objective justification are, firstly, that the discrimination has a legitimate aim and, secondly, that it is an appropriate and proportionate means of achieving that aim. The 2005 DTI consultation document accompanying the draft Regulations stated that it will not be easy to meet the requirements for objective justification, but also admits that 'most other discrimination legislation only allows direct discrimination in cases of genuine occupational requirements', and that for age 'it will be possible to objectively justify direct discrimination in the same way as indirect discrimination'.

The last sentence of Regulation 3(1) provides that direct and indirect discrimination are unlawful subject to the fact that A cannot 'show the treatment or, as the case may be, the provision, criterion or practice to be a proportionate means of achieving a legitimate aim'.

In the 2005 draft Regulations some specific examples of treatment which 'depending upon the circumstances' may be a legitimate and proportionate aim and being justified exceptions to the rule on direct discrimination were included. In the 2003 DTI consultation exercise a number of specific aims had been suggested and the consultees were asked whether the list should be expanded. Some 42 per cent of the respondents said no, whilst 40 per cent said yes and suggested a number of other potentially legitimate aims.[12] The Government decided not to have an exhaustive list, as this would prove 'too

---

10   Employment Rights Act 1996, section 156
11   See now *Rutherford v Secretary of State* [2006] IRLR 551 HL
12   *Equality and Diversity: Coming of Age* (2005)

restrictive and prescriptive'. IT then put in a statement which might perhaps have revealed the true scope of the Age Regulations. It stated:

> We would not want to prevent employers or providers of vocational training from demonstrating that age-related practices could be justified by reference to aims other than those in such a list.

It would not be conceivable for the Government to make this statement about sex or race discrimination, but somehow it is possible with age discrimination.

In the event these examples were left out of the final Regulations but it is likely that any Court might first turn to Article 6 of the Framework Directive, which permits exceptions in a way that it does not to other forms of discrimination.[13] According to the 2005 consultation document[14] 'a wide variety of aims may be considered legitimate'. Two examples of legitimate aims are 'business needs' and 'considerations of efficiency'. In themselves, of course, these are meaningless phrases but the scope that they imply are potentially of concern. The word 'proportionate' is, it is claimed, the same as the Directive's requirement that the means of pursuing the legitimate aim are 'appropriate and necessary'.[15] The 2005 consultation document states that the requirement of proportionality has three aspects:

- The provision, criterion or practice must actually contribute to the pursuit of the legitimate aim; an example of this is if an employer or other person wants to use an age-related provision, criterion or practice to encourage loyalty, then they must show that it actually does so.

- The importance of the legitimate aim should be weighed up against the discriminatory effects.

- One should not discriminate more than is necessary; if there is a choice of means of achieving the aim, then the one with the least discriminatory effect should be used.

There are, therefore, likely to be numbers of exceptions which allow direct as well as indirect discrimination. The specific examples in Article 6 of the Directive are:

1. the setting of special conditions on access to employment and vocational training, employment and occupation, including dismissal and remuneration conditions, for young people, older

---

13 Directive 2000/78/EC
14 *Equality and Diversity: Coming of Age* (2005)
15 Framework Directive 2000/78/EC, Article 6.1

workers and persons with caring responsibilities in order to promote their vocational integration or ensure their protection. It is not altogether clear what the scope of vocational integration;

2.   the fixing of minimum conditions of age, professional experience or seniority in service for access to employment or to certain advantages linked to employment;

3.   the fixing of a maximum age for recruitment which is based on the training requirements of the post in question or for a need for a reasonable period in the job before retirement. Of course, there would not be a need to have this second exception if there was no mandatory retirement age contained in the contract or in law.

Other justifiable exemptions are discussed below.

DISCRIMINATION BY WAY OF VICTIMISATION

Regulation 4(1) provides that victimisation is less favourable treatment by A on the grounds that B had done something in relation to the Age Regulations, such as bringing proceedings or giving evidence or information. This protection is subject to something done, being done or said in good faith[16] and is identical in wording to the provisions in other measures on discrimination.

INSTRUCTIONS TO DISCRIMINATE

If A instructs B to carry out an act which is unlawful under the Age Regulations and B does not carry out the instruction, or complains to A or another about the instruction, then any less favourable treatment of B by A would amount to discrimination on the grounds of age.

HARASSMENT ON THE GROUNDS OF AGE

Throughout the Age Regulations there are statements that it is unlawful to subject a person to harassment.[17] Harassment is then defined in Regulation 6(1). There now seems to be a standard definition of harassment in all the anti-discrimination measures. The Age Regulations adopt this standard approach. Thus, harassment on the grounds of age takes place when A engages in unwanted conduct which has the effect of violating B's dignity, or creating an intimidating, hostile, degrading, humiliating or offensive environment for B. There is also a reasonableness test, including taking into account B's perception, in Regulation 6(2).

---

16   Regulation 4(2)
17   Regulation 7(3) in relation to employees and regulation 9(2) in relation to contract workers

Harassment is always unlawful and there is no possibility of justification. The 2005 consultation document points out that any harassment of an older person will automatically be harassment on the grounds of age. The reason for the harassment must be the person's age for the Regulations to have effect, although it is interesting that there is no mention of harassment with regard to a person's perceived age as elsewhere.

PART 2   DISCRIMINATION IN EMPLOYMENT AND VOCATIONAL TRAINING

APPLICANTS AND EMPLOYEES

Regulations 7(1) and 7(2) set out what an employer may or may not do in relation to age discrimination in employment.[18] Two limitations are that it is only the employer's actions in relation to employment that count and only employment at an establishment in Great Britain.

Insofar as applicants are concerned, it is unlawful for an employer to discriminate in the arrangements made for the purpose of deciding to whom employment should be offered, in the terms on which the person's employment is offered or by not offering employment.[19] As far as those who are employed at an establishment in Great Britain: an employer may not discriminate in the terms of employment offered; in offering promotion, transfers or training; or in receiving any other benefits or refusing or deliberately stopping such opportunities; or by dismissing[20] or subjecting to any other detriment[21]. These provisions are identical (apart from the exception mentioned below) to those Regulations concerned with sexual orientation and religion or belief.

Regulation 7(4), however, does allow discrimination on the basis of age for those applicants who would be employees if recruited or in Crown employment and who are older than the employer's normal retirement age or 65 years of age if the employer does not have such an age. This exception also applies to applicants who would reach such an age within a period of six months from the date of the application. In such cases it will be permissible for employers to discriminate in the recruitment process on the basis of age. An employer may

18   For a further definition of employment see notes on Regulation 10 below
19   Regulation 7(1)(a)–(c)
20   Regulation 7(7) ensures that those on fixed-term contracts and those who effect a constructive dismissal are included in the definition of dismissal from employment
21   Regulation 7(2)(a)–(d)

decide not to offer employment or may decide to offer less favourable terms than to other employees.

This exception, of course, goes to the heart of the problems with these Regulations. A blanket rule which says that it is legitimate to discriminate against applicants of 65 years and over is not a rule based upon the individual rights of potential employees. It is a rule which is based upon a commercial imperative, yet is in opposition to all the arguments in favour of ending age discrimination at work. Why is it permissible to discriminate against a 65-year-old person but not to discriminate against a 64-year-old person? Why not set the age limit at 60 or 70?

These are the same questions that one can apply to the issue of the default retirement age of 65 (see below). Of course, the provision in Regulation 7(4) is closely connected to the age limit on retirement. It would not be logical to have a default retirement age of 65 and then not allow the employer to discriminate, so that they did not recruit a replacement who was the same age or older. If an employee was forcefully retired at the age of 65 and the employer advertised the post, receiving an application from someone aged 66, it would be absurd if the employer were not allowed to discriminate against that person. The problem really starts with having a default retirement age in the first place. It this were removed, then there would not be a logic in having this age limit on recruitment.

The 2005 consultation document stated that, in the 2003 consultation, it was 'proposed to include a provision for employers to be able to apply an upper age limit if they can justify doing so. Some 73 per cent of respondents agreed with this proposal'.[22] This is a poor rationale for the inclusion of this exception. There is no requirement for the employer to justify this discrimination. They are just to be allowed to discriminate. The 73 per cent quoted, therefore, did not vote for the final result.[23]

The consultation document did state that recruitment, selection and promotion decisions should be made on the skills required, rather than age, but there are situations where direct or indirect discrimination can be justified. Some examples of where there might be issues are:[24]

---

22   Page 39
23   Nor, of course, does a figure which equates the TUC and the CBI as individual respondents and gives them the same weight as an individual person have much meaning.
24   These are taken from the 2005 consultation

- birth dates on job application forms might help an employer to make decisions based upon age;

- requiring a certain length of experience for recruitment or promotion might need to be objectively justified as it is likely to discriminate against young people;

- requiring a certain qualification might put people at a disadvantage. The example given is of an older person who may never have had the opportunity to take media studies;

- graduate recruitment schemes might need to be open to students of all ages or open to other sources of recruitment;

- vocational training; any age limits concerning access will need to be objectively justified;

- employment agencies will need to justify any age limits or specialisms related to age.

Regulation 7(3) makes harassment in relation to those employees or those who are applicants unlawful. Regulation 7(6) provides that benefits provided by the employer to the public, or to part of the public, from which the employee benefits as being a member of the public or that part are not covered by the Regulations. This is unless there are differences in the benefits given to the employees and the public, or whether the benefits are regulated by the contract of employment or are concerned with training.

EXCEPTIONS FOR GENUINE OCCUPATIONAL REQUIREMENT

This Regulation is identical to the equivalent provisions contained in the Sexual Orientation and the Religion or Belief Regulations. It provides that all the provisions, except those relating to terms of employment, in Regulation 7(1) and 7(2) concerning applicants and those in employment do not apply where 'possessing a characteristic related to age is a genuine and determining occupational requirement'.[25]

The example given in the 2005 consultation is that of an actor who might need to be of a certain age, but even that would need objective justification to show that it was 'proportionate to apply that requirement in the particular case'.[26] The same consultation pointed out that it is unlikely to be a great issue for age discrimination. This Regulation is used in the other statutes and regulations concerning discrimination because it is an exception to the rule that there can

25 Regulations 8(1) and 8(2)(a)
26 Regulation 8(2)(b)

be no justification of direct discrimination. As we have seen above, somewhat depressingly, this rule does not apply in the case of age discrimination, where it is permissible to justify such discrimination generally.

CONTRACT WORKERS

This Regulation provides for contract[27] workers to be given similar rights in relation to Regulations 7 and 8, where relevant, to those workers in employment. Thus, Regulation 9(1) makes discrimination against a contract worker by a principal unlawful in respect of the terms on which he allows him or her to do the work, by not allowing him or her to do it or continue to do it, in the way access to benefits or refusing the same, or by subjecting the contract worker to any detriment.[28] A principal is defined as 'a person who makes work available for doing by individuals who are employed by another person who supplies them under a contract made with the principal', contract work is the work which is made available and a contract worker is an individual supplied to the principal to do the work.[29]

Regulations 9(2) to 9(4) provide the same protection as before concerning harassment, genuine occupational requirement and benefits supplied to workers and the public, as in Regulation 7(6).

MEANING OF EMPLOYMENT AND CONTRACT WORK AT ESTABLISHMENTS IN GREAT BRITAIN

Regulation 10 is identical to Regulation 9 of the Religion or Belief Regulations and the Sexual Orientation Regulations. It is concerned with the geographical location of the employment or contract work. An employee is to be regarded as working at an establishment in Great Britain if the work is done wholly or mainly in Great Britain, or, if it is work done wholly outside Great Britain, then the employer must have a place of business at an establishment in Great Britain and the work is for the purposes of the business carried out at that establishment. The employee will also need to be ordinarily resident in Great Britain at the time they apply for employment or is offered it, or at any time during the course of employment.[30] Employment[31] includes employment on board a ship, if the ship is registered at a port of registry in Great Britain, and

---

27 For further definition of contract work see note on Regulation 10 below
28 Detriment does not include harassment, Regulation 2(2)
29 Regulation 9(5)
30 Regulations10(1) and 10(2)
31 Regulation 10(7) provides that this Regulation also applies to contract work; for employee, employer and employment, read contract worker, principal and contract work

employment on an aircraft or hovercraft if the vehicle is registered in the United Kingdom and is operated by a person who has his principal place of business in, or is ordinarily resident in, Great Britain.[32]

Regulations 10(4) to 10(6) are then concerned with employment in the Continental Shelf and the Frigg Gas Field.[33]

TRUSTEES AND MANAGERS OF OCCUPATIONAL PENSION SCHEMES

The Government is taking advantage of Article 6.2 of the Framework Directive which allows the use of age criteria to continue with regard to certain aspects of occupational social security schemes. Such exceptions will not, according to the Directive and the UK Government, constitute age discrimination. According to the 2005 consultation, although employers and pension scheme managers will have to examine the rules of their schemes, 'we expect pension schemes to be able to operate largely as they do now'.[34]

Regulation 11(1) states that it is unlawful, except for rights accrued and benefits payable related to length of service before the Age Regulations come into force, for trustees and managers of occupational pension schemes to discriminate against members or prospective members, in particular their functions relating to admission and treatment of members. It is also unlawful for them to subject a member or prospective member to harassment.[35] It then provides, in Regulation 11(3), that Schedule 2 shall have effect for a number of purposes including 'exempting certain rules and practices in or relating to occupational pension schemes'.

Section 2 of Schedule 2 introduces a non-discrimination rule into all occupational pension schemes. There are then a list of exempted rules, practices, actions and decisions relating to occupational pension schemes.[36] The Government has effectively excluded the workings of occupational pension schemes from the coverage of the Age Regulations.

OFFICE HOLDERS

Regulation 12 applies to any office or post to which appointments are made to discharge their functions under the supervision of another, and from which

---

32 Regulation 10(3)
33 Schedule 1 to the Age Regulations is also concerned with the Frigg Gas Field
34 *Equality and Diversity: Coming of Age* (2005)
35 Regulation 11(2)
36 Schedule 2, Part 2

they are entitled to remuneration. It also applies to any office or post to which appointments are made by a Minister of the Crown.[37]

The Regulation concerns the application of the Age Regulations to office or post holders. Thus, it is unlawful to discriminate in the recruitment and selection process, in the terms of the appointment, opportunities for promotion, transfers or training and termination.[38] There is also a genuine occupational requirement exception available in Regulation 12(5). An exception to this rule is political office holders which includes Members of Parliament and local authority councillors.

POLICE, BARRISTERS, ADVOCATES AND PARTNERSHIPS

Regulation 13 ensures that members of the police force are included in the scope of the Regulations. Regulation 15 concerns barristers and barristers' clerks in England and Wales and ensures that pupillages and tenancies are included. Regulation 16 ensures that the same rules apply to advocates in Scotland. Regulation 17 applies the Regulations to partnerships. These provisions are identical to those contained in the Regulations concerning sexual orientation and religion or belief.

TRADE ORGANISATIONS

Trade organisations are defined as 'an organisation of workers, an organisation of employers, or any other organisations whose members carry on a particular profession or trade for the purposes of which the organisation exists'.[39]

Such organisations may not discriminate in the terms for membership or for joining or leaving. Nor may they discriminate in the way an individual has access to the benefits of membership. All these Regulations include the non-harassment clause also.

QUALIFICATIONS BODIES

Regulation 19 refers to any body, apart from the governing bodies of educational establishments[40] and school proprietors[41], which can confer professional or trade qualifications. Such bodies may not discriminate in the conferring of awards, or in refusing or withdrawing them. Regulation 18(2) also provides

---

37 Regulation 11(8)
38 Regulations 12(1)–(3)
39 Regulation 18(4)
40 These are dealt with in Regulation 23
41 Regulation 19(3)

that it is unlawful to subject to harassment a person who holds or applies for a qualification.

Interestingly, the draft Regulations had provided for a religious exception to this. It had provided that a professional or trade qualification for the purposes of an organised religion, where there is an age requirement to 'comply with the doctrines of the religion or to avoid conflicting with the strongly held religious convictions of significant number of the religion's followers', is an exception. This exception was dropped in the final version.

PROVISION OF VOCATIONAL TRAINING

It is unlawful for a training provider to discriminate against a person seeking or undergoing training: in the arrangements made for the purpose of who should be offered training; in the terms on which the training provider affords access to any training; by refusing access; by terminating the training or subjecting the applicant or person to be trained to any other detriment during the training.[42] Regulation 20(2) also makes harassment of an applicant or a person undergoing training unlawful.

Training here means:

- all types that help fit a person for any employment;

- vocational guidance;

- facilities for training;

- practical work experience;

- assessment related to the award of a professional or trade qualification.

There is a problem with defining vocational training as including all types that help fit a person for any employment. As NATFHE said in its response to the 2005 consultation:

> *Part of the problem arises from the use of the term 'vocational training' in common parlance and in these (and earlier sets) of Regulations. The national debate around education sees a divide between 'vocational' courses and 'academic' ones. A student taking three A levels at a further education college, or a degree in philosophy at a university would be unlikely to see themselves as undergoing 'vocational training'. Yet*

---

42   Regulation 20(1)

> *these Regulations, like their predecessors, define all courses provided by institutions falling within the further and higher education sector as set out in the Further and Higher Education Act 1992, as being 'vocational training' and thus covered by the Regulations. We believe that only the cognoscenti will be aware of this usage, and it needs to be made much more explicit that everything provided by colleges and universities is covered. A complete list of all the institutions falling under the Regulations, as provided when the Race Relations Amendment Act was introduced, is needed.*

There is one exception in the Regulations. This is that it will not be unlawful to discriminate if the training is for employment for which the trainee or potential trainee would not get because the employer could lawfully refuse to offer employment on the grounds of Regulation 8 (genuine occupational requirement).[43] This might seem clear as there seems no point training someone for a job which they are not going to obtain, on the grounds of the employer claiming a genuine occupational requirement that the potential trainee cannot fulfil. It is not clear, however, what happens to someone who is turned down because some employers might decide that a person is too old under Regulation 3(2)(c), which allows a maximum recruitment age based on the 'need for a reasonable period in post before retirement'. If the employer thinks that they can objectively justify a retirement age which would not allow them to get a sufficient return on their investment in training, then it would seem pointless providing relevant vocational training. This point is not covered in the Regulations, however.

EMPLOYMENT AGENCIES

This Regulation applies to employment agencies, which includes guidance on careers or any other service related to employment.[44] It is unlawful for an employment agency to discriminate in the terms on which it offers its services, or by refusing to provide its services, or in the way it provides its services, as well as subjecting a person to harassment.[45]

There is also an exception in Regulation 21(3) which provides that it is not discrimination if it concerns employment for which the employer will claim a genuine occupational requirement. An employment agency will not be liable for a claim of discrimination if it can show that it relied upon a statement by the employer that the genuine occupational requirement exception applied, and

---

43   Regulation 20(3)
44   Regulation 21(6)(b)
45   Regulation 21(1)–(2).

that it was reasonable for them to rely on the statement. They will, therefore, still have to exercise their own judgement, although it is difficult to see how they could avoid relying on an employer's statement. There is provision, though, in Regulation 21(5) for a person who knowingly or recklessly makes such a statement to be liable to a fine.

ASSISTING PERSONS TO OBTAIN EMPLOYMENT

It is unlawful for the Secretary of State, Scottish Enterprise and Highlands and Islands Enterprise to discriminate[46] in the provision of facilities or services under various statutory requirements.

INSTITUTIONS OF FURTHER AND HIGHER EDUCATION

The Regulations also apply to institutions of further and higher education in relation to students[47] and applicants at those institutions. It is unlawful for an educational establishment included here to discriminate against a person in the terms on which it offers to admit them as a student or by refusing or deliberately not accepting an application. It is also unlawful, in relation to students: to discriminate in the way that access to any benefits is afforded; to refuse or not afford them those benefits; to exclude the student from the establishment; or to make them suffer from any detriment or harassment.[48] The exception to this, as elsewhere, is training for which an employer might refuse employment because of a genuine occupational requirement as in Regulation 8. The balance of this Regulation then goes on to define which institutions are covered.

There is unhappiness about the level of preparation for this. NATFHE's response to the 2005 consultation repeated its response to the 2003 one:

> NATFHE is extremely concerned about the overwhelming silence from Government about the meaning and implications of the new legislation for further and higher education institutions. This is now a matter of most urgent concern. Now is the time to begin looking at the implications of the age legislation for colleges and universities. There is a need for consultation, advice and guidance, codes of practice and training programmes. It is simply not good enough to say that the legislation will apply to colleges and universities, and do absolutely nothing to ensure that they understand and can meet their new responsibilities. We would reiterate the point we have made in all previous consultations –

---

46 Regulation 22; by subjecting the person to a detriment or harassment
47 Regulation 23(6); student means any person who receives education at an institution to which Regulation 23 applies
48 Regulations 23(1)–(2)

> *that there needs to be a consultation group set up with all the interested parties involved in post-school education, in which NATFHE would be happy to participate*

RELATIONSHIPS WHICH HAVE COME TO AN END

If, during a relationship, an act of discrimination has taken place against B, then it is unlawful for A to discriminate against B, by subjecting him or her to detriment, or to subject B to harassment, after their relationship has ended, if this discrimination 'arises out of or is closely connected to the relationship'.[49] This is true even if the relationship came to an end before the Age Regulations came into force in October 2006, provided that the original act of discrimination would have been unlawful if it had taken place after the commencement date of the Age Regulations.

This same provision applies to the Sexual Orientation and Religion or Belief Regulations and is designed to stop continuing discrimination or harassment, such as inhibiting a person's attempts to get another job.

PART 3   OTHER UNLAWFUL ACTS

LIABILITY OF EMPLOYERS AND PRINCIPALS

Anything done by a person in the course of their employment is to be regarded as having been done by the employer as well as the person. It is not relevant whether the employer had knowledge of the things done or approved them. Similarly, anything done by an agent for another person with the authority[50] will be treated as having been done by the original person as well as the agent. There is a defence in Regulation 25(3) where a person such as an employer can prove that they took steps 'as were reasonably practicable to prevent the employee from doing that act or acts in the course of employment'.

AIDING UNLAWFUL ACTS

If a person knowingly aids another person to do an act that is made unlawful by the Age Regulations, then that person is to be treated as having done an unlawful act of 'the like description'. A person may have a defence to the provisions of this Regulation if they rely upon a statement by the other person that the act done would not be unlawful by virtue of some aspect of the Age Regulations and that it is reasonable for them to rely on the statement. Again, if a person

---

49   Regulation 24(1)–(2)
50   Regulation 25(2) whether express or implied and whether precedent or subsequent

knowingly or recklessly makes such a statement which 'in a material respect is false or misleading' then that person will be liable to a fine on conviction.

PART 4   GENERAL EXCEPTIONS TO PARTS 2 AND 3

The Regulations on Religion or Belief have three general exceptions.[51] These are exceptions for:

- national security

- positive action

- the protection of Sikhs in connection with requirements as to wearing safety helmets.

The Regulations concerning Sexual Orientation also contain three general exceptions.[52] These are exceptions for:

- national security

- benefits dependent upon marital status

- positive action.

The Age Regulations 2006 contain eight general exceptions.[53] These are exceptions for:

- statutory authority

- national security

- positive action

- retirement

- national minimum wage

- the provision of benefits based on length of service

- the provision of enhanced redundancy payments

- the provision of life assurance cover for retired workers.

An extra number of exceptions for age, of course, could be just a reflection of an increased complexity when compared to other grounds of discrimination.

---

51 Employment Equality (Religion or Belief) Regulations 2003, Regulations 24–26
52 Employment Equality (Sexual Orientation) Regulations 2003, Regulations 24–26
53 Regulations 27–34; this is an improvement on the Draft Regulations 2005 which contained 11 such exceptions

Indeed, the Sex Discrimination Act 1975 and the Race Relations Act 1976 also have a greater number of general exceptions.[54] It is part of the argument of this book, however, that the numbers reflect a greater willingness to countenance exceptions which are based upon a pragmatic and business approach rather than an individual human rights one.

EXCEPTIONS FOR STATUTORY AUTHORITY AND NATIONAL SECURITY

These provide that nothing in Parts 2 or 3 shall make unlawful any act done in order to comply with a statutory provision or for the purpose of safeguarding national security. An obvious statutory example quoted in the 2005 consultation document, is the Licensing Act 1964 which prohibited the employment of persons under the age of 18 years in a bar when it is open for the sale of alcohol.

EXCEPTIONS FOR POSITIVE ACTION

Because of the availability of the test of objective justification in direct and indirect discrimination, the need for something more is seen only narrowly by the Regulations and the 2005 consultation. There are only two areas described in the Regulations as fulfilling a less-demanding test for positive discrimination: allowing persons of a particular age or age group to have access to facilities for training which will help them find particular work; AND encouraging persons of a particular age or age group to take advantage of opportunities for doing particular work. There is an additional proviso that this action is possible:

> *where it reasonably appears to the organisation that the act prevents or compensates for disadvantages linked to age suffered by those of that age or age group doing that work or likely to take up that work.*[55]

The same approach is taken to trade organisations[56] for measures to encourage membership by persons of a particular age or age group where it reasonably appears to prevent or compensate for disadvantages linked to age.[57]

---

54 Sex Discrimination Act 1975, sections 42A–52A; Race Relations Act 1976, sections 35–42. Both of these pieces of legislation cover a much wider field than employment, as in the Age Regulations
55 Regulation 29(1)
56 Within the meaning of Regulation 18 as being an organisation of workers, an organisation of employers, or any other organisation whose members carry on a particular profession or trade for the purposes of which the organisation exists
57 Regulation 29(3)

The test here, of course, is reasonableness rather than the much stricter test of objective justification requiring the having of a legitimate aim being achieved by an appropriate and proportionate means.[58] In the case of positive action the legitimate aim is the preventing or compensating for disadvantages linked to age. The subsequent requirement is to show reasonableness.

How this may be done without too much difficulty was shown in the 2005 consultation document where two examples are given. The first is an employer placing a recruitment advertisement only in a magazine read by young people, in order to encourage applications from young people. This might amount to indirect age discrimination unless it can be shown to come within the terms of Regulation 29 on positive discrimination, by reasonably appearing to the employer that it helps compensate for disadvantage suffered by that age group within the organisation. The second example is an employer asking a headhunter to search for candidates in a particular age group which is under-represented in the workforce. According to the consultation document 'as long as applications from people in other age groups are not excluded, this is covered by the positive action provision'.

This approach is identical to that adopted in the Religion or Belief and Sexual Orientation Regulations. When it comes to age, however, it may well have a much more profound effect than in the other Regulations and may well be used much more commonly by employers. Whilst it is difficult to argue that such measures should not be allowed, there is the potential for abuse; for example, if an organisation has few younger workers or older workers, is it permissible for them only to use the positive action exception to recruit young people or should they be required to look at all age groups if they are to use this exception? If not, the effect of having a positive action exception in this case is to add discrimination against older workers.

EXCEPTION FOR RETIREMENT AND THE DUTY TO CONSIDER WORKING BEYOND RETIREMENT

Regulation 30(1) is concerned with the exception for retirement and states that:

> *Nothing in Part 2 or 3 shall render unlawful the dismissal of an employee at or over the age of 65 years where the reason for the dismissal is retirement.*[59]

---

58   See Regulation 3 above
59   According to Regulation 30(1) employee has the same meaning as in Employment Rights Act 1996, section 230(1)

This also applies to those in Crown employment and relevant members of the House of Commons and the House of Lords staff.[60]

What this means, of course, is that provided the employer follows the rules (see below), the employee may be dismissed for reasons of retirement at any age on or after the age of 65. Thus, despite the Government repealing those parts of the Employment Rights Act 1996 which took away a person's right to complain of unfair dismissal or to qualify for a redundancy payment (see below) once they had reached retirement age, employers are still to be freely allowed to dismiss people almost at will. It is worth remembering that retirement is not always a voluntary event; as has been shown in the previous Chapters of this book it is not always welcomed and not only means the compulsory removal of an employee from their individual workforce, but usually means the removal of any opportunity to work anywhere in the future as the chances of them returning to the workforce after 65 are very low. Such a return is even more unlikely as a result of Regulation 7(4) which provides that an employer may discriminate against applicants aged 65 and above in deciding whether to recruit them or not.

Section 98(2) of the Employment Rights Act 1996 had a new subsection (ba) inserted, wherein the retirement of the employee was made an additional 'fair' reason for dismissal. There was also a new Section 98(2A) which made this fairness subject to Sections 98ZA to 98ZF. Section 98(3A) also provides that the question of fairness or unfairness of a dismissal related to retirement shall be determined in accordance with Section 98ZG of the Employment Rights Act 1996.[61]

The first part of the amended Employment Rights Act 1996 deals with two categories of employees: those with no normal retirement age and those with a normal retirement age.

Firstly, if the operative date of termination for such an employee is before the employee's 65th birthday, then retirement shall not be taken as the reason for the dismissal.[62] If the operative date of termination falls on or after the employee's 65th birthday and the employer has followed the correct notification procedure (see below) then retirement is the only reason that can be taken for dismissal, provided that the employment does terminate on the intended date

---

60 Regulation 30(1)
61 See Schedule 6 amendments to unfair dismissal legislation
62 Employment Rights Act 1996, section 98ZA

of retirement.[63] If, despite following the duty to notify procedure, the contract is terminated before the intended date, then retirement cannot be the reason for dismissal.

If the employee has a normal retirement date and the operative date of termination falls before this date, then retirement cannot be the reason for dismissal. As one would expect, if the normal retirement age is 65 years or more and the operative date is when the employee reaches the normal retirement date and the employer follows the correct procedure, then retirement is the reason for dismissal. If the employer has not followed the correct procedure or if the contract of employment terminates before the intended date of dismissal, then retirement cannot be the reason for dismissal.[64]

The same principles apply if the normal retirement date is below the age of 65, provided that such a date does not constitute unlawful discrimination under the Age Regulations. In this latter case retirement could not be taken as the reason for the dismissal.[65]

There are particular matters to be considered with regard to the fairness of the reasons for dismissal.[66] These are:

- whether or not the employer has notified the employee in accordance with paragraph 4 of Schedule 6.[67] This paragraph is concerned with an employer's continuing duty to notify the employee of the intended retirement date and the employee's right to make a request (see below);

- if the employer has notified the employee, in accordance with paragraph 4, how long before the notified retirement date the notification was given;

- whether or not the employer has followed, or tried to follow, the procedures in paragraph 7 of Schedule 6. Paragraph 7 is concerned with arranging and holding a meeting to consider the employee's request.

It is clear that employers' procedures will need to be robust in order to ensure that events take place at the correct time and that all the procedures are correctly followed. A retirement dismissal will be unfair if the employer

---

63 Ibid., section 98ZB(1)
64 Employment Rights Act 1996, section 98ZC–98ZD
65 Ibid., section 98ZE
66 Ibid., section 98ZF
67 Schedule 6 is concerned with the duty to consider working beyond retirement

fails to comply with obligations under paragraph 4 (notification of retirement if not already given under paragraph 2), paragraphs 6 and 7 (duty to consider employee's request not to be retired) and paragraph 8 (duty to consider the appeal) of Schedule 6.[68] The one-year qualifying employment period for protection against unfair dismissal does not apply in these cases and, of course, the upper age limit on being able to make a claim for unfair dismissal was removed.[69]

Schedule 6 of the Age Regulations is about the duty to consider working beyond retirement. The 2005 consultation document confidently asserted that 'in many cases retirement is an occasion for which the employee has planned and to which the employee is looking forward'. This must be true, but the consultation document then states that these occasions take place by mutual agreement or by the employee giving notice. This is less likely to be true. In many cases the date has been set by the employer using the employer's normal retirement age or the default retirement age. To say that someone happily retires at their default retirement age by mutual consent is less than honest. Many people retire and will retire, happily, but on a date established by the employer and, now, by the Age Regulations 2006. The 2005 consultation emphasised that the Age Regulations do not oblige an employer to retire employees at 65 years and that they can delay the retirement date to a later age if they wish. However, the document also states that the introduction of a default retirement age is 'because a significant number of employers use a set retirement age as a necessary part of their workforce planning'. It seems an odd expectation to then assume that these employers, given a choice in the matter, will not choose to use the default retirement age of 65 as a continuing part of their workforce planning.

Compulsory or mandatory retirement is the worst form of age discrimination in employment. It is the worst because it is not just a dismissal at one instance. It is a life sentence for those affected because the chances of them obtaining a new job at the same level are remote. The employer response to consultations have been to rationalise the event as being necessary for staff planning purposes and for the dignity of the individual concerned, who can retire instead of being dismissed for incapability or competence. This will be the subject of legal challenge.

---

68   Employment Rights Act 1996, section 98ZG
69   Age Regulations 2006, Schedule 5, paras 24–25,

Schedule 6

The Schedule imposes two duties upon an employer. Firstly, there is the duty to inform the employee of his or her intended retirement date and of his or her right to make a request. This information must be given not more than one year and not less than six months before the dismissal. This is a continuing duty of the employer and such an obligation exists until the fourteenth day before dismissal.[70] The employee may make a request to the employer not to retire on the intended retirement date. The employee must propose that, following the intended date of retirement, their employment should continue indefinitely, for a stated period or until a stated date. This request must be in writing and can only be made once under this paragraph.[71] In a case where the employer has complied with their duty to notify, the employee's request must be made more than three months but not more than six months before the intended retirement date; in a case where the employer has not complied with the duty, then within the six months before the intended date.[72]

There then occurs the employer's second duty, which is to consider the request.[73]

According to paragraph 6, considering a request means:

- holding a meeting with the employee to discuss the request;

- the employer and employee taking all reasonable steps to attend the meeting.

In the 2005 draft Regulations there had also been a requirement for the employer to 'act in good faith'. These words disappeared from the final version!

The meeting is to be held within 'a reasonable period' after the request has been received. In the draft Regulations there was a time limit of 14 days for the employer to notify the employee of the decision. In the final Regulations this changed to 'as soon as reasonably practicable'. The decision, which needs to be in writing, is either to grant the request, stating whether the employee's employment will continue indefinitely or whether it will continue for a specified period, or to refuse it and to confirm the date of dismissal as well as informing the employee of their right to appeal.[74]

---

70 Schedule 6, paras 2 and 4
71 Ibid., para. 5
72 Ibid., para. 5(5)
73 Ibid., para. 6
74 Schedule 6, para. 7(3)

It is possible for the decision to be given in writing without a meeting taking place, if it has not proved reasonably practicable to hold one within a period that is reasonable (again there was a time limit of two months in the draft).[75] The appeals procedure, contained in paragraph 7, follows a similar procedure and, again, time limits for decision making were removed. Employees have a right to be accompanied to the first meeting and any subsequent appeal meeting.[76] The accompanying person must be a fellow employee, which excludes trade union representatives who are not employees. The accompanying employee may address the meeting and confer with the employee, but not answer questions on behalf of the employee.

If the employer dismisses the employee after the request has been made but before a decision has been reached, then the contract of employment will continue in force for all purposes including the purpose of determining the period for which the employee has continuity of employment until the day after the date of the employer's notice of the decision is made.[77] It is not altogether clear why an employer would dismiss an employee under these circumstances when all they had to do was reach a decision to retire the employee. Where an employer fails to inform the employee of the retirement date or of their right to make a request, then an employment tribunal may award compensation of a maximum eight weeks' pay from the employer to the employee. [78]

The 2005 consultation document stated that the procedure was part of changing the culture which 'retires people without regard to the contribution that they can still make to the labour market'.[79] It further stated that the duty to consider procedure would be modelled on the right of parents with young children to request flexible working.[80] It then states that, of course, there is a real difference in that parents who have a request turned down may continue working. Those who have a request to continue working, instead of being retired, turned down will become unemployed. There are other differences also, in that an employer, in the case of a request for flexible working, may only turn down the request for a number of possible reasons as listed in Section 80G(1)(b) of the Employment Rights Act 1996. These reasons are fairly broad

---

75 Ibid., paras 7(4) and 7(5)
76 Ibid., para. 9
77 Ibid., para. 10; the continuation of employment contained here does not count for the purposes of Employment Rights Act 1996, sections 98ZA to 98ZH
78 Ibid., para. 11; the rule on calculating a week's pay contained in Employment Rights Act 1996, Part XIV and the limit in section 227(1), apply here; see Schedule 6, paras 11(3)–(5)
79 The Government has committed itself to reviewing the provisions on a default retirement age in 2011
80 See Employment Rights Act 1996, Part VIIIA

and open to exploitation, but they are a significant improvement over the situation with regard to the Age Regulations. Here, there is no list of possible reasons for turning down a request not to retire, nor is there any obligation upon the employer to give any reasons for turning down the request. The only obligation is to notify the employees of the decision and their right of appeal.

EXCEPTION FOR THE NATIONAL MINIMUM WAGE

This allows for differential rates of pay related to age. This is in relation to the hourly rate set by the Secretary of State[81] or in relation to differential pay for contracts of apprenticeship.[82]

There are, of course, two lower bands for young people: one for those aged 16 and 17 years; the other for those aged between 18 and 21 inclusive. This measure only applies to the age bands and pay levels established by the statutory measures on the national minimum wage. Objective justification would be needed to pay a 16-year-old at a different rate to a 17-year-old. Similarly, if an employer were paying rates which were above the levels of the national minimum wage, they would need to justify this, even if the same age bands were used.

According to the 2005 consultation the justification for this was to encourage young people to stay in full-time education or to encourage employers to employ young people. This measure does exploit young people and is an example of age discrimination written into statute with a business motivation outweighing any individual rights considerations. Why shouldn't employers be expected to provide objective justification for paying some people less according to their age. They could probably do so in numbers of cases, but why is it necessary to undermine the Age Regulations in this way?

EXCEPTION FOR PROVISION OF CERTAIN BENEFITS BASED ON LENGTH OF SERVICE

Regulation 32 is concerned with the issue of benefits related to length of service and seniority. It is not uncommon for employees to be given extra benefits related to length of service with an organisation. Holiday entitlement is one example of a benefit that might be linked to length of service. Without further provisions such benefits might constitute unlawful age discrimination, because it will tend to mean that older (and longer serving) employees receive greater benefits than less-experienced (and often younger) employees.

---

81   National Minimum Wage Act 1998, section 1(3)
82   National Minimum Wage Regulations 1999, Regulation 12(3)

It will not be unlawful for A to award a benefit to employee B less than that awarded to employee C, when the reason for the difference is the relative length of service.[83] There is a further proviso relating to service that is longer than five years. In this case it must reasonably appear to A that the way in which the criterion of length of service is used 'fulfills a business need of his undertaking (for example, by encouraging the loyalty or motivation, or rewarding the experience, of some or all of his workers)'.[84] It is difficult to see why the Government bothered with this proviso for service over five years when it has such a broad justification that will be almost impossible to disprove.

Obvious benefits that are linked to service include pay scales, entry into health and employee discount schemes. It is for the employer to decide which formula to use to calculate length of service. It may be either the length of time a worker has been working at or above a particular level or it can be the length of time the worker has been working for the employer in total.

This distinction is important because it means that the five-year rule can be used again and again. Thus, if a worker is employed as a shop-floor operative for a few years, doing work of a like nature, and is then promoted to being supervisor, then the five-year period can start all over again whilst they do work of a like nature which is different to that done previously. The 2005 consultation gives a legal example:[85]

> A law firm uses a four-year pay scale for trainees, a five-year pay scale for junior associates, and a five-year pay scale for senior associates. The natural progression for lawyers at this firm is to rise automatically through each of these scales in turn.

> The question arises whether, for the purposes of the five-year exemption, they should be seen as a single pay scale of 14 years (in which case the last nine years would not be covered by the five-year exemption). In order to use the five-year exemption for all three scales, the employer would have to demonstrate, if challenged, that all three apply to sufficiently different kinds of work. It might be argued for instance that the responsibilities of the trainees, junior associates and senior associates are different.

---

83   Regulation 32(1)
84   Regulation 32(2).
85   Para. 5.1.17

Presumably this would not be difficult for the firm to do. Thus, the five-year blanket exemption would apply to each of these pay scales, allowing them to continue without the need for further justification.

EXCEPTION FOR PROVISION OF ENHANCED REDUNDANCY PAYMENTS

The subject of statutory redundancy payments has been discussed elsewhere in this book. The payments are calculated using a combination of the length of service and age. The older the redundant employee the higher the rate of payment, at least until the age of 64 when there was a severe tapering off of benefit. The Government was clearly of the view that this would be discriminatory on the grounds of age and put forward a proposal to level out the payment to one week's pay per year of service up to a maximum of 20 years. This would clearly have amounted to a regression in the rights of those over the age of 40 who would have suffered a drop in payments as part of the implementation of the Directive and this undoubtedly would have led to an indefensible legal challenge as such regression is specifically excluded by the Directive. In the final version of the Regulations there was a retreat to the standard formula, but employers are to be allowed to pay more so long as they follow the same formula. The age restrictions at either end are also removed.

It is difficult to see how this can be an adequate implementation of the Directive.

EXCEPTION FOR PROVISION OF LIFE ASSURANCE COVER TO RETIRED WORKERS

Regulation 34 provides that where a person arranges for workers to be provided with life assurance cover after their early retirement for ill health, it will be permissible to end that cover when they reach normal retirement age or, if none, then 65 years.

PART 5   ENFORCEMENT

The new Commission for Equality and Human Rights will include age diversity and age discrimination within its scope. It will have similar roles in relation to advice and guidance on age as with regard to other grounds of discrimination, as well as powers to investigate and challenge discrimination itself and through support of others. ACAS will issue guidance on the Age Regulations.

JURISDICTION

Complaints, in relation to employment and vocational training, should be submitted to an Employment Tribunal. Disputes concerning institutions of further and higher education are dealt with by county or sheriff courts. There is also, of course, a requirement to follow the statutory grievance procedure before legal action is taken.

BURDEN OF PROOF

The burden of proof is the same in both types of court. The complainant needs to prove facts from which the court could infer discrimination in the absence of an adequate explanation. It is for the respondent to prove facts showing that age discrimination was not the reason or part of the reason for the action. Alternatively, the respondent may show objective justification for the difference in treatment in the case of direct and indirect discrimination. There is no justification defence for victimisation or harassment.

REMEDIES ON COMPLAINTS TO EMPLOYMENT TRIBUNALS

An Employment Tribunal may make an order declaring the rights of the complainant, award damages[86] and make a recommendation to the respondent to take action within a specified period obviating or reducing the adverse effect complained of. If the respondent proves that the application of a provision, criterion or practice was done without the intention of treating the complainant unfavourably, any orders directed at the respondent or recommendations for action need to be done as if the Tribunal were not awarding damages. Such damages, if any, that are awarded if such orders or recommendations are made should only be awarded as well as the orders or recommendations if the Tribunal thought it 'just and equitable' to do so.[87] This is the same approach as is adopted in the Regulations on Religion or Belief and Sexual Orientation.

HELP FOR PERSONS IN OBTAINING INFORMATION

Like the other anti-discrimination Regulations there is a procedure for sending a questionnaire to respondents or prospective respondents.[88] The questionnaire is contained in Schedule 3 and there is provision within Regulation 41(1) for the questions to be varied 'as the circumstances require'. The form is simple and invites the questioner to give a factual description of the circumstances

---

86 As with other areas of discrimination there are no statutory ceilings to the amount that can be awarded
87 For remedies connected to failure to inform employees about retirement see the notes on Schedule 6 above
88 Regulation 41

and the treatment received and why such treatment was unlawful. It then asks the respondent whether they agree with the facts and whether they agreed that this amounted to unlawful discrimination or harassment. If the respondent disagrees, then they are invited to say why not, what was the reason for the treatment and how far did considerations of age affect the treatment of the questioner. Question 4 is then simply a statement of any other questions to be asked. Schedule 4 merely asks the respondent to reply to these questions or, if they refuse to do so, to give reasons for not answering.

There are time limits for serving such questionnaires[89] and rules about how they may be served.[90] The questions and answers, subject to the time limits, are admissible as evidence in the proceedings and the court will take into account, and may draw inferences, if it appears that the respondent deliberately failed to reply (without a reasonable excuse) within eight weeks of the questions being served or if it appeared that the replies were evasive or equivocal.[91]

PERIOD WITHIN WHICH PROCEEDINGS TO BE BROUGHT

Regulation 42 states the normal periods for submission: three months for an Employment Tribunal and six months for a county or sheriff court beginning when the act[92] complained of was done, with discretion to extend these periods if it is just and equitable to do so.

PART 6   SUPPLEMENTAL

VALIDITY OF CONTRACTS, COLLECTIVE AGREEMENTS AND RULES OF UNDERTAKINGS

Regulation 43 gives effect to Schedule 5 of the Age Regulations. Schedule 5 is divided into two parts: one on validity and revision of contracts and one on collective agreements and rules of undertakings.

Schedule 5 Part 1: Validity and revision of contracts

A term of a contract is void if:[93]

- the making of the contract is, by reason of the inclusion of the term, unlawful by virtue of the Age Regulations. This does not

---

89   Regulations 41(3)–(4)
90   Regulation 41(5)
91   Regulation 41(2)
92   Including omission to act
93   Schedule 5, Part 1, para. 1(1)

include a term which constitutes unlawful discrimination or harassment against a party to the contract, although the term will be unenforceable against that party;[94]

- it is included in furtherance of an act which is made unlawful by the Age Regulations;

- it provides for the doing of an act which is unlawful by virtue of the Age Regulations.

Similarly, any term in a contract which aims to exclude or limit any part of the Age Regulations is unenforceable by any person in whose favour the term would operate. The contents of compromise agreements reached with the assistance of conciliation officers[95] or which follow the rules for regulating compromise agreements[96] are excluded from these provisions.[97]

Schedule 5 Part 2: Collective agreements and rules of undertakings

This part applies to any term of a collective agreement[98], any rule made by an employer which applies to those employed and those who apply to be employed, or any rule made by a trade association with respect to its current and prospective members and any upon to whom it has given qualifications or who seek its qualifications.[99] Any term of such agreements or rules are void where:

- the making of the collective agreement is unlawful because of the inclusion of such a term;

- the term or rule is included or made in furtherance of an act which is unlawful by virtue of the Age Regulations;

- the term or rule provides for the doing of an act which the Age Regulations make unlawful.

APPLICATION TO THE CROWN

These Regulations apply the Age Regulations to acts of Ministers of the Crown, Crown employees and staff of the House of Commons and House of Lords.

---

94 Ibid., para. 1(2).
95 See Employment Rights Act 1996, section 211
96 Schedule 5, Part 1, para. 2(2)
97 Ibid., para. 2(1)
98 Collective agreement means any agreement relating to matters contained in Trade Union and Labour Relations (Consolidation) Act 1992, section 178(2), which includes terms and conditions of employment, engagement or non engagement, or termination or suspension of employment, or allocation of work, or matters of discipline
99 Schedule 5, Part 2, para. 4(1)

The major exception is that they will not apply to 'service in any of the naval, military or air forces of the Crown'. This seems an unnecessarily harsh approach as there must be many jobs in the forces which need not be age related.

AMENDMENTS TO UNFAIR DISMISSAL LEGISLATION

Regulation 47 enacts Schedule 6, which amends the Employment Rights Act 1996. Retirement is added to the potential fair reasons for dismissal contained in Section 98(2) of the Act.[100] Section 109, which placed an upper age limit on the tight not to be unfairly dismissed, is omitted

AMENDMENTS TO OTHER LEGISLATION

Regulation 49(1) enacts Schedule 8 and Regulation 49(2) enacts Schedule 9. The Employment Rights Act 1996 is further amended by:

- amending Section 126, acts which are both unfair dismissal and discrimination, to add to the Age Regulations. This means that awards cannot be made under one or other headings if the loss or other matter has already been taken into account in another tribunal hearing;

- repealing Section 156 which placed an upper age limit on the entitlement to a redundancy payment;

- repealing Section 158 concerning the right to receive a full redundancy payment when there is an entitlement to a pension, gratuity or superannuation allowance;

- amending Section 162 concerning the amount of redundancy payment; Sections 162(4) and 164(5) which applied a severe tapering of redundancy pay entitlement after the age of 64 are repealed;

- repealing Section 211(2) which ensured that a person's continuous employment did not start until their eighteenth birthday and thus effectively stopped any person under the age of 20 having an entitlement to a redundancy payment.

Other amendments to statute are to the:

- Social Security Contributions and Benefits Act 1992

- Employment Tribunals Act 1996

---

100 Employment Rights Act 1996, section 98(2)(ba)

- Employment Tribunals (Interest on Awards in Discrimination Cases) Regulations 1996[101]

- Employment Act 2002

- Employment Protection (Continuity of Employment) Regulations 1996.

Schedule 9 also contains a number of repeals and revocations.

101 SI 1996/2803

Bibliography

ARTICLES

Duncan C. and Loretto W. (2004), 'Never the right age? Gender and age-based discrimination in employment', *Gender Work and Organisation* 11:1, 95–115

Eglit, Howard E. (1999), 'The ADEA at Thirty', *U.Rich.L.Rev.* 31, 579

Fredman, Sandra (2001), 'Equality: A New Generation?', *Industrial Law Journal* 30:2, 145–168

Gaullier, Xavier (1988), 'La deuxieme carriere, Seuill', cited in 'Ageing of the working population and employment', *EFILWC* 1991

Gunderson, Morley (2003), 'Age discrimination in Canada', *Contemporary Economic Policy* 21:3, 318–328

Handley, Keith (1993), 'The case for legislation on age discrimination', *Personnel Management*

Hannett, Sarah (2003), 'Equality at the Intersections: The Legislative and Judicial Failure to Tackle Multiple Discrimination', *Oxford Journal of Legal Studies* 23:1, 65–86

Hepple, Bob (2001), *Age discrimination in employment: Implementing the framework directive*, Paper presented to the IPPR seminar, 11 December 2001 at the Nuffield Foundation

Hurley, Amy E. and Giannantonio, Christina M. (1999), 'Career attainment for women and minorities: the interactive effects of age, gender and race', *Women in Management Review* 14:1, 4–13

Jolls, Christine (1996), 'Hands-Tying and the Age Discrimination in Employment Act', *Tex. L. Rev.* 74, 1813–1846

Lewis, J. (2001), 'Does the law begin at 40?', *Law Society Gazette* 98:02

Marsh, Alan and Sahin-Dikmen, Melahat (2003), 'Discrimination in Europe', *Eurobarometer*

McGregor, Judy (2002), 'Stereotypes and Older Workers', *Journal of Social Policy New Zealand* 18, 163–177

Mitchell, David E. (2001), 'Recent cases affecting the role of ADEA in protecting older workers', *Duq. L. Rev.* 39, 437

Taylor, Philip and Walker, Alan (1994), 'The Ageing Workforce: Employers' Attitudes Towards Older People', *Work, Employment and Society* 8:4, 569

Sargeant, Malcolm (2004), 'Age Discrimination in FE and HE', *Education Law Journal*, 5:2, 91–97

Sargeant, Malcolm (2005a), 'Age discrimination: equal treatment with exceptions', *International Journal of Discrimination and the Law* 6, 251–266

Sargeant, Malcolm (2005b), 'Age Discrimination: multiple potential for discrimination', *International Journal of Sociology of Law* 33, 17–33

Sargeant, Malcolm (2005c), 'For Diversity: against discrimination – the contradictory approach to age discrimination in employment', *International Journal of Comparative Labour Law and Industrial Relations*, 21:4, 627–642

Sargeant, Malcolm (2006), 'The Employment Equality (Age) Regulations 2006: A Legitimisation of Age Discrimination in Employment', *Industrial Law Journal* 35, 209–227

Schiek, Dagmar (2002), 'A New Framework on Equal Treatment of Persons in EC Law?', *European Law Journal* 8:2, 290–314

Smith, Allan and Twomey, Brenda (2002), 'Labour market experiences of people with disabilities', *Labour Market Trends*, Labour Market Division Office of National Statistics, 415–427

Weber, Beth M. (1998), 'The effect of O'Connor Consolidated Coin Caterers Corp on the requirements for the establishing of a prima facie case under the age discrimination in employment Act', *Rutgers Law Journal* 29: 3

Whiting, Elizabeth (2005), 'The labour market participation of older people', *Labour Market Trends 2005*, Office for National Statistics

Whittle, Richard (2002), 'The framework directive for equal treatment in employment and occupation; an analysis from a disability rights perspective', *European Law Review* 27: 3, 303–326

BOOKS AND PAMPHLETS

Cormack, Janet and Bell, Mark (2005), *Developing Anti-Discrimination Law in Europe* (European Commission)

Dine, Janet and Watt, Bob (1996), *Discrimination Law* (Longman)

Drury, Elizabeth (1993), *Age Discrimination against older workers in the European Community* (Eurolink Age)

Fredman, Sandra and Spencer, Sarah (eds) (2003), *Age as an Equality Issue: Legal and Policy Perspectives* (Oxford: Hart Publishing)

Friedman, Lawrence M. (1984), *Your time will come: the law of age discrimination and mandatory retirement* (New York: Russel Sage Foundation)

Grattan, Patrick (2002), *Short guide to pensions, retirement and work* (Third Age Employment Network)

Gregory, Raymond F. (2001), *Age Discrimination in the American Workplace: Old at a Young Age* (New Brunswick: Rutgers University Press)

Hirsch, Donald (2003), *Crossroads after 50: Improving choices in work and retirement* (York: Joseph Rowntree Foundation)

Hornstein, Zmira (ed) (2001), *Outlawing age discrimination: Foreign lessons, UK choices* (Bristol: The Policy Press in association with the Joseph Rowntree Foundation)

Lissenburgh, S. and Smeaton, D. (2003), *Employment transitions of older workers: The role of flexible employment in maintaining labour market participation and promoting job quality* (Bristol: The Policy Press in association with the Joseph Rowntree Foundation)

McEwen, Evelyn (1990) (ed), *Age: the unrecognised discrimination* (Age Concern England)

Morris, Anne and O'Donnell, Thérèse (eds) (2000), *Feminist Perspectives on Employment Law* (Cavendish Publishing)

O'Cinneide, Colm (2005), *Age discrimination and European Law* (European Commission)

Sargeant, Malcolm (1999), *Age Discrimination in Employment* (London: Institute of Employment Rights)

Wedderburn, Lord (1986), *The Worker and the Law* (Penguin Books)

BOOK CHAPTERS

Ashiagbor, Diamond (2000), 'The intersection between gender and race in the labour market: lessons for anti-discrimination law', in Morris and O'Donnell

Evans, John Grimley (2003), 'Implications of the ageing process', in Fredman and Spencer

Gunderson, Morley (2001), 'Age discrimination legislation in Canada', in Hornstein

Henwood, Melanie (1990), 'No Sense of Urgency: Age Discrimination in Healthcare', in McEwen

Robinson, Janice (2003), 'Age Equality in Health and Social Care', in Fredman and Spencer

Schuller, Tom (2003), 'Age equality in Access to Education', in Fredman and Spencer

Walker, Alan (1990), 'The Benefits of Old Age? Age Discrimination and Social Security', in McEwen,

REPORTS

The Older American Worker-Age Discrimination in Employment (1965), report to the US Congress

Demographic Ageing - consequences for social policy (1988), Maria Maguire, OECD

Older workers: Employers' attitudes and practices (1990), Metcalf, Hilary and Thompson, Mark , Institute of Manpower Studies report no 194

Stereotyping (1995), Robert Jelking and Emanuelle Sajous, Public Services Commission of Canada (monograph)

The demographic situation in the European Union (1995), European Commission, Brussels

The National Committee of Inquiry into Adult Education report 2 (1997) (*The Dearing Report*)

The Dynamics of Retirement (1997), Disney, R., Grundy, E. and Johnson, P., Department of Social Security Research Report 72

Action on Age: Report of the Consultation on Age Discrimination in Employment (1998), Department for Education and Employment (DfEE), HC 4 November 1993

Ageing and the Labour Market: Policies and initiatives within the European Union (1998), Report of a European conference at the University of Twente, Netherlands, Eurolink Age

Characteristics of Older Workers (1998), Researchers: Stephen McKay and Sue Middleton, Centre for Research in Social Policy, Loughborough University, Research Report RR4 and RR45, DfEE

Tackling age bias: code or law? (1998), EOR no 80, July/August

Age Discrimination is Alive and Well, Submission to the House of Representatives Standing Committee on Employment, Education and Workplace Relations Inquiry into issues specific to workers over 45 years (1999), Drake Personnel Limited, available at www.aph.gov.au/house/committee/eewr/OWK/subslist.htm

EU Proposals to combat discrimination (1999), House of Lords Select Committee on European Union, Ninth Report

Towards a Europe for all Ages (1999), Communication from the Commission, COM (1999) 221

Age discrimination in health and social care (2000), Emilie Roberts, Kings Fund Briefing Note at www.kingsfund.org.uk

Age Matters; a report on age discrimination (2000), Human Rights and Equal Opportunity Commission (Australia)

Evaluation of the Code of Practice on Age Diversity in Employment Interim Summary of Results (2000), Deborah Jones, DfEE

Entry in the legal professions (2000), Research Study No 39, The Law Society, cited in *Occupational age restrictions sector review: Law* (2001), DWP

Winning the Generation Game (2000), Performance and Innovation Unit, Cabinet Office, April

Replacement migration: is it a solution to declining and ageing populations? (2000), Population Division, Department of Economics and Social Affairs, New York, United Nations

Age Discrimination in Employment (2001), House of Commons Education and Employment Committee Seventh Report Session 2000-01, HC 259

Ageism: Attitudes and Experiences of Young People (2001), Department for Education and Employment

Age discrimination at work Survey Report (2001), Chartered Institute of Personnel and Development

Disability and social participation in Europe (2001), European Commission, Eurostat

Evaluation of the Code of Practice on Age Diversity in Employment Final Report (2001), Department for Work and Pensions

Occupational age restrictions sector review (2001), Department for Work and Pensions

Significance of age in the workplace (2001), South London Training and Enterprise Council

The employment situation of people with disabilities in the European Union (2001), Executive Summary of Research Paper, written by European Experts Group on employment for disabled people, commissioned by the DG Employment and Social Affairs

Towards Equality and Diversity; Implementing the Employment and Race Directives (2001), Department for Trade and Industry

Winners and Losers in an expanding system (2001), Fiona Aldridge and Alan Tuckett, NIACE survey on adult participation in learning

Increasing labour force participation and promoting active ageing (2002), COM (2002) 9

National Adult Learning Survey (2002), Rory Fitzgerald, Rebecca Taylor and Ivana Lavalle, National Centre for Social Research, Research Report 415, Department for Education and Skills

National Service Framework for Older People: Interim Report on Age Discrimination (2002), NHS

Policy on discrimination against older persons because of age (2002), Ontario Human Rights Commission

Simplicity, Security and Choice: Working and Saving for Retirement (2002), Department for Work and Pensions

Uncovered: workers without pensions (2002), TUC

Working and Saving for Retirement (2002), Department for Work and Pensions

Age Discrimination in Employment; survey of retired members of NATFHE and PCS (2003), Malcolm Sargeant, Centre for Legal Research, Middlesex University Business School

Aspects of the Economics of an Ageing Population (2003), House of Lords Select Committee on Economic Affairs, 4th Report, Session 2002-03, HL Paper 179-1

Discrimination in Europe (2003), Alan Marsh and Melahat Sahin-Dikmen, Eurobarometer

Equality and Diversity: Age Matters (2003), Department for Trade and Industry

Ethnic Minorities and the Labour Market (2003), Cabinet Office Strategy Unit

Factors affecting the labour market participation of older workers (2003), Alan Humphrey, Paddy Kostigan, Kevin Pickering, Nina Stratford and Matt Barnes, Department for Work and Pensions, Research Report No 200

Immigration, integration and employment (2003), COM (2003) 336

Ontario Human Rights Commission Year-end Results 2002–2003, Ontario Human Rights Commission

Retirement ages in the UK: a review of the literature (2003), Pamela Meadows, DTI Employment Relations Series No 18

Towards Equality and Diversity: Report of Responses on Age (2003), Department for Trade and Industry

Advancing women in the workplace: statistical analysis (2004), Michael Lewis, Linda Miller, Fiona Neathey, IRS Research Working Paper Series No 12, Women and Equality Unit, Equal Opportunities Commission

Ageing and employment policies: United Kingdom (2004), OECD

An intersectional approach to discrimination addressing multiple grounds in human rights claims (2004), Ontario Human Rights Commission

Critical Review of Academic Literature Relating to the EU Directives to Combat Discrimination (2004), Bell, Mark and Kjellstrand, Sara, European Commission

Early retirement schemes still the norm in final salary schemes (2004), IDS Pensions Bulletin 160

Employment in Europe 2004, European Commission

Equality and non-discrimination in an enlarged European Union (2004), Green Paper, European Commission, Brussels

Equality Authority Annual Report (2004), Equality Authority Ireland

Facing the challenge: the Lisbon strategy for growth and employment (2004), Report from the High Level Group chaired by Wim Kok, November, European Commission

First annual report on migration and integration (2004), COM (2004) 508

Focus on Older People (2004), Office for National Statistics

Green Paper on an EU approach to managing economic migration (2004), COM (2004) 811

Implementing Equality for Older People (2004), Equality Authority of Ireland

Older Workers; statistical information booklet (2004), Department for Work and Pensions

Pensions: Challenges and Choices The First Report of the Pensions Commission (2004), TSO, Norwich

Protecting Young Workers: the national minimum wage (2004), Low Pay Commission Report Cm6152

Simplicity, Security and Choice: Working and Saving for Retirement (2004) DWP

Time for Action: Advancing Human Rights for Older Ontarians (2004), Ontario Human Rights Commission

A New Pension Settlement for the Twenty-First Century: The Second Report of the Pensions Commission (2005), TSO, Norwich

Age and...multiple discrimination and older people (2005), Age Reference Group on Equality and Human Rights, Age Concern England

Age at Work: the definitive guide to the UK's workforce (2005), Employers Forum on Age

Changing Priorities, Transformed Opportunities? (2005), Jane Parry and Rebecca Taylor, Policy Studies Institute, London

Confronting demographic change: a new solidarity between generations (2005), COM (2005) 94, Green Paper

Equality and Diversity: Age Matters Age Consultation 2003: Summary of Responses (2005), DTI

Equality and Diversity: Coming of Age (2005), Department of Trade and Industry

European anti-discrimination law review no 2 (2005), European Network of Legal Experts, produced by Human European Consultancy on behalf of the European Commission

Facts about Women and Men in Great Britain 2005, Equal Opportunities Commission

How Ageist is Britain? (2005), Age Concern

Opportunity Age (2005), Department for Work and Pensions; vol. 1 – *Meeting the challenges of ageing in the 21st century*; vol. 2 – *A social portrait of ageing*

Part time working is no crime – so why pay the penalty (2005), Equal Opportunities Commission

Tackling age discrimination in the workplace (2005), Chartered Institute of Personnel and Development and the Chartered Management Institute

The age dimension of employment practices: Employer case studies (2005), Stephen McNair and Matt Flynn, Centre for Research into the Older Workforce; Employment Relations Research Series No 42, Department of Trade and Industry

Women and Pensions the evidence (2005), Department for Work and Pensions

Equality and Diversity Coming of Age Report on the Consultation on the draft Equality (Age) Regulations 2006 (2006), Department of Trade and Industry

Live Longer, Work Longer (2006), OECD

Survey of employers' policies, practices and preferences relating to age (2006), Hilary Metcalf with Pamela Meadows, Research report 325, DTI Employment Relations Research Series No 49, Department for Work and Pensions

LAW

CASES

Agco Ltd v Massey Ferguson Works Pension Trust Ltd [2003] IRLR 783

Application by Badeck and others Case C-158/97 [2000] IRLR 432 ECJ

Banks v Ablex Ltd [2005] IRLR 357 CA

Beith v Nitrogen Products Inc. 7 F.3d 701 (8th Cir. 1993)

Bentley v Secretary of State for Trade and Industry [2002] IRLR 768 Employment Tribunal

Brian McLoughlin v Bus Éireann Equality Officer Decision No: DEC-E2004-059

Burton v De Vere Hotels [1997] ICR 1 [1996] IRLR 596

Carroll v Monaghan Vocational Guidance Education Committee DEC-E/2004/003

Commission v United Kingdom [1984] IRLR 29

Commonwealth of Australia v Human Rights and Equal Opportunity Commission [1999] FCA 1524

Canada (A.G.) v Mossop [1993] 1 S.C.R. 554 at 645-646

Cross v British Airways [2005] IRLR 423

E.E.O.C. v Insurance Co. of North America 49 F.3d 1418 (9th Cir. 1995)

Equality Authority v Ryanair Equality Officer Decision DEC – E/2000/14

Gillen v Department of Health and Children DEC-E2003-035

Greater Vancouver Regional District Employees' Union v Greater Vancouver Regional District [2001] BCCA 435

Hazen Paper Co v Biggins 113 SCt 1701, 16 FEP 793 (1993)

Holley v Sanyo Manufacturing Inc. 771 F.2d 1161

Hughes v Aer Lingus Equality Officer's Decision No: DEC-E2002-49

Igen Ltd v Wong [2005] IRLR 258 CA

James v Eastleigh Borough Council [1990] IRLR 288 HL

Loeb v Textron Inc 600 F.2d 1003 (1979)

MacDonald v Advocate General for Scotland; Pearce v Governing Body of Mayfield School [2003] IRLR 512

Mahoney v Trabucco 574 F.Supp. 955 (1983)

Majrowski v Guy's and St Thomas's NHS Trust [2005] IRLR 240

Mangold v Helm Case C-144/04 [2006] IRLR 143

Marschall v Land Nordrhein-Westfalen Case C-409/95 [1998] IRLR 39 ECJ

Massachusetts Board of Retirement v Murgia 427 U.S. 307 (1976)

McDonnell Douglas Corp v Green 411 US 792

McKinney v University of Guelph [1990] 3 SCR

Metz v Transit Mix Inc. 828 F.2d 1202 (7th Cir 1987)

Nash v Mash/Roe Group Ltd [1998] IRLR 168

O'Connor v Consolidated Coin Caterers Corp 517 U.S. 308 (1996)

O'Flynn v Adjudication Officer Case C-237/94. [1996] ECR 2617

Quantas Airways Ltd v Christie [1998] HCA 18

Pearce v Governing Body of Mayfield School [2003] IRLR 512

R v Secretary of State for Employment, ex parte Seymour-Smith and Perez (No 2) [2000] IRLR 263 HL.

Rutherford v Secretary of State for Trade and Industry (no 2) [2004] IRLR 892

Rutherford v Secretary of State [2006] IRLR 551 HL

Smith v City of Jackson, Mississippi 544 U.S. (2005)

Spence v Maryland Casualty Co 995 F.2d 1147 (2d Cir 1993)

Stanley Edward Griffin v Australian Postal Corporation. Industrial Relations Court of Australia 980001 September 15 1998

Superquinn v Barbara Freeman AEE/02/08 Determination No 021

Taggart v Time Inc 924 F.2d 43 (2d Cir. 1991)

Taylor v Secretary of State for Scotland [2000] IRLR 503

Trans World Airlines v Thurston 469 U.S. 111 (1985)

Usery v Tamiami Trail Tours Inc. 531 F.2d 224 (1976)

Venebles v Hornby [2004] 1 All ER 627

Waite v Government Communications Headquarters [1983] IRLR 341

Western Airlines Inc. v Criswell 472 U.S. 400, 105 S.Ct. 2743, 86 L.Ed.2nd 321 (1985)

Woroski v Nashau Corp 31 F.3d 195 (2nd Cir. 1994)

X v Department of Defense [1995] EOC 92-715

Zafar v Glasgow City Council [1998] IRLR 36 HL

DIRECTIVES

Directive 76/207 EEC on the implementation of the principle of equal treatment between men and women; subsequently amended by Directive 2002/73/EC

Council Directive 94/33/EC concerning certain aspects of working time OJ L216/12 23-11-1993

Council Directive 97/80/EC on the burden of proof in cases of discrimination based on sex OJ L14/6, 20 January 1998

Proposal for a Council Directive establishing a general framework for equal treatment in employment and occupation COM (1999) 565

Directive 2000/43/EC of 29 June 2000 implementing the principle of equal treatment between persons irrespective of racial or ethnic origin OJ L180/22

Directive 2000/78/EC of 27 November 2000 establishing a general framework for equal treatment in employment and occupation OJ L303/16

STATUTORY INSTRUMENTS

Transfer of Undertakings (Protection of Employment) Regulations 1981 SI 1981/1794

Working Time Regulations 1998 SI 1998/1833

The National Minimum Wage Regulations 1999 SI 1999/584

Part-time Workers (Prevention of Less Favourable Treatment) Regulations 2000 SI 2000/1551

The Employment Equality (Religion or Belief) Regulations 2003 SI 2003/1660

The Employment Equality (Sexual Orientation) Regulations 2003 SI 2003/1661

The Employment Equality (Age) Regulations 2006 SI 2006/1031

LEGISLATION

Old Age Pensions Act 1908

Widows, Orphans and Old Age Contributory Pensions Act 1925

Old Age and Widows Pensions Act 1940

National Insurance Act 1948

Licensing Act 1964

Age Discrimination in Employment Act 1967 (USA)

Equal Pay Act 1970

European Communities Act 1972

Sex Discrimination Act 1975

Social Security Act 1975

Race Relations Act 1976

Anti Discrimination Act 1977 (New South Wales)

Canadian Charter of Rights and Freedoms 1982

Equal Opportunity Act 1984 (South Australia)

Older Workers Benefit Protection Act 1990 (USA)

Civil Rights Act of 1991 (USA)

Further and Higher Education Act 1992

Trade Union and Labour Relations (Consolidation) Act 1992

Disability Discrimination Act 1995

Employment Rights Act 1996

Workplace Relations Act 1996 (Australia)

Protection from Harassment Act 1997

Employment Equality Act 1998 (Ireland)

National Minimum Wage Act 1998

Disability Rights Commission Act 1999

Equal Status Act 2000 (Ireland)

Age Discrimination Act 2004 (Australia)

Equality Act 2004 (Ireland)

Equality Act 2006

Index